THE SILENCES OF HAMMERSTEIN

THE
SEAGULL
LIBRARY OF
GERMAN
LITERATURE

HANS MAGNUS ENZENSBERGER

THE SILENCES OF HAMMERSTEIN

TRANSLATED BY
MARTIN CHALMERS

LONDON   NEW YORK   CALCUTTA

This publication was supported by a grant
from the Goethe-Institut India

Seagull Books, 2019

Originally published in German by Suhrkamp Verlag
Frankfurt/Main 2008
as *Hammerstein oder Der Eigensinn*

© Suhrkamp Verlag, Frankfurt am Main, 2008

First published in English translation by Seagull Books, 2009

English translation © Martin Chalmers 2009

ISBN   978 0 8574 2 703 8

British Library Cataloguing-in-Publication Data

A catalogue record for this book is available
from the British Library

Typeset by Seagull Books, Calcutta, India
Printed and bound by WordsWorth India, New Delhi, India

Fear is no philosophy of life
K. v. H.

Contents

THE SILENCES OF HAMMERSTEIN

The marriage of General Kurt von Hammerstein-Equord was blessed with seven children, four daughters and three sons. This book is about him and his family.

A difficult day

On 3 February 1933, the general left his apartment in the east wing of the Bendler Block in Berlin punctually at seven o'clock, as he did every morning. He didn't have far to go to his office. It was on the floor below. There, that same evening, he would sit at the same table with a man called Adolf Hitler.

How often had he encountered him before? He's supposed to have met him already, in the winter of 1924–25, in the house of the piano-maker Edwin Bechstein whom he had known for a long time. That's what Hammerstein's son Ludwig says. Hitler had not impressed his father. At the time, the general described him as a muddle-head, albeit an adroit muddle-head. Frau Helene Bechstein had been a great admirer of Hitler from the start. She had not only subsidized him during his Munich years—there was talk of loans and jewels—but also introduced him to

Kurt von Hammerstein, about 1934

what she considered to be good society. She gave big dinners in Hitler's honour to introduce him to influential friends, and taught him how to hold a knife at table, when and where to kiss a lady's hand and how to wear tails.

Then, a couple of years later, in 1928 or 1929, Hitler had called at the general's private home in Hardenbergstrasse, not far from Zoo Station, in Berlin's west end, presumably to sound out the views of the General Staff about him. Franz von Hammerstein, about seven or eight at the time, remembers how his father received the guest: 'They sat on the balcony and talked. My father's opinion of the man: He talks too much and what he says is much too confused. He gave him the cold shoulder. Hitler nevertheless made an effort with him and sent him a free subscription to a Nazi periodical.'

At Hitler's request, there was a third meeting on 12 September 1931 at the home of a Herr von Eberhardt. By then, Hitler was leader of the second-largest party in the German parliament. 'Hammerstein said on the telephone to his friend Kurt von Schleicher, the Minister of Defence: "The great man from Munich wants to talk to us." Schleicher replied: "I'm afraid I can't." ' The meeting lasted four hours. Apart from an interjection by Hammerstein, Hitler spoke without interruption for the first hour. In the remaining three there was an exchange of views, and Hammerstein— according to this Herr von Eberhardt—is supposed to have concluded by saying: 'We want to move more slowly. Aside from that, we're really in agreement.' Did he say that? It would be an indication of the profound ambivalences produced by a crisis to which even the most intelligent minds were not immune.

After the conversation, Schleicher asked Herr Eberhardt: 'Now what do you think of this man Hitler?'—'Even if some of what he says should be rejected, he can't be ignored, because of the masses that are behind him.'—'What am I supposed to do with the psychopath?' Schleicher, both a major-general and one of the most influential politicians in the country, allegedly responded.

In less than a year, the 'psychopath' had come to power in Germany. On 3 February 1933, he appeared before the commanders of the Reichswehr for the first time to expound his plans to them and, if possible, to win them over. His host that evening was General Kurt Baron von Hammerstein-Equord.

It was his fifty-fourth birthday that day, and it very much looked as if he had reached the peak of his career. In 1929, he had been appointed Chief of the Truppenamt—the Troop Office—with the rank of major-general. Truppenamt was a cover name for the General Staff of the Reichswehr, which officially, because of the Versailles Treaty, was not allowed to have such a staff. One year later, he was promoted to full general and appointed Chef der Heeresleitung Chief of Army Command—the highest rank in the German army. The decision was very controversial:

the right-wing parties were fiercely opposed to Hammerstein and accused him of being insufficiently 'national'. The Defence Ministry, labelled him 'the Red General', presumably because his personal experience provided him with a good knowledge of the Red Army. He was impressed by its close ties with the mass of the population, whereas the Reichswehr was completely isolated from the working class. Nevertheless, to attack Hammerstein as being left-wing, as the Nazi daily *Völkischer Beobachter* did, was absurd. Ultimately, as far as his general background was concerned, he was an aristocratic officer of the old school. At a commanding officers' conference in February 1932, he expressed himself quite unequivocally: 'By conviction we all of us stand on the Right, but we must be clear in our minds who is to blame for the current internal political shambles. And that is the leaders of the right-wing parties. *They* are responsible.'

Yet, although he could look back on a successful career, one year later Hammerstein had had more than enough of his post.

The exemplary career of a cadet

1888   Cadet School Plön

1893   Central Cadet School Lichterfelde, Berlin

1898   Second Lieutenant in the Third Guards Foot Regiment in Berlin

1905–07 In Karlsruhe

1907   Military Academy in Berlin

1909   First Lieutenant

1911   Mobilization Section of the Great General Staff

1913   Captain in the General Staff

1913   Adjutant to the Quartermaster-General

1914   Company Commander in Flanders

1915   First General Staff officer on the General Staff
         of the VIII Reserve Corps

1916   On the Great General Staff

1917   Major

1918   First General Staff officer on the General Staff
         of the General Command

1919   On the General Staff of the Lüttwitz Korps

1919   attached to the staff of Group Command I
         in Berlin

1920   Lieutenant-Colonel

1920   Chief of Staff of Group Command II in Kassel

1922   Commander of Third Battalion of the 12
         Infantry Regiment in Magdeburg

1924   Chief of Staff of the 3 Division in Berlin

1925   Colonel

1929   Major-General, Chief of Staff of Group
         Command I in Berlin

1929   Lieutenant-General, Chief of the Troop Office

1930   General of Infantry, Chief of Army
        Command

A very ancient family and a suitable marriage

The Barons von Hammerstein are a widely ramified
family, descended from ancient Westphalian nobility,
which has divided, as the *Almanach de Gotha* tells us,
into two lines and four branches. A thousand years ago
they were settled in the Rhineland, and a ruined castle
near Andernach still bears their name; later, they were
to be found in Hanover, in Austria and in Mecklen-
burg. There were among them landowners, officers,
district administrators and forest superintendents; the
daughters made matches appropriate to their rank or
ended their lives as canonesses or abbesses.

The general's father was a forest superintendent
in Mecklenburg-Strelitz. He sent his son, of whom it
is said he would rather have been a lawyer or a
Bremen coffee trader, to the cadet school. Because he
had two more children, but no financial means, he
could not afford any other education. Apart from that,
young Hammerstein occasionally had to do service as
a page at the imperial court in Potsdam, something he
enjoyed just as little as drill. It was during this period
of training that he got to know Kurt von Schleicher,
later Reich Chancellor. At twenty, they both got their
commissions and joined the Third Guards Foot

Regiment as lieutenants. The unit was highly regarded; it produced several generals, including, unfortunately, Paul von Hindenburg.

In order to prepare for military academy, Hammerstein had himself attached to the field artillery in Karlsruhe. He travelled there with all his possessions packed in two laundry baskets, having auctioned off the rest at his regiment. This decision was to have far-reaching consequences—because in Karlsruhe he once again met a lady whose father, Baron Walther von Lüttwitz, was chief of staff. In fact, Hammerstein had chosen the place to be close to her. Her name was Maria. He had got to know her in Berlin in 1904 and did everything he could to marry her.

Lüttwitz came from an old Silesian noble family of land owners and civil servants. His wife, a Countess von Wengersky from Hungary, was said to have gypsy blood in her veins and was quite different from most German women; one of her ancestors was a dancer, Catarina Filipacci, whom the King of Saxony had brought to his court.

There was no sign of such extravagances in the big house that the Lüttwitzes kept in Berlin. In the Wilhelmine society in which they moved, they were 'in the favour of both Their Majesties'. The daughters took gavotte lessons, spoke fluent French and were carefully prepared for their first season; that was especially true of the second daughter, Maria, of whom it is said that she 'was pleasing and had many suitors'.

It was not unusual for there to be a hundred guests at the house for balls. The gentlemen invited belonged to the right families and the right regiments.

In his diary, Lüttwitz writes:

Naturally, Lieutenant Kurt von Hammerstein frequented our house as a comrade of my old regiment. He also played a great deal of tennis with our two daughters. At first, we had no idea that he had an eye on our Mietze [Maria]. But it gradually became clear to us, and, since in our view, there was not enough there for a marriage, so that she could live without worries, I put that to the suitor when, shortly after, he approached me with a proposition. I demanded withdrawal, he acknowledged my arguments, but requested to be allowed to maintain social relations so that it did not attract attention. I consented; that had the result, however, which I should have known, that the flirtation continued.

Maria von Hammerstein remembers: 'We knew each other from the winter of 1904, Kurt and I. He struck me as particularly calm and serious, different from the other men. At a fancy dress party, he was a Magyar and I was Old-Strassburg. We danced quite a lot together. I always felt so strange in his presence.' They met again at the tennis club. 'On the way home Herr von Hammerstein always carried my shoes. He had brought four bottles of sparkling wine to our farewell party. In November, we met at a bazaar in the

Karlsruhe Fest-halle. I was dancing there as a Sèvres figurine painted entirely in white and wearing a white gown. I faced the future with apprehension.'

Herr von Lüttwitz was not very taken with all this. Poor officer families were not wanted in the army, never mind in one's own family. And Hammerstein had no money. He could not bring much more to the marriage than a file labelled 'For orderly settlement of debts'. Only when a grandfather helped Hammerstein out did Lüttwitz give up his resistance.

Another impediment will also have played its part in Lütwittz's reservations. The von Lüttwitz family was strictly Catholic, while Hammerstein, who anyway showed little interest in religion, had been baptized a Protestant. In such circles, a 'mixed marriage' was considered problematic. Later, too, the question gave rise to all kinds of annoyances for the parents of the couple, which Kurt finally ended by putting his foot down.

> In any case [he wrote to his wife] *I* am of the opinion that children must be baptized in accordance with the mother, because it is she who must teach them the rudiments of religion. Any further chatter is superfluous, therefore. For all I care they can stand on their heads and wave their feet in the air in shock. *You* need not put up with any arguments whatsoever about it. If anyone wants something, he should talk to *me*.

Notwithstanding all the problems, a splendid wedding was celebrated in 1907 in Karlsruhe. There's even an official photograph. Although the father of the bride complained that he had to organize the festivities 'on a modest scale', the gathering appears altogether impressive. All the guests, among them the later Chancellor of the Reich, Kurt von Schleicher, belong to the military nobility; the men in full-dress uniform, wearing their decorations, the ladies all in floor-length white dresses and elaborately adorned hats.

The sinister general

A later photo shows Maria's father as a general, white-haired, thin, gazing coldly, displaying the Pour le mérite, the highest Prussian military honour, his right hand on his hip as he challengingly inspects the viewer.

His granddaughter Maria Therese remembers him as rather unpleasant.

> He was not very close to us, and he represented a world that had disappeared and which he had futilely tried to conjure up again. To us, his world was a shadow world, the cold splendour of his official apartment as much as the feudal estates. Most of us couldn't bear him.

Maria and Kurt von Hammerstein.
Wedding picture, 1907

Walther von Lüttwitz, 1920s

One day, he commissioned a painter to do portraits of my two sisters and myself. The pictures still exist. Three pastels with Butzi [Marie Luise] on the left, looking at Helga, who's sitting in the middle and with me on the right. My grandfather sent Helga's portrait back to the painter because he thought she looked Jewish in it. Probably, he had read Chamberlain's book which was very much in fashion then. [Houston Stewart Chamberlain's *Foundations of the Nineteenth Century*, published in 1899, is considered to be one of the central texts of German anti-Semitism.]

In my grandfather's house there was no family life in which we participated. His eldest daughter always lived at home, because her father had forbidden her to marry the man she loved. We children were never allowed to eat at the same table as the adults; we were fed in the pantry. My grandmother always sat on the veranda on the second floor, surrounded by wisteria. We were never allowed to go up to her because she had TB. She died in Switzerland in November 1918.

A little later, there was a major family upset.

When we returned to Berlin, in autumn 1918, after the summer holidays, the revolution had broken out. Grandfather Lüttwitz was still the general in command in Berlin. He lived in Hardenbergstrasse. My brother Ludwig was also born there, and my mother remained in grandfather's house with the baby. One day, Field Marshal Hindenburg called to talk to my grandfather. Mother, perhaps out of her naïve ambition, had the idea that he should be my brother's godfather. I wanted to be in her good books, and, unlike my older sisters, who would never have been willing to do anything so silly, I promised to ask Hindenburg for this favour. With a bouquet in my hand, I stepped up to him, curtsied and made the request.

A couple of weeks later, when I came to the house with my mother, we found it deserted. Where was he? We looked in his study and couldn't find him. I had the feeling that there was a pursuer lurking behind every chair. The house felt creepy. We couldn't know that he had fled and was staying with his relatives in Hungary. How did my mother bear it all? She was so close to her father that all his life he wrote her a postcard every day in his tiny, space-saving hand-writing.

Lüttwitz remarked in his laconic, brusque way: 'Later, unfortunately, a tension arose between me and Kurt Hammerstein. After the war, he became an opportunist and we then came into conflict.' And Smilo, Hammerstein's brother-in-law, says: 'A line had been drawn. An almost classical tragedy in the immediate family circle. My sister Maria suffered greatly from this conflict.'

A couple of anecdotes

The eighteenth century was the heyday of a short form which today has gone out of fashion: the anecdote. Authors like Chamfort, Fontenelle and Lichtenberg made use of it. It doesn't have a good reputation as a historical source. A pity, because anyone interested in characters and maxims should at least give it a hearing, even if not unquestioningly believe it.

In her delightful, completely unpretentious memoirs, Hammerstein's daughter, Maria Therese, relates of her father:

> He has two huge index fingers, Butzi [Marie Luise] holds one and I hold the other and he goes with us to the Südwestkorso [in Berlin], to the horses which have been brought there from Moabit Barracks, places a piece of sugar on each of our hands and shows us how thumb must be firmly pressed against index finger, so that the horse doesn't snap at it. Before 1914, that's the only thing I can remember my father teaching us. (1913)

> My parents are running round the breakfast table, which I've crawled under. She has the morning paper in her hand, and father is chasing after her because he wants it. I found that very unusual. Although I was only four years old, I understood that it wasn't good news. The newspaper announced mobilization. (1914)

One morning, my father looks through the door into our dark bedroom. He's wearing his helmet with the big white plume and is taking leave of us, before travelling to headquarters on the Emperor's special train. He was then a captain on the Great General Staff. (1914)

Maria Therese's younger sister, Helga, adds a less idyllic story:

In the big dining room with the green damask-covered chairs from some castle or other and a very ugly table that didn't match them at all. Papus [their father] is angry with us (Butzi and me), I no longer know what about, and hits us with the riding whip. The only time we were hit—not very nice. (1921)

Maria Therese again:

One summer, my father had rented a place for us in Steinhorst near Celle. A part of the house, however, was occupied by a family that didn't want to move out and had barricaded themselves in it. They didn't want to give up the kitchen and were defending their home by force of arms. My father entered their dining room, likewise with a weapon in his hand. That's the only time I saw him in a civil war-like situation, and in his own house at that. He had to go through a wearisome lawsuit, in order finally to get them to move out. And he had even leased the house in order not to be burdened in the Berlin of those years with his big family. (1921)

A removal van has driven up: I run out and help the men by carrying in the dining room chairs. Afterwards, I hear Papus say about me: 'Good-natured but stupid.' It must have pained him that I didn't run into the new garden like the others. The impulse, not to be waited upon, was quite foreign to him, the last 'grand seigneur'. (1924)

From Berlin, he takes us to Lake Stechlin. He shows us his father's head forester's house—it's quite close. He knows all the trees and tells us their names: elm, alder, ash . . . He takes the forest seriously. He gets hold of collapsible canoes and goes paddling with us. He's happy in the countryside in which he spent his childhood and we are too. (1920s)

We only ever heard him talking at length when there were visitors. He always let us sit and listen. I admired his knowledge, but, when it came to it, he always took Mummy's side. Once he came into my room, which was between floors, to apologize—in the Tiergarten park, he had got so angry on one occasion that he had hit out at me with his walking stick. Because of the long separation during the war and after, he and Mummy hadn't learned to accommodate one another. Perhaps that also explains his complete silence at table. (1926)

He wanted a united Europe, was friends with Coudenhove-Kalergi. In a second world war, he said, Germany would be partitioned. 'Communism will come, but I shall try to

prevent its coming for as long as possible.'
(1929)

His son-in-law Joachim Paasche relates:

> He definitely had a taste for luxury. He loved
> his cognac and a good cigar. In the Bendler-
> strasse, he sat at the head of the family dinner
> table without saying a word, without moving
> a muscle. But he had to laugh when I didn't
> realize that we were served game and thought
> it was beef. I heard him say to the servant:
> 'Let him bring me . . .' I had never heard this
> eighteenth-century form of command before.
> (1931)

> His seven children were known for their
> wildness and rebellious nature. And nor did
> he bear any similarity to the typical, hard-
> working and conscientious German. He liked
> people, often simply left his work lying and
> went hunting. (1931)

> His self-irony, as anti-Semitism became
> rampant: 'I hope we'll soon be rid of this
> Hitler, so that I can insult the Jews again.' At
> that time, one could still permit oneself such
> a remark. (1931)

Margarethe von Oven, his secretary, later Countess Hardenberg, remembers: 'When I entered his
office the morning after the Reichstag Fire, he welcomed me with the words: "Of course they set it alight
themselves!" I was shocked and at first disbelieving.
His response brought me down to earth: "So you've

fallen for them too?" He and my mother were the only ones who didn't let themselves be taken in.' (1933)

And Maria Therese recalls: 'My father kissed me twice in his whole life: once in the hall, during the First World War, when he came home on leave, and the second time, when I said goodbye to him in 1935, before emigrating to Japan.'

A posthumous conversation
with Kurt von Hammerstein (I)

H: You wanted to talk to me?

E: Yes. If you have a moment.

H: Time is something I've plenty of. But what is it you want to talk to me about?

E: General Hammerstein, I have come across your name everywhere — in Berlin, in Moscow, in Canada . . . Your family . . .

H: My family is of no concern to anyone else.

E: But history, Herr von Hammerstein, in which you played an important part.

H: Do you seriously believe that? For two or three years perhaps, then it was over and done with. Are you a historian?

E: No.

H: A newspaper journalist?

E: I am a writer.

H: Aha. I fear I don't understand anything about literature. In my parents' house, no one read any novels. And as for me, some Fontane, and, when I was in hospital, *War and Peace*. That was all.

E: I am writing a book about you.

H: Must you?

E: Yes. I hope you haven't got anything against it.

H: My old Latin teacher always said that the poets lie.

E: That's not my intention. On the contrary. I want to know exactly how it was, in so far as that is at all possible. That's why I am here. Besides, it's your birthday today. I have taken the liberty of bringing you a box of Havanas. I know that you have a weakness for good cigars.

H (laughs): So you want to bribe me. Thank you very much. I don't mind. Come in. As you see, my desk is bare. I have no secrets to keep any more. What do you wish to know?

E: Perhaps you can tell me something about your father-in-law, Herr von Lüttwitz?

H: He was completely lacking in imagination and politically a hopeless case. That was clear to me the first time I met him.

E: In 1904, in Berlin.

H: Correct. And then in the war, during my time on the General Staff. He was my superior after all.

E: You had difficulties with him.

H: You can say that again. Already in December 1918 — he was commandant in Berlin — he took quite big risks.

E: The revolution.

H: If you want to call that mess a revolution. You can imagine that I didn't have much time for the Spartakus people; but the marauding Freikorps were even worse, and the old man allied himself with them.

E: He put down the uprising. Is it true that his troops were involved in the murder of Rosa Luxemburg and Karl Liebknecht? Your daughter

Maria Therese remembers that you rushed into the dining room and shouted: 'Soldiers have thrown a woman into the Landwehr Canal by her red hair.'

H: Quite possible. The fact is at the time I was First General Staff Officer at Berlin Group Command, and Lüttwitz was my boss. His favourite unit was the Ehrhardt Naval Brigade, an altogether demoralized troop, and it has the murders on its conscience.

E: The Army Minister at the time was the Social Democrat Gustav Noske, who coined the notorious motto: 'Someone has to be the bloodhound.'

H: Yes, the Communists liked to quote that sentence. They wanted to set up council republics on the Soviet model. That would have meant civil war, which was, of course, out of the question for me and my friends.

E: You were the 'three majors'.

H: Where did you get that phrase from?

E: Brüning uses it in his memoirs.

H: Did he? By that he presumably means Kurt von Schleicher and Bodo von Harbou, whom I knew from Military Academy and the First World War.

E: He writes about you: 'In the first half of 1919, these three majors, who were in constant contact with one another, had a great, perhaps even dominant influence on all important issues linked to military matters.' He means that as great praise. You prevented a descent into chaos.

H: Well, he's exaggerating a little there.

E: A year later, Noske, as laid down by the Versailles Treaty, finally wanted to disband the Freikorps who were leading him a merry dance. That didn't suit your father-in-law.

H: Of course not. He refused to obey orders. At that the minister suspended him, that is to say, kicked him out. So then the old man mounted a *coup d'état*. That was on 12 March 1920. I remember very well, how he ordered the Ehrhardt Brigade to march on the capital and overthrow the government. He absolutely wanted me to join him.

E: Difficult for you!

H: Why?

E: You refused.

H: Naturally. A brainless operation!

E: You apparently did everything you could to dissuade him.

H: It was pointless.

E: At the time, your friend Schleicher was an important man in the Defence Ministry. He warned you against refusing to obey orders. 'Think very carefully, you have five children.' And you are supposed to have replied: 'Let them go begging, if they are hungry.'

H: Who says that?

E: Your son Kunrat.

H: It may be so.

E: In the end, your father-in-law even had you arrested.

H: Three or four hours, then my people got me out.

E: And how did things go on?

H: He used a figurehead by the name of Kapp. An insignificant, plump civil servant with pince-nez and a wing collar, who had cosied up to Ludendorff (who incidentally was also a flop).

E: Nevertheless, Lüttwitz and his Freikorps people occupied Berlin.

H: Mutiny.

E: The chancellor and his cabinet fled.

H: Bauer was his name. No genius either.

E: And then this Wolfgang Kapp installed himself as chancellor.

H: Had no say. Lüttwitz had assumed supreme command of the Reichswehr, he wanted to play at
military government. The army of course didn't
join in. And the civilians certainly didn't
either. They then organized a general strike.

E: But there were 2,000 dead.

H: Dirty business. It was all over in four days.
High treason! Fifty thousand marks reward for
his capture — he was proud of that. Wasn't
easy for Maria, the whole thing. Kapp, poor
fellow, decamped to Sweden, and the old man
took to his heels. First to Breslau, then with
a relative's passport to Slovakia; passed himself off as a Herr von Lorenz. From there with
a horse and cart over the border to Hungary.
Once a border guard who thought his passport
was suspicious wanted to stop him. Galloped
past and was gone. In the place where he found
refuge, he met a cousin of my deceased mother-
in-law and promptly married her. Heaven knows
how he got hold of a genuine passport. With
that he went back to Germany a few years later
and hid with a priest in the Eulengebirge
hills in Silesia. One day, the CID turned up,
fifteen strong. 'Where is the general?' — 'No
idea.' —'His bed is still warm.' Probably they
weren't that interested in finding him. But
why am I telling you all this?

E: Go ahead!

H: Naturally three weeks later, as sure as fate,
came the amnesty. Hindenburg had just been
elected President of the Reich and he made
sure of that. My father-in-law even had the
nerve to sue for back payment of his pension.
And do you know what? He got it too. A bit
thick. After all, he had been sentenced by a
court for high treason. He kept his mouth shut
for a while after that, until 1931. Then he
saw a ray of hope again. The Harzburg Front
suited him down to the ground, and, in 1933,
he congratulated the Nazis on taking power.

E: That doesn't surprise me. He couldn't stand
    Jews either.

H: He wasn't the only one. It was quite normal in
    the army. You should have heard the jokes of
    the officers in my regiment! No one thought
    it out of the ordinary. The French and the
    English were no different by the way. It
    wasn't fanaticism — more a bad habit. By the
    time they realized where it led, it was too
    late.

E: Some never learn.

H: You can say that again! But you misjudge old
    Lüttwitz. In 1934, after the Night of the Long
    Knives, there was a change. That's when most
    of the old guard grasped what Hitler was capa-
    ble of. And we went hunting again, Lüttwitz
    and I, as in the old days. You probably don't
    understand that.

E: Perhaps not quite. But I'm doing my best.
    Nevertheless, may I ask you another question?

H: Go on.

E: What was your state of mind, thirteen years
    later, on 3 February 1933, as you were waiting
    for your guest at the Bendlerstrasse?

H: My mood more than seventy years ago? Probably
    I felt like throwing up.

First gloss.
The horrors of the Weimar Republic.

We should be grateful that we weren't there.

The Weimar Republic was a fiasco from the start.
That's not merely a smart judgement made with the
benefit of hindsight. Ernst Troeltsch already described
it thus in his *Spectator-Briefen* (Spectator Letters) of

1918–22, and he wasn't the only one. A glance at Joseph Roth's early novels and reports should be enough to convince anyone who has doubts. It wasn't only that the old elites were not prepared to put up with the republic. Many who came home from the lost war were unwilling to give up 'battle as inner experience' and schemed revenge. They invented the legend of the 'stab in the back'; then, later, for a whole decade, there was the slogan: 'Yet you were victorious'. The judges and the police clung to their Wilhelmine norms and habits. The universities were dominated by authoritarian, anti-parliamentary and anti-Semitic sentiments. More than once, the tense atmosphere erupted in dilettante coup attempts and plans to overthrow the government.

Things didn't look much better on the Left. They too didn't think much of democracy, and their cadres planned revolt.

The desperate economic situation contributed to the instability of German society. War debts and reparations payments were a heavy burden on the republic's budget. The inflation ruined the middle classes and the petty bourgeoisie. Then there was the endemic corruption, which went right up to the highest levels of the state and of the political parties and had direct political consequences. The case of Reich President Hindenburg is notorious. The only economic breathing space, which allowed hopes of recovery, lasted little more than five years, from 1924 to 1929. Then it was brutally brought to an end by the Great Depression.

The economic collapse and resulting mass unemployment led to bitterness on the part of wage-earners and to massive fears of proletarianization.

On top of that there were the foreign policy burdens which, at times, seemed unbearable. The Versailles Treaty, far removed from the intelligent peace which the British and Americans envisaged after the Second World War, aroused fierce resentment in German society. The occupation of the Ruhr and separatism and ethnic conflicts fostered and exacerbated chauvinist opinions. Immediate neighbours, in particular the French and the Poles, did everything in their power to further humiliate the Germans, and the Soviet Union, too, tried to destabilize the republic as best it could.

In a word, the country was in a state of latent civil war, which was not only conducted by political means but which also repeatedly assumed violent forms. From the Spartakus Uprising to the armed aggression and murders of left-wing and liberal figures by the Freikorps and the 'Black Reichswehr', from the March 1921 fighting in central Germany to the march of the National Socialists on the Feldherrnhalle in Munich (in 1923), from the failed workers' uprising in Hamburg, also in 1923, to 'Bloody May' in Berlin in 1929, democracy was repeatedly caught in a pincer movement by the militants on both sides.

Today, the word 'system' is a largely innocent one, particularly popular in computer terminology. In the 1920s and 1930s, the term was interpreted differently—

On Civil War. Periodical of the M-Apparatus
of the KPD (German Communist Party), 1923–25

it was a battle slogan coined in the Weimar years (and which had a strange renaissance in 1968), and deployed against the republic by Right and Left, by Goebbels as by Thälmann.

In the years 1932 and 1933, the divisions in society, not only in Germany but also in Austria, assumed almost Lebanese forms. Militias—Nazi SA (Sturmabteilung—Storm Troops), Communist Rotfrontkämpferbund (Red Front Fighters' League), Stahlhelm (Steel Helmet—Conservative veterans), Hammerschaften (Hammer Squads—trade unions), Reichsbanner (Social Democrats), Schutzbund and Heimwehr (Social Democratic and Catholic reactionary paramilitary organizations in Austria)—fought in the streets, and the agony of the Weimar Republic reached crisis point.

It's puzzling that the lie about the 'Golden Twenties' could ever have been believed by later generations. This cannot be excused either by ignorance or by a lack of historical imagination. Instead, this fragile myth is nourished by a mixture of envy, admiration and kitsch: by envy of the vitality and admiration of the achievements of a generation of great talents, but also by cheap nostalgia. We watch the thousandth production of *The Threepenny Opera*, are astonished by the prices fetched by Beckmann, Schwitters and Schad in the auction houses, are full of enthusiasm for replicas of Bauhaus furniture and revel in films like *Cabaret* which show a hysterical, polymorphous perverse, 'disreputable' Berlin. A bit of decadence, a pinch of risk and a strong dose of avant-garde send pleasant thrills down the spines of the inhabitants of the welfare state.

This blossoming of a minority culture allows us to forget the swamp on which it flourished. Because the intellectual and artistic world of the 1920s was far from immune to the emotional excitement of civil war. Writers and philosophers like Martin Heidegger, Carl Schmitt or Ernst Jünger, but also Bertolt Brecht, Max Horkheimer and Karl Korsch, set the pathos of resolve against the faintheartedness of the political class—and it was quite secondary to them *what* one was resolved on. Their fellow-travellers, too, on the Right as on the Left, indulged in gestures of absoluteness.

Moderate politicians were unable to keep up— they appeared colourless and helpless, and entirely lacked the capacity to mobilize the fears, the resentments, the capacity for enthusiasm and the destructive energy of the masses. And so, without exception, they underestimated Hitler, who understood how to do that better than anyone else. In the end, there was nothing else the political class could do except manoeuvre between panic and paralysis.

A feeling of impotence led much of the population to take flight to extremes. People believed that protection and security were only to be found in organizations like the KPD (German Communist Party), the NSDAP, the Reichsbanner or the SA.   The masses swung between left and right, and the fluctuation between the two poles took on epidemic forms. Out of fear of isolation people sought the   collective—they fled to the community of the nation (*Volksgemeinschaft*) or Soviet Communism. Paradoxically, for many this flight ended in total isolation: in exile, in the concentration camps, in the purges, in the Gulag or in expulsion from their homes.

A posthumous conversation
with Kurt von Schleicher

E: General, thank you for receiving me.

S: I don't mind if you leave out the general. It's of no account any more. What is it you want to know?

E: You didn't write any memoirs.

S: You can have three guesses why not. A dead man doesn't write memoirs.

E: But he doesn't need to mince words either.

S: That's true.

E: It's about your friend Kurt von Hammerstein.

S: I see. Did you know him?

E: No. He only survived you by nine years.

S: Tell me more.

E: He knew that he had failed, but he never gave way to resignation nor did he ever go along with what was taking place.

S: That was just like him. Yes, you can say that we were friends. For a very long time. Like him, I was a cadet in Lichterfelde, then lieutenant in the 3rd Regiment of Guards, then military academy, Great General Staff and so on,

virtually the same career. One gets to know a
man that way. Hammerstein was someone who could
be relied on, he was down-to-earth, very intelligent and, above all, utterly loyal.

E: Which one cannot unreservedly say about you.

S   (laughs): Yes, if you like, we always played
different parts. An ideal team, really.

E: After the end of the World War, you were
transferred to the Army Ministry and took over
as head of the political section in the Troop
Office, an influential position, whereas
Hammerstein was sent to Lüttwitz.

S: Yes, to his straitlaced father-in-law. I
stayed in the Ministry.

E: You rose fairly rapidly there.

S: There was no one else there who could be
relied on.

E: By 1929, you were already major-general and
permanent undersecretary.

S: Well, Hammerstein didn't do so badly either. He
too was promoted in the same year, Chief of the
Troop Office, and the following year Chief of
Army Command. I made sure of that.

E: You?

S: One does what one can.

E: You were never exactly fastidious in these
matters.

S: What do you mean?

E: Cronyism, nepotism, patronage.

S: Nonsense! He was quite simply the right man.
Most of the old comrades from the war were
useless. Couldn't come to terms with the
republic and wanted to do nothing more than
organize *coups d'état*. And the young ones —
inexperienced, clumsy and full of hate. I only
need to say one word: Versailles! No prospects
of advance, no money for promotions. No, what
was needed was a cool head, someone with

General Staff experience, no dilettante and no adventurer! And if the right man was a friend — then all the better.

E: Nevertheless, neither the Left nor the national Right was pleased with the decision.

S: Do you think that bothered me? One has to let the mob howl.

E: Things are altogether a little awkward as far as your posthumous reputation is concerned, Herr von Schleicher.

S: That doesn't surprise me. What else do people still say about me?

E: It's said that you were a master of the political game. 'Desk general. Infantile recklessness. Polished and amusing smoking-room conviviality. Cunning and shrewd. Without inhibition.'

S: Who says that?

E: Blomberg, your successor as Defence Minister.

S: Just jealous. My own people saw me quite differently.

E: Well, who?

S: Hammerstein, for example. But also Eugen Ott. It was he, I think, who said, I was 'a good comrade with a warm heart, which he frequently hid under sarcasm'. And he wasn't the only one. Apart from him Ferdinand von Bredow, my man at military intelligence, and of course Erwin Planck as Undersecretary in the Reich Chancellery were my most important helpers. I could trust them, and they could also trust me.

E: That doesn't seem to have been the case with most others. You were opportunistic, unreliable, disloyal, is what I hear again and again. You pulled the strings behind the scenes and stayed out of the public eye yourself. 'A manhunter is about. His eyes sparkle ironically. It's as if there was a greenish veil in front of his iris. A deep line around his mouth suggests a great and far from innocuous reserve,'

writes a former SA leader, who fled from his
Führer after the June 1934 massacre. Presumably
before that he was once involved in negotiations with you. 'To be a leader of men,' you
advised him, 'you need not cheap scepticism,
but a degree of cynicism.'

S: Doesn't surprise me. But it's nice of you to
tell me all this. It's so long ago! Wouldn't
have thought posterity is interested in these
old stories. Go on, let's hear more!

E: Even more favourable observers were not without
their reservations with respect to you, Herr
von Schleicher. 'Cunning and very flexible,
sometimes erratically so,' writes Brüning.

S: Aha.

E: Admittedly, he allows that your position
shaped you, your constant dealings with the
secret service, the need to dissemble, and so
on. But, above all, he also commented on your
friendship with Hammerstein, and did so, I
would say, very sympathetically.

S: What does he say, then?

E: 'In terms of temperament, Schleicher was the
opposite of Hammerstein. Hence — as so often
in life — they got on very well together. Hammerstein was averse to politics in so far as
it was a matter of mere party tactics. In that
respect, he relied on Schleicher who felt like
a fish in water in politics but often had to be
brought back to a clear and calm course by Hammerstein. The latter brought everything back
to firm, simple lines, as a good General Staff
officer must. Schleicher was very sensitive,
had a quick and nimble imagination, was easily
offended and equally easily influenced. As a
result, he often made quite unpredictable
leaps. He sensed every danger, and silently
suffered from these dangers. Outwardly, that
is towards the officer corps, he hid it all
under a show of cynicism. Near him he needed a

Kurt von Schleicher, Heinrich Brüning,
Kurt von Hammerstein (left) in Wildbad, 1930

Kurt von Schleicher with Franz von Papen, 1932

calm, clear, steady character, such as Hammerstein's, on whom he could rely.'

S: Not bad. I would never have expected it from
Herr Brüning.

E: Well, you also had a hand in his fall. And,
before that, you had already cleared another
chancellor out of the way, the decent Hermann
Müller, to say nothing of your patron and superior Defence Minister Wilhelm Groener who considered you his 'political cardinal', which was
perhaps a mistake since you ousted him as well.

S: I'm supposed to have been that powerful? You're
turning me into an absolute Machiavelli.

E: I've got it all from the archives. And, in
Groener's place, you installed your own candidate, Herr von Papen, while always remaining
in the background. 'Who trusts you now?'
Groener wrote to you. 'Almost no one. The
riding whip manners have to stop. Hitler can
do that too. No one needs you for that.'

S: Spare me your Hitler.

E: It's not my Hitler.

S: I didn't even meet him until 1931.

E: At the time, you said he was 'an interesting
man with outstanding gifts as an orator. In
his plans he loses himself in higher spheres.
Then one has to pull him down to earth by the
coat-tails.' Unfortunately, the earth turned
out not to be so firm after all.

S: Who could know that then?

E: You're right there. There's a poem by Gottfried Benn in which he says: 'Easy to say:
wrong politics./ Wrong when? Today? After ten
years? After a hundred?' In your case, it
didn't take that long — less than a year was
needed to refute you. In 1932, you were convinced that you had great influence over
Hitler, indeed, that he was really enthusiastic about you and would do nothing against you
and the Reichswehr.

S: So?

E: Your friend and helper Erwin Planck, the son of the physicist, testified to that. And in August of the same year, you are even supposed to have recommended Hitler's chancellorship to Hindenburg.

S: I only proposed him in order to outmanoeuvre him. For a while, I even succeeded in doing so.

E: And then it was Papen's turn. In June 1932, you pressed him on Hindenburg behind Brüning's back. Others maintain you wanted to reintroduce the monarchy. Or was that only one of your jokes?

S: Much ado about nothing.

E: Nevertheless it's quite unbelievable all the things you instigated as a mere under-secretary. I wonder how you could have exercised such influence. Admit it, Papen was no more than your front man.

S: A conceited dandy! I soon regretted that I had made him a candidate.

E: Why didn't you take power yourself?

S: I never wanted to take the stage myself. You know, basically I always operated behind the scenes. I was familiar with the way military intelligence worked. That was of advantage to me in politics. Delicate matters should never be committed to paper. Remember that!

E: In the end, however, you did step out of the shadows, removed Papen and became Reich Chancellor yourself.

S: But only for a few weeks.

E: You were the first and only chancellor who didn't deliver his inaugural policy statement to the Reichstag but had it read out on the radio.

S: That's true. But by then the Reichstag didn't have much say any more. I certainly wouldn't

Erwin Planck, around 1932

Kurt von Schleicher, radio address, 1932

THE SILENCES OF HAMMERSTEIN

have been able to rely on it, anyway. Hindenburg had promised me it would be dissolved. I would then have been able to continue governing without a parliamentary majority. But, in the end, he dropped me. He came to an arrangement with Papen, that nonentity, behind my back. I was already finished on 22 January, and I resigned on the 28th.

E: Hammerstein, I think, didn't want to know about all your complicated manoeuvres. He was reluctant to be drawn into such political backroom business. 'As Chief of Army Command I had no reason to concern myself with politics during the 56-day government of Reich Chancellor Schleicher.'

S: Are those his exact words?

E: I find the way he relied on you quite touching, Herr von Schleicher. Defence Minister Groener, whose protégé you were and whose benevolence you repaid so meanly, used to say: 'Hammerstein, the apolitical soldier and huntsman, follows his friend Schleicher like a well-trained hound.'

S: That's nonsense. He had a strong character and knew very well what he wanted. But it's also true that my activities relieved him. 'Spare me your tricks,' he often said. In the last years of the republic, of course, that was no longer possible.

E: He always complained about the politicians. He wasn't suited to pulling strings behind the scenes.

S: No. Hammerstein was anything but the classic schemer. Not like me — that's what you're trying to say, isn't it?

E: I can't judge that. I'm only repeating what the historians say. For years, you tried to play off the destructive forces at work against one another. You thought you could bind Hitler and his people — those were your words weren't they? — and tame them by allowing them to take over the government. Your words!

S: You obviously enjoy rubbing it in. Yes, I thought I could take the wind out of the Nazis' sails by getting them involved in parliament. But one could only have eliminated them by force, and I didn't have the strength to do that.

E: And perhaps the conviction?

S: It's easy for you to talk, my friend! I tried to save what could be saved. Had a hopeless hand! In fact, Germany had already been ungovernable since 1930.

E: Is it true that, at the end of January, you negotiated with Hindenburg, without Hammerstein knowing anything about it?

S: Nonsense.

E: Even before Hitler's famous talk in Hammerstein's apartment, it was already settled that he would be deprived of power. That is, at least, what Brüning maintains.

S: Well, Brüning . . .

E: Your friend could hardly suspect what was going on in the background.

S: Well, perhaps suspect. But he never held my behaviour against me. A generous man, unlike myself.

Second gloss.
A tangle of manoeuvres and intrigues.

How the Weimar Republic came to an end is something historians have researched in every detail, from day to day, indeed from hour to hour. The files and the minutes have been sifted, the speeches collected, the diaries and memoirs analysed and the letters deciphered. Despite that, indeed perhaps even because of it, the more the non-expert becomes absorbed in the sources, the less he understands how it happened. It makes for dispiriting reading. One gets lost in an impenetrable jungle of rumours, backstairs gossip, intrigue and manoeuvring. Contradictions, versions, excuses and lies and propaganda wherever one looks. That's perhaps true of most of the unpredicted turning points of world history.

Rarely, however, is the helplessness of the political figures as evident as in this case. All of them, starting with President Hindenburg, who was no longer capable of formulating a clear thought, appear incomprehensibly weak and out of their depth, swinging irresolutely between hysteria, illusion and panic. But the executive politicians (Brüning, Schleicher, Papen, Meissner) and background figures (like Hugenberg or Gregor Strasser) also disappear in a jumble of speculations, vanities, wheeling and dealing and would-be clever calculations. Their half-hearted efforts to 'tame' the Nazi Party, attest to a blindness which in retrospect is hard to understand. In the end, parliament was sidelined by emergency decrees which effectively created a state of emergency, and presidential dictatorship was a fact. The army, which had never really supported the republic, adopted a supposedly 'apolitical' position, and those who were willing to defend the republic could never make up their minds to intervene—they were paralysed by fear of civil war which they wanted to avoid at all costs.

In the country as a whole, confidence in the institutions of the state had in any case been exhausted long ago, and the standing of the political class had sunk to zero. The economic situation was desperate. The streets were dominated by the militias, and the democrats, few enough in number, looked on at the terror—the Nazi SA alone had over 450,000 men—as if hypnotized.

The only actor who from the beginning had pursued a clear goal was Adolf Hitler. Everyone else, and not least the Communists, underestimated his destructive energy, his ruthlessness and his ability to mobilize the desperate masses.

Difficult times

General von Hammerstein not only had political worries but also private ones. His long absence in the war had affected his relationship with his children. After the birth of the fourth child, his wife was exhausted and, for the time being, did not want to risk any further pregnancy. Her husband, however, regarded the growth of the family more as something akin to a natural event. In a letter from the front, he described Maria's reservations as 'stuff and nonsense'.

It was the mother, however, who had to ensure the survival of the family. 'She felt lonely and was

overwhelmed by too much work and too many children, without help,' says her daughter Maria Therese.
It was their mother who made sure that the children
spent as much time as possible in the country where
at least there was enough to eat. That was hard enough
in the famine winters of 1917 and 1918. 'What was hap-
pening in the world didn't reach us children, although
it was the winter of the revolution. The adult world
didn't exist for us and we didn't exist for our father. It
was as if he hadn't returned from the war at all. He
was there again, almost without us noticing,' Maria
Therese was still complaining almost four decades
later.

Shortly afterwards she, like her elder sister Marie
Luise, was put in a 'stupid, backward convent school'
in Kassel.

> My father should have intervened and made
> sure that we weren't sent to this hidebound
> school, which we *had* to break out of. If he had
> realized that, he would have saved us and him
> a great deal of grief. But he didn't show the
> least bit of interest in us. He didn't talk to us.
> At the time the estrangement, even from my
> mother, which had arisen because of the war,
> was total.

In those years, the children were simultaneously
subject to the most curious social shifts and changes.
On the one hand, they received invitations to the
estates of aristocratic families acquainted with their

Maria and Kurt von Hammerstein,
summer 1914

parents, where, as in the case of Silesian relatives of the Lüttwitz clan, there were coach rides and horse-riding. 'As soon as I was big enough,' relates Maria Therese, 'I was sitting on a horse, without a saddle and without reins. All the old aunts came out to the meadow to give their expert opinions on me. I didn't know fear.' Often the children—there were by now three daughters and two sons—were guests of friends of their father, the von Asseburg-Neindorf family, at their castle near Magdeburg. On the other hand, they spent long months in rented village cottages where, in order to get by, hens and ducks were kept. (Hammerstein never owned a house.)

Under these circumstances, there could be no question of an aristocratic or even bourgeois upbringing. As was to be expected, Maria's father, old Lüttwitz, was very displeased: 'How Maria, without ever a word of complaint, resigns herself to the modest circumstances into which she has come through her marriage. Almost always without servants she as good as looks after her six children and the household alone.' Lüttwitz also missed in the daughters what he considered to be good manners. Instead, Maria von Hammerstein had got used to a great measure of independence.

In her memoirs, her second daughter Maria Therese, known as Esi, asks herself: 'After the end of the First World War, would [my father] rather have changed careers, like most of his friends? During the war, he twice had shingles, no doubt because of worry. At any rate, there was often talk of worry, never of the

Maria von Hammerstein with Marie Luise,
Maria Therese and Helga, around 1918

pain which was certainly also involved.'

In any case, one should not imagine the salaries of officers during the First World War as being too generous. The old soldier's adage held good: 'The King's coat keeps you warm, but it's tight.' In the Weimar Republic, things were no less frugal; first the inflation and, later, the economic crisis. It is said that, in the 1920s, the general nonchalantly travelled fourth class on his trips. 'In the early days we never had money,' relates Helga von Hammerstein.

> Ama [her mother] wasn't particularly good with money either. By the 20th of every month, the salary had been spent and then we had to get through the last ten days without [any money]. Once, in Kassel, as the inflation was starting, we took dried hare skins we had from hunting to a junk shop in the old town and sold them. Later on, fortunately, there were usually some aunts or uncles who helped us out. Such difficulties were always tackled very casually. In Berlin, when I once lost 100 marks—a huge sum then, with which I wanted to pay the monthly bill at the grocer's—my very wealthy godmother was informed, and I could fetch the money from her. Great relief!

For a long time, the rule at the Hammersteins' was that the older children had to look after the younger ones—no doubt, this contributed to their independence even if there were the usual rivalries. Each of the three sisters was charged with taking care of one of the brothers. Helga later maintained 'I had no youth,' because Franz was entrusted to her, a responsibility that she experienced as a burden.

The likeable chaos of this household only changed somewhat when Hammerstein was promoted to major-general. Lüttwitz, however, was still dissatisfied with the pattern of his son-in-law's life:

> We stayed with them in Hardenbergstrasse, in the house I had occupied as commander-in-chief. Whereas I, however, lived in state-rooms, now we had to make do with modest accommodation, because the Hammersteins only occupy about a quarter of the rooms which I had at my disposal then. Instead of coming in by the main entrance, we had to use the back stairs.

And not until Hammerstein advanced to Chief of Army Command in 1930 was old Lüttwitz to some degree satisfied, though still unable to let go of his prejudices:

> He has a large salary and a fine apartment, but he is now in a politically exposed position and, as a consequence of some mistakes made previously, was immediately closely scrutinized and attacked. I fear that the government of the Right, which is inevitably coming with time, will wring his neck as it will that of his friend and patron, Herr von Schleicher.

Indeed, at army headquarters in the Bendler-strasse, Hammerstein had at his disposal a personal chauffeur as well as the imposing official apartment spread over three floors. His offices, also intended for use on social occasions, were below; the floor above that was for the family; and in the attic was a refuge with its own entrance, where the three daughters were at home along with Fräulein Else Caspari from Osterburg (known as Pari), the indispensable wet-nurse and confidante who had been present at their births. Otherwise, they went from one castle to another and knew how to keep silent about all the family secrets into which they had been initiated.

Even at the Bendlerstrasse, Hammerstein stuck to his rather modest way of life. As before, there was a lack of servants. The mistress of the house is said to have burst into tears when they moved into the new home, out of fear of all the social obligations that came along with it. 'Invitations three times a day, changing, making conversation—it was a terrible strain.' A guest list which has survived leaves no doubt about that. On the one hand, half the *Almanach de Gotha* is represented, from Louis Ferdinand, Prince of Prussia, to the Stolbergs, Brühls, Dohnas and Hardenbergs; then, of course, the senior army officers and the politicians, starting with Hindenburg, Schleicher and Papen, followed by the ambassadors and envoys of almost all the powers represented in Berlin. Indicating that Hammerstein's position had a political weight which would be inconceivable for senior generals today. It is significant that the long list includes names from China and Egypt but not a single one from the Soviet Union. Evidently, the host exercised discretion in this respect. In any case he attached no great importance to prestige. Perhaps he preferred Herr von Arnswaldt to all their excellencies—the former was a head forester by trade and knew something about hunting.

So Maria von Hammerstein had charge of a complicated household. The inventory of the dining room alone is good evidence of that: 24 oak chairs, 48 oyster forks, 238 table knives, 133 sherry glasses, and so on and so on . . . If there were no official guests present, life was all the more homely. A relative remembers that, at the Hammersteins', there was often only sausages and potato salad to eat. Really, Maria already had enough to do. After all, she had to take care of the children. And, as far as the general was concerned, even if one loves them, indeed especially then, he may have thought that seven children—that's how many there were by then—were not always easy to bear in a house.

A large number of children, however, was more the rule than the exception in such aristocratic families. One was used to big houses in the country, where one went for the summer holidays. Both parents had many siblings—a tradition which has continued in the Hammerstein family to the present day.

Still, his work offered the general the possibility at any time of absenting himself from the family. In

Maria Therese, Helga, Ludwig,
Franz and Kunrat von Hammerstein,
about 1925

Kunrat, Hildur, Franz and Ludwig von Hammerstein,
around 1929

his office he was 'protected'—as it was put in those days. In the anteroom, his secretary, Margarethe von Oven, who was later to work for the 20th July conspirators, kept guard over him. He had hardly any idea what his daughters were up to. He did not know the worlds in which they moved.

Three daughters

The oldest of the daughters, Marie Luise, known as Butzi, was twenty-five in January 1933. Her sister, Maria Therese, was twenty-four. The third, Helga, had just turned twenty. The four youngest children, Kunrat, Ludwig, Franz and Hildur, were still at school.

Maria Therese had still picked up something of the roaring Twenties. There's a photo of her posing in the middle of a country road somewhere in Brandenburg, on her heavy new motorbike (owed to the generosity of a wealthy aunt): straddling the bike, hair in the wind, grasping the handlebars, elbows at shoulder height, she gazes at the viewer with a provocative smile.

But that's deceptive. In 1926, she had already followed the example of her older sister and joined a Wandervogel youth group. 'We go on walking tours with our rucksacks, until I drop half-dead. In the unheated youth hostels, we wash ourselves from top to bottom in icy water. We are Spartans, nothing else counts.' Youth movement, 'natural living', Rilke's call: 'You must change your life'—all of that was in accord with her idealistic leanings. Maria Therese had also come in contact with Anthroposophy quite early on.

But then her older sister decided that they were too old for the harmless excursions with the Wandervogel; one had to now be politically organized. It was not a need that Maria Therese, who 'didn't have a clue' about politics, felt; yet, just like Helga, the youngest sister, she followed this advice—a decision that proved momentous for all three.

Maria Therese had, very soon after joining, left the Catholic school, and took her leaving certificate at the liberal Auguste Viktoria Grammar School in Nürnbergerstrasse. That was also where she got to know her lifelong friend, Wera Levin. The latter's family was not religious but very interested in Zionism, the father a well-known Jewish doctor, cancer researcher and specialist in occupational illness. Wera also liked coming to the Hammersteins', until:

> one day she saw a big swastika on our front door. My brother Kunrat, who was then ten years old, had scrawled it there with chalk. Probably he had read too much of the *Völkischer Beobachter* which, in our home, was always in the waste-paper basket because Bechstein, the piano-maker, sent my father the Nazi paper for years. My relationship with Kunrat remained bad until I left Germany. He criticized everything I did. I was

Maria Therese, 1932/33

glad when I heard that later he risked his life in the resistance.

From that day, Wera never again came to us. We always met at her home in Fasanenstrasse. Dr Lewin played piano and Wera the violin. In his library, there was the whole of world literature. That was an entirely new phenomenon to me, because in my father's world no one talked about novels. On the walls were pictures by then still unknown painters, Klee and Kirchner. How different from our apartment!

From now on, Maria Therese also went to the concerts at the Singakademie on Unter den Linden, was interested in Max Reinhardt's theatre productions, listened to Bruno Walter, Wilhelm Furtwängler and Otto Klemperer in the old Philharmonic hall, learned Russian and read Leo Tolstoy; she is even said to have gone to some Yiddish theatre performances.

'Despite my friendship with Wera I still followed my political thread. I penetrated as far as [working-class] Neukölln, poked my nose into everything, but remained an outsider.' Nathan Steinberger, known as 'Nati', a Jewish Communist who later emigrated to Moscow, had got to know her in the Socialist School Students League. 'We met,' he said, 'at the railway station, camouflaged as a sports club in a pub, by the banks of the Spree or in the Girl's Grammar School on Weinmeister Strasse for what were called home afternoons, where outside speakers addressed pupils with revolutionary views.' He describes Maria Therese as 'silent, like a sphinx'. She went on extended trips with the School Students League

> to a nudist camp, which was very decorous, however. We slept in a tent with workers without being exposed to suggestive remarks of any kind. Nati, with whom I spend the night in the hay, loves me but I don't love him. I still see his sad face. I think he was studying philosophy.
>
> I read the Marxist classics, including Engels, also Ludwig Feuerbach, *The German Ideology* and even *Das Kapital*, and suddenly thought I understood the world, that I had found a key to understanding a mixed-up world. I had the feeling that with historical materialism I had firm ground under my feet, and was, for the first time, as happy again as I had been at fourteen when the world began to open up to me. For a while, I saw my parents and their friends principally as representatives of their class, and, although I was still living with them, I stopped taking part in their life.
>
> Above all, I avoided everything which to me seemed to smack of luxury—horse racing, for example, which until then I had loved very much. I did not want to be one of those people dancing at the edge of the precipice. Apart from my sisters and me, only the children of Berlin intellectuals felt the same way. So we were the black sheep.

Maria Therese, 1933

My father never asked about our school-friends or our teachers. Berlin was like a great ocean in which one could disappear. Did he know we wanted to explore the whole city and not only its western part? Or had he resigned? Did we feel the precipice at whose edge we were standing more than he did? It was an advantage that our absence usually went unnoticed, because the house was still full of little brothers and a little sister.

Living in two worlds which had nothing to do with one another was not so simple. Once, later on when I was afraid of the Gestapo—I had been summoned to the secret police's headquarters in Prinz Albrecht Strasse—I said to him that I had close Jewish friends. To which he replied: '*Personal* relations you can have.' By that he meant that only political relations were dangerous. That gave me strength. Not a word about me having to be more careful.

Maria Therese's enthusiasm for historical materialism soon waned; unlike her sisters, she missed a spiritual dimension in this doctrine, an aspect that mattered to her. Also she was not, in the long run, prepared to give up her independence and join a party.

She did not enjoy university—the lectures bored her. 'I didn't want to pore over old, venerable books. I wanted to live.' She travelled to Budapest, Barcelona and Prague and worked as a temporary teacher on a

Marie Luise von Hammerstein, around 1928

North Sea island. In 1932, her godfather, Kurt von Schleicher, found her a position as secretary in a mysterious office on Lützowplatz of which a certain 'Baron Roland' or 'Rolland' was in charge. It was said that he had been working for German military intelligence since 1914. Ostensibly, it was a Spanish import company trading in tropical and subtropical fruits but the place more resembled a political salon where mysterious people from the world of the intelligence services met each other. How far Maria Therese was initiated into what was going on is unclear. It's possible, however, that her sister Helga monitored her for information.

It wasn't Maria Therese's restlessness that worried the general, but the adventures of Marie Luise and her younger sister Helga. Even if he didn't betray anything, it had not escaped him that, by the standards of the family, the two of them were leading rather permissive lives.

What excited them was not the fashionable life of the metropolis. The slightly hysterical atmosphere of the late Weimar years had for them no appeal. Marie Luise was the first to take an interest in explicitly political questions. In an autobiographical statement that she composed in 1951, she writes: 'Through the youth movement escaped the feudal-bourgeois sphere of my birth, friendly contact with proletarians. Left the church at the age of 16.' In 1927, immediately after her school-leaving certificate, she began to study law at Berlin University and, as early as her first semester, became a member of the Communist Party. In the lecture theatre, she got to know a fellow student whom she liked. Werner Scholem was a Jew, a charmer and a man who could already look back on a long political career. One of the founders of the Spartakus League, member of the Reichstag and of the Politburo, and organization head of the Communist Party. Expelled as an 'ultra-leftist' in 1926, he at first withdrew from political work but, as a Communist without a party, remained true to his convictions. In 1927, he took up his legal studies once again. This is the period of his liaison with Marie Luise von Hammerstein. It speaks for the generosity and the inner freedom of the general that he passed over such a relationship in silence.

In addition to her university studies, which she concluded in 1931 with the state examination, Marie Luise also learned Russian and, from 1930, took on 'Party duties' (about which there will be more to say) which ultimately led to a police investigation. Influential friends of her father ensured that the inquiries were abandoned. After the Nazi seizure of power, however, the files fell into the hands of the Gestapo.

Marie Luise's sister Helga also confronted the family with all kinds of problems. The fact that she had no desire to complete her school-leaving certificate was the least of it. On the one hand, her mother set store by her daughters getting a good education; she suffered because as a young girl she had only been allowed to attend the convent school of the Ursulines in Breslau, but never to study. On the other hand, she was extremely liberal as far as school was concerned. 'We were allowed to play truant as often as we wanted,' relates Helga. 'We always got an excuse note from her, and she wasn't in the least interested in the details of our marks or how we looked.' Her father told everyone, 'My children are free republicans. They can say and do what they want.'—'Which is what we then did, which didn't always please him,' remarks Helga, who stopped attending school in spring 1930. Looking back from the 1950s Maria Therese is better able to appreciate Hammerstein's attitude: 'He had such unshakeable confidence in us, which is something I envy him for, now that I have children of the same age.'

He cannot always have found it easy. Helga, like Marie Luise, came in contact with Communism while she was still at grammar school in Charlottenburg, in Berlin. At first, it was relatively harmless. 'Although as a result of Marxist theory and ideology, which we followed, we knew it all as far as the development of world history was concerned, we accepted Papus's analyses of the present, his characterization of politicians and situations.'

But it didn't stay that way. In May 1928, on a trip with the Socialist School Student's League, Helga fell in love with a man who called himself Leo Roth. If her parents believed that this was no more than a harmless crush of a fifteen-year-old (who in the family was always called 'the delicate little one'), then they had underestimated Helga's seriousness and her strength of will.

Roth, the son of a Jewish clothes dealer from Rzeszów in Polish Galicia, who had emigrated to Berlin before the First World War, was expelled from school several times and had completely fallen out with his authoritarian father. A rebel by nature, at the age of thirteen he had already joined a Jewish youth organization; he started an apprenticeship as a mechanic, because he wanted to emigrate to Palestine, where there was a shortage of good craftsmen. By 1926, at the latest, he had turned to Communism and joined the Communist Youth Organization (KJVD). From the very beginning, he was involved in the movement's faction-fighting. Political instruction, changing party lines, splinter groups, cliques, suspicion and accusations were inescapable on the militant Left. In that same year, Roth became a follower of Karl Korsch the Marxist theorist, also Brecht's teacher, was declared a 'Trotskyist' and expelled from the youth organization of the KPD; three years later, in October 1929, he was readmitted because the Party could make use of him. He had broken off all contact with his family, and, from then on, he was a professional revolutionary holding a position in the 'Apparat', the section of the Communist Party which operated illegally.

So what was this legendary apparatus or organization for? As a reminder: in Lenin's time, the Soviet Union placed its hopes in the Communist revolution also taking place in the West. To this end, the Third International, also known as the Comintern, was set up in Moscow. Subsequently, it gathered together up to sixty parties. Dominated from the start by the Bolsheviks, the following goals were laid down in its statutes: 'the overthrow of capitalism, the establishment of a dictatorship of the proletariat and the creation of an international Soviet republic and the complete annihilation of all classes'.

Among the foreign Communist parties at that time, the KPD was considered the most important; it had many loyal supporters in Germany and a substantial representation in parliament. In Moscow, a 'German October' was already planned for 1923, but an attempted uprising in Hamburg was a sorry failure. The Comintern had instructed the parties outside the Soviet Union to set up parallel illegal apparatuses under military discipline—these were financed by Russian gold roubles and the sale of diamonds from the Kremlin treasure.

Under Stalin, the Comintern developed into the controlling body of the movement. Its nerve centre was the Executive Committee, usually known as the ECCI, which also maintained its own intelligence, spy and sabotage organization. The Red Army, which of course had its own classic secret service, the Fourth Section, to some extent pursued separate interests and employed its own agents, whereas the Comintern, particularly in Germany, worked with the German party's 'military apparatus'. Rivalries and petty jealousies, such as often occur in espionage work, were inevitable. Nevertheless, their activities were complementary, particularly in the fields of industrial and military espionage.

The Comintern ran its own military academy in Moscow, which instructed KPD cadres in radio and code techniques and in the use of weapons and explosives for future insurrections. From 1930, Leo Roth worked in this M-Apparat, as it was called, which was directly answerable to the Politburo and outwardly carefully separated from the Party.

And Helga? According to the family story, she had then 'already broken the rules'. In plain words, she had, at seventeen, left the family home and moved in with her boyfriend Leo Roth in the Polish-Jewish Scheunenviertel of Berlin. Like Roth, who had been born in the *shtetl*, she wanted to take leave of the milieu from which she came. In 1929, shortly after she got to know Roth, she became a member of the youth organization of the KPD; in May 1930, she joined the Party. From that moment on, she bore the cover name Grete Pelgert.

Official duties

Opinions of Hammerstein's qualities as commander-in-chief are divided. Some talk of a gulf between 'office' and 'front'; of him being more a political than a soldierly general; of the lack of close contact with the garrisons; of his interest in the men and their concerns being extremely limited.

Leo Roth. Passport photo taken before 1933.
From a Gestapo photo album of members
of the M-Apparatus

The opinions of those who knew him from his service during the First World War are quite different. His brother-in-law, Smilo von Lüttwitz, said this of him:

> I have never again encountered a General Staff officer who derived such a clear idea of the overall situation from the frequently contradictory reports of the units, and was then able so succinctly to sum up in a brief order, in a manner comprehensible to all, the measures needed to address it. The whole thing was often a matter of a few minutes, in which he worked with absolute calm and composure, and without allowing himself to be distracted in the least by telephone calls or excited people coming into the room. Hammerstein was the stabilizing influence on this staff. The trust in him was based simply on his outstanding ability, his clear, very concrete assessment of the situation.

The numerous official trips and tours of inspection that he undertook as Chief of Army Command also speak for themselves, and his connections from the First World War, like his close contacts with the intelligence services, meant that he was always very well informed.

Nonetheless, he was accused of 'excessive indolence and an unusual degree of aversion to normal work'. (Even at the age of twenty, when he received his first commission, his report stated that he was 'of productive indolence'.) General Hermann Foertsch, a major in the Defence Ministry before 1933, accused at Nürnberg of war crimes but acquitted, appointed by Konrad Adenauer as an adviser on the setting up of the new West German armed forces in 1955, commented in retrospect on Hammerstein's departure from his post as follows:

> On the one hand, political reasons, opponent of the National Socialists out of a proper recognition of the extremism of the movement. In addition, there was the fact that H. was a man who shied away from any normal kind of work. He was brilliant, shrewd, casual also in outward appearance, very critical, a little pessimistic (bone idle), so that the impending tasks with respect to the army demanded a different personality. Not only political reasons. In the first instance, Hitler, then certain circles in the army, who said that brilliance alone wouldn't do.
>
> Hammerstein came from the same regiment as Schleicher, was a close friend. He was furthermore branded a republican. [Before taking up his post in 1930] he is supposed to have said: 'For heaven's sake, Schleicher, don't do that, then I'll have to do some work.' The National Socialists rightly saw in him an intellectually far superior opponent and a sceptical, mocking observer of their words and deeds. No one expected this general to be long in command under Hitler.

Schwerin von Krosigk, Finance Minister under Hitler and sentenced as a war criminal at Nürnberg, wrote after the war:

> Experts say he was one of the best strategic talents of the German army. He was only able to display this talent in war games and on manoeuvres. That bored him. So, the higher he rose, a failing in him appeared ever more prominent: Hammerstein was lazy—there is no other more polite way of putting it. He himself was aware of it and justified the trait by saying that every man in a leadership position must have the courage to be lazy. But he overdid the rest necessary to collecting one's thoughts when he, a passionate huntsman, went hunting from late summer well into the winter, only turning up in Berlin from time to time like a passing comet. We were neighbours in Dahlem. When I met him on the street in 1933, after his removal [actually 1934], and asked him what he was going to do with himself, he replied that he would now make hunting and fishing his principal occupations. I knew him well enough to be able to respond: 'So not much will change in your daily life,' and he had enough of a sense of humour to laugh.

Efforts to retain his post were not in Hammerstein's line; he abhorred the idea of lobbying Hitler, Goering or Blomberg. He went his own straight way, kept to the direction he had recognized as imperative, and didn't care if he found favour or disfavour.

In his memoirs, Erich von Manstein, later Field Marshal, also sentenced as a war criminal in 1949 and, like General Foertsch, subsequently an adviser on the setting up of the West German army, assessed Hammerstein as follows:

> Like me, he had come from the Third Regiment of Foot Guards and was, next to General von Schleicher, who had also served in our regiment, probably one of the cleverest people I've ever met. The saying 'Regulations are for the stupid,' by which he meant all average people, was his and was characteristic of the man. He would have been an outstanding commander in wartime. As Chief of Army Command in peace time, he lacked a feeling for the importance of detail just as he viewed 'diligence' with a feeling of pity, since this virtue was indispensable to the average person. He himself made modest use of it, something he could also afford to do given his quickness of mind and his keen intelligence. His military talent was complemented by a markedly clear political judgement, formulated on the basis of a sober examination of the political situation and its conditions. He probably had less time for the imponderables of psychological factors. From the start, his mental attitude, related to the fact that his whole frame of mind was that of a grand

Kurt von Hammerstein as Chief of Army Command

seigneur, inevitably made him a firm opponent of the clamorous National Socialists.

All his military collaborators also agree that,
while he didn't love paperwork, he had the rare gift of
grasping situations with lightning speed and in an
uncomplicated way and of expressing his thoughts
in writing with classic brevity. To his adjutant, as
Hammerstein's son Ludwig notes, he characterized
the mode of working of a commander-in-chief, like
this: 'Free yourself of work on the details. Make sure
you have a few clever people for that. But leave yourself plenty of time to have ideas and to be quite clear
in your own mind. Only then can you lead properly.'

Once, when he was asked according to what crite-
ria he judged his officers, he said:

I divide my officers into four groups. There
are clever, diligent, stupid and lazy officers.
Usually two characteristics are combined.
Some are clever and diligent—their place is
the General Staff. The next lot are stupid and
lazy—they make up 90 per cent of every army
and are suited to routine duties. Anyone who
is both clever and lazy is qualified for the
highest leadership duties, because he possesses the intellectual clarity and the compo-
sure necessary for difficult decisions. One
must beware of anyone who is stupid and
diligent—he must not be entrusted with any
responsibility because he will always cause
only mischief.

There is an English translation of these maxims, which turned up in a surprising place. Eric M. Warburg was an American officer detailed to a secret command post of the British army, navy and air force, which had established itself on Lord Latimer's estate in Buckingham-shire. 'I was not a little surprised,' he reports, 'when I saw in big letters on the wall behind the desk of the duty officer a quote from Colonel General von Hammerstein: "*I divide my officers into four groups*" '. . . In the middle of the war, the British had adopted the principles of a German General Staff officer.

Cover-up

While front-stage the Communists had been planning the German Revolution since 1919, instigating uprisings and denouncing German militarism, in the background the Red Army was collaborating closely with the Reichs- wehr. Karl Radek, arrested in February 1919 as the Bolsheviks' emissary, received German officers in his cell and made the first contacts. One year later, then Chief of Army Command, General von Seeckt, argued that help in building up a new German army could not be expected from the victors but only from Bolshevik Russia: 'Germany and Russia are dependent on each other, as they were before the war. And if Germany allies itself with Russia it cannot be defeated. If Germany opposes Russia, then it loses the only hope in the future that is left to it.' Seeckt dispatched his old friend Enver Pasha, former Turkish Minister of War living in exile in Berlin, to Moscow. He reported that Trotsky supported cooperation with Germany and was even prepared to accept Germany's eastern borders of 1914. One year later, Lenin approached Berlin with a request for help in building up the Red Army.

The first serious negotiations took place in autumn 1921, and were, of course, top-secret. In 1922, a Special Group R was set up in the Defence Ministry and provided with an undeclared budget of 250 million Reichsmark. In summer 1923, the head of the Soviet air force signed an agreement with Generals von Seeckt and von Schleicher in Berlin to expand the Russian armaments industry and to produce war matériel for Germany. Beyond that, it concerned participation in manoeuvres, General Staff training of Russian officers with their German colleagues, and the development and testing of new weapons, particularly of the air and tank forces. Allegedly also present at the signing were Karl Radek, Kurt von Hammerstein and Ferdinand von Bredow. On the General Staff, which outwardly was not allowed to bear that designation, a secret headquarters was set up, which took over the planning and worked out the system of deception in every detail.

Radek, at that time still on the Executive Committee of the Comintern, bluntly explained to the German ambassador in Moscow: 'I am convinced that the

Soviet government can work together well with a German reactionary government. That is also the wish of General von Seeckt, who has declared that it is necessary to throttle the Communists in Germany but to make common cause with the Soviet Union.'

The successes did not fail to materialize. In 1927, the Soviet ambassador in Berlin wrote to the Foreign Ministry in Moscow:

The attendance at German manoeuvres and the lectures at the German academies are useful to us. All the military people, without exception, who have come here have confirmed that. What we offer the Germans in exchange costs us nothing, since they pay for everything themselves, and, in the depths of the Soviet Union, it is easy to find a place for every kind of school and other small German training establishments.

The installations concerned could hardly be described as small. At an air base near Lipezk, 120 German pilots and 100 observers were trained between 1925 and 1933 and 100 fighter planes from the Junkers and Fokker plants tested. The Tomka base at Wolsk on the Volga served, from 1929, for joint 'special tests' to develop gas and chemical weapons for combat use. Stresemann, the leading German statesman of the short stable period of the Weimar Republic, had already declared himself in agreement with this project years ago. Internally, the Reichswehr invented the cover names 'Refinement of Chemical

Raw Materials' and 'Development of Pesticides' for these secret experiments. A school for tank troops was set up in Kazan, and the German Defence Ministry established a headquarters office in Moscow to direct these activities.

The military alliance of convenience was on both sides based on a quite clear calculation of interest. The Versailles Treaty had imposed a number of restrictions on Germany: the armed forces limited to 100,000 men (while France alone maintained a million men under arms), no air force, no tanks, no submarines, no chemical weapons, no heavy artillery, no General Staff, no universal conscription. The Soviet Union for its part was militarily weakened after the civil war and did not have a modern arms industry. The training of senior officers also left something to be desired. Both powers were internationally isolated: Germany because of the defeat of 1918; the Soviet Union as a pariah state and country of origin of the 'Communist menace'. In foreign policy, their cooperation was aimed above all at France but also against a Poland resurrected after a long period of partition and which had inflicted a heavy defeat on Soviet forces in 1920. Polish fears of a new dismemberment of their country were by no means unjustified, as would be demonstrated in 1939.

The diplomatic guarantee of Russo-German cooperation was provided in 1922 by the Treaty of Rapallo. Four years later, Social Democratic politicians opposed to the treaty leaked information about the secret military collaboration to the Berlin correspondent of the *Manchester Guardian*. Publication led to heated debates. In the Reichstag, Philip Scheidemann, also in the SPD, confirmed the existence of the agreements; his speech led to a vote of no confidence and the fall of the Social Democratic-led government. In part, the right-wing parties were enraged because of the prohibited brotherhood in arms with the Bolsheviks; in part, they saw in its disclosure a 'bottomless pit of treason'. The KPD resorted to denial and described all those who talked of a cooperation between the Red Army and the Reichswehr as 'slanderers of the Russian proletariat'. The Western powers kept in the background; presumably their secret services had long known all about the treaty-breaching activities of the German army. Finally, Stresemann declared the cooperation to be a military policy necessity. He had recognized that it was vital to the German armed forces—without modern air and tank forces, they would have been in a completely hopeless position in any conflict. In spite of the protests, the illegal activities of the Reichswehr were resumed and even considerably expanded.

On the Russian side, it was stated that 'the German army is a force whose command structure possesses the traditions of the best army of the world war. This alone forces us to value highly the contact with it, all the more so, since until now it's the only air-hole for the Red Army, its window to Europe.'

Between 1924 and 1932, groups of high-ranking Soviet officers repeatedly visited Germany. Mikhail Tukhachevsky, for example, later Marshal of the Soviet Union, came to Germany several times between 1923 and 1932. As Joachim von Stülpnagel relates, the Russian guests 'usually spoke fluent German and were astonishingly well-versed in military history. Every one of them had studied the works of Clausewitz.'

In the Moscow military archive, there is a report by the Leningrad Chief of Staff, Feldman, about just such a visit to manoeuvres, in which prominent commanders of the Red Army participated. 'Everywhere,' it states, 'in the car, during the exercise, at table—Tukhachevsky was always in the place of honour.' There follow details about the course of the manoeuvres and about the deployment of units. Hindenburg and Schleicher turned up at an Oder crossing-point; they were also present at the manoeuvre critique.

Likewise, many senior German officers, among them Generals von Blomberg, Adam, von Brauchitsch, Paulus, von Manstein, Keitel and Guderian, travelled to Russia. One of the Red Army's most important guests was Kurt von Hammerstein.

A strange pilgrimage

In August 1929, Hammerstein travelled to Russia in strict secrecy for a lengthy tour of inspection, to

Red Army manoeuvre visit in Germany, early 1930s.
Tukhachevsky to the left of Hindenburg (*back to the camera*)

conduct negotiations and to be present at joint manoeuvres. Even on the boat from Stettin to Leningrad he had to travel incognito. Also on the ship, incidentally, was Max Hoelz, a famous workers' leader, who had organized an armed uprising in the impoverished Vogtland in Saxony in 1920. Sentenced to life imprisonment, he had only been allowed to emigrate to the Soviet Union after an amnesty. He came on board, as Hammerstein writes, 'accompanied by several hundred supporters. Leave-taking with the Internationale and police surveillance.' (Hoelz was probably murdered by the GPU in 1933.)

Hammerstein's letters to his wife reveal that he very much enjoyed his stay in Russia: 'Both in Petersburg as here [in Moscow] I was received at the ship or the railway station by the heads of the Operations Section of the General Staff of the Military Districts.' The most important address for him was 'Headquarters Moscow' on Vorovskogo Street, the secret office of the Reichswehr which supervised all the training and test facilities in the interior of Russia. Two German officers there looked after the delivery of matériel, took care of cash transfers and guided the many German officers through the Russian provinces.

The planning for Hammerstein's three-month stay was perfect.

> For rail journeys, I have for the whole time a very good saloon car with sleeping compartments and kitchen with attendants provided

by the Russian government. Usually, the People's Commissar of Transport travels in it. The carriage is so fine that later on, in the eastern towns and on manoeuvres in the Ukraine, we'll simply go on living in it. Once a day there's sure to be caviar, often twice.

By way of Nizhni Novgorod, Kazan and Samara, he went on to the test and military training area in Tomka on the Volga and to Saratov.

Deepest and remotest Russia. But then a Russian training area of 500 square kilometres, dimensions which are astonishing. Everywhere I arrive, the appropriate senior Russian specialist from Moscow is already there; on the one hand to negotiate, on the other hand to supervise. Today, before my departure, I still have a difficult discussion with one of the smartest minds from Moscow. But I have already become good friends with him and will probably get the better of him.

The trip, which is recorded in a private photo album, took Hammerstein back to Germany via Kharkov, Sebastopol, Yalta, Odessa and Istanbul.

In his letters to his family, the general's Russian visit appears harmless but his intentions in connection with it were far-reaching. He thought it 'foolish and dangerous' if Germany of all countries were to refuse the Soviet Union that equality of status which France and Britain did not wish to grant it. 'As much as we reject and oppose the revolutionary endeavours,

Germany must at the same time not forget that Moscow is home not only to the Communist International but in the first instance to the government of Russia, which even today remains an economic and political factor, which every European state has to take into account.'

General Kliment Voroshilov, later Marshal of the Soviet Union, with whom Hammerstein negotiated on his trip, was entirely of the same opinion. Extracts from a secret transcript of a conversation on 5 September 1929 speak volumes about the harmony which was achieved there.

VOROSHILOV: I am interested in your overall impression of this trip.

HAMMERSTEIN: My impression is that much remains to be done here. But the work was begun with a great deal of idealism.

VOROSHILOV: I don't want to disguise the fact that there were some points of friction in our relationships, but, on the whole, the results were positive. You, General, I welcome as a man who has a good relationship with the Red Army. That's why we don't need to waste time talking about trust or distrust but about whether we can find new additional ways of further concretizing our relations.

HAMMERSTEIN: In spring, we plan to carry out tests with new tanks. We will train ten participants in the course in tank technology in German factories and deliver the tanks.

VOROSHILOV: I know that, as a consequence of the Versailles Treaty, Germany is not allowed to manufacture any tanks. The USSR is not bound by any treaties, and we can make tanks not only for ourselves but also for others. We would also like to establish good relations with German industry so that, in the near future, we can get technical support for our army.

HAMMERSTEIN: It also has to be taken into consideration, however, that the German companies are carrying out their work in contravention of the Versailles Treaty, so that, to mention only one example, Krupp is anxious that it should not be harmed as a result.

VOROSHILOV: We believe that the German chemical industry is unsurpassed in the world. Do you intend to acquaint us with the new chemical weapons which the Reich has at its disposal?

HAMMERSTEIN: The pace of supply and research into these weapons in particular is of primary importance. None of us knows when a war can break out. We intend to intensify research activity in Tomka and to enlarge the technical base.

VOROSHILOV: Just a couple of words on political questions. Our starting point must be the fact that, in socio-political terms, our two states are antipodes. But it is quite superfluous to involve the Third International or the Party in our quite practical relations. One does not have to love the Bolsheviks, but one should respect our people who are conducting a life-and-death struggle for survival.

To the Politburo, the marshal justified his line in terms of the 'systematic and total exploitation of the German military and technicians to increase the fighting power of the Red Army'.

At the German Foreign Office, for that very reason, Hammerstein made few friends with his 'Eastern course'. He was fiercely attacked in the nationalist press. He didn't let himself be swayed by that and stuck to his views until he left his post. At the end of 1932, he told Jacob Wuest, the American military attaché in Berlin, what he thought of the Red Army, an assessment that was to be proved right ten years later.

> It is a good force, disciplined and well-trained, which will fight well when it is on the defensive and can count on the support of the Russian population. The Russians know that they cannot conduct a war of aggression, because they lack the necessary infrastructure. The roads and railways are in such bad condition that they can only fight within the borders of their own country. They have prepared for that and established two zones of defence, one around Moscow and the other in the Urals at Perm. If they are pushed that far back, they can maintain themselves for an unlimited period of time in these regions. They only need to withdraw—then, no enemy can defeat them.

There was a final meeting with Soviet officers on 1 July 1933(!). Hammerstein held a reception for them in the Hotel Kaiserhof and declared that the Reichswehr would 'continue to be prepared to cultivate such a fruitful military exchange'. In June, he had to order the winding-up of the Lipezk flying school, and, by September 1933, all the German bases in Russia had been shut down.

A veteran's story

It would be wise to treat the stories of the illegal activities of the general's daughters with a certain amount of scepticism. The following report by Comrade Hermann Dünow is good evidence of that. Dünow had been working for the KPD's intelligence service from 1923 until he was arrested in December 1933. Two years later, he was sentenced to life imprisonment and did not get out of prison until 1945, after which he played a part in building up the Volkspolizei (People's Police) of the GDR.

In his memoirs, he relates the following about the infiltration efforts of the Party's M-Apparatus:

> With the help of a young comrade we picked (student at Berlin University), we were able to get to know the three daughters of General von Hammerstein-Eckurt [!], the head of the Reichswehr. With the help of this comrade, we succeeded in politically convincing these three girls so that they became secret members of the Communist Youth Organization. I then got them into the Party Congress in Wedding, as guests. With the help of these girls, we had access to General von Hammerstein-Eckurt's safe. There we could, at our leisure, take out the secret documents, photograph them and put them back again, so that nothing was noticed. Then, one fine day, on the basis of this material the Communist Deputy Kippenberger spoke in the Reichstag

about the Black Reichswehr, etc. By chance, in the early morning of that day, General Hammerstein had destroyed these documents —torn them in little pieces and thrown them in the waste-paper basket. The cleaning woman then put them in the dustbin, which was emptied at about 11. At 2 p.m. of the same day, Deputy Kippenberger spoke in the Reichstag about this Black Reichswehr. That very evening, a conversation took place between General Hammerstein-Eckurt and a General von Stülpnagel, the two were very good friends, in which General Hammerstein expressed his admiration for the Communists' organizational talents. He said that the Communists might be unpleasant fellows but organizing was something they could do. He was full of admiration—at 11 a.m. he had seen the dustmen taking the stuff away, and at 2 p.m. Deputy Kippenberger was already speaking on the subject!

Virtually nothing in this cock-and-bull story is correct. Quite apart from the fact that the author is not even capable of spelling the general's name properly, the term Black Reichswehr is ambiguous to say the least. Originally, it meant the paramilitary formations, the Freikorps above all, of the early years of the Weimar Republic, which Hammerstein had nothing at all to do with. As far as the Communist Youth Organization is concerned, Dünow has completely invented the recruitment of the three daughters by one and the same 'young student'. In his memoirs, he maintains that, before his arrest, he had been in charge of the KPD's intelligence service. That, too, is not true. Anyone who believes the memoirs, related in old age, of veteran comrades without checking them has no one to blame except themselves.

Herr von Ranke's adventure

Someone who really did meet Helga von Hammerstein at that time was called Hubert von Ranke and was related to the great historian Leopold von Ranke. His life, full of abrupt changes of direction, would be worth a study in itself. At the age of nineteen he joined the Freikorps Oberland and participated in the storming of the Annaberg in Silesia; after that he worked for a number of years for Lufthansa and its precursor companies. In 1932 he was recruited by Hans Kippenberger, the head of the KPD's military organization. His code name was 'Moritz' His wife, also willing to cooperate and said to have had important social and family connections, was given the name 'Olga'.

It was important to the Apparatus that such sympathizers kept silent about their relationship with the KPD or even apparently broke off contact with it again. These people, according to Kippenberger, concerned themselves with contacts which the Party could not otherwise reach:

Government offices, business and industrial circles, diplomats, party leaders, military departments. Special circles had to be established for that or salons exploited or brought into being and 'names with a ring to them' put to use. Over the years, a group of comrades had come into being whose members could be successfully deployed in this branch of the Apparatus's work.

(Incidentally Heinrich Blücher, later husband of Hannah Arendt, also worked for Kippenberger. The historian Reinhard Müller is preparing a detailed study of this activity, which Blücher passed over in silence in his—unpublished—account 'An Average Life'.)

If it proved that they had not yet exposed themselves too greatly with their Party membership (with respect to their previous milieu), they received the instruction to detach themselves once again from the general Party organization. That often involved great psychological difficulties, and a certain skill was required to keep them in line. The most difficult thing was to prevent them thinking that the Party regarded and used them as agents.

In 1933, Ranke was arrested for a short time. His secretary had seen Marxist literature in his desk and betrayed him. His father, an elderly officer, came to see Himmler in Berlin and secured his son's release.

After that, Ranke lived illegally in Berlin for a while. But Kippenberger thought it better that he leave Germany immediately—it was likely that he would be accused of high treason—and sent him to Paris where he was placed in charge of the external base of the intelligence apparatus.

Kippenberger's secretary and long-time companion had been born into an aristocratic family by the name of Lenderoth, but, as the divorced wife of a Communist provincial MP, she bore the name Anna Kerff. She used the cover names Lore or Christine Brunner, and, long after Kippenberger's death, married a Bulgarian who had suffered as she had; from then on, she signed herself Christina Kjossewa. This throng of names is characteristic of the chaos in which she and her comrades lived. Lore then—let's stick with that name—relates of Ranke's first exile:

> On our arrival [in Paris], half-starving, we found one of our earlier, most valuable agents, Hans Hubert von Ranke, who had been in charge of flight arrivals and departures at Tempelhof Airport. He knew all about the illegal build-up of the German Luftwaffe after the First World War. Naturally, we immediately struck up a friendship. He told us that he knew a circle of well-placed people—French anti-Fascists, who invited him for dinner from time to time. He spoke fluent French. Moritz offered to talk to the daughter of the Norwegian writer Bjørnstjerne Bjørnson, and

Hubert von Ranke, about 1930

ask whether she was willing to put us up for a couple of days. We lived with her for a while. It was all very grand. In other ways, too, he was very helpful to us.

In 1936, with Herbert Wehner's agreement, Ranke went to Spain as one of the first volunteers. There, he was deployed on the Aragon Front and in the Republican Secret Service. In 1938, he broke with the Communist Party. After the outbreak of the Second World War, he was in Paris again, this time working for the French intelligence service. Then he fled from the Germans to North Africa; later, he went underground in the unoccupied zone of France and joined the Resistance as an expert in conspiratorial techniques. After the Liberation, he once again served as an officer in the French secret service. He did not return to Germany until 1960.

This biography, rich in dangerous twists and turns, is related here because Ranke is one of the few witnesses who can say something from the early 1930s about Leo Roth and Helga Hammerstein, known as Grete.

Soon after our first meeting at Hallesches Tor [Halle Gate, a district in Berlin] in 1931, Alex, alias Kippenberger, phoned me again, to arrange a meeting with Rudi, one of his people. His real name was Leo Roth. After that, Rudi became my immediate contact man, a friend; he remained so until his recall

Leo Roth, Moscow 1936

to Russia. Grete, his companion at the time, is probably one of the few survivors.

[Leo] looked very Jewish, was always impeccably dressed, invariably wore leather gloves and usually named vegetarian restaurants, cafes, cake shops or secluded bars as rendezvous. He had got to know his companion, Grete, whom I did not meet at first, in the Socialist Youth Organization. Once, we were walking past the Kaiser Wilhelm Memorial Church, when Rudi pointed to the spire and said he had worked up there as a roofer. To look at him, one would really never have connected him with such a job.

Entrance of a lady from Bohemia

Neindorf Castle near Magdeburg, with its big park and its pheasant-run, had been a familiar refuge for the Hammerstein children since their childhood. They particularly liked to spend their summer holidays at the castle, where there were other children of the same age. The master of the house, Maximilian von Asseburg-Neindorf, known as 'Uncle Max', was an old friend of the general, who had already been a guest there with his parents when he was young and had gone hunting hares.

On New Year's Eve 1930, at Neindorf Castle, Ruth von Mayenburg 'met an elderly gentleman in evening dress, tall and very good-looking, just the way I loved elderly gentlemen, for whom I've always had a weakness'. She was the daughter of a Bohemian mining director from Teplitz-Schönau. As she says, she 'was not a good girl' and didn't want to put up with the 'aristocratic nonsense'. She went to Vienna, where, in the 1920s, there were many points of contact between *bohème* and left-wing politics. The parallels with Helga Hammerstein's Berlin experiences are evident.

There was no mention of any of that when she appeared at Neindorf; on the contrary, her hosts had prepared everything for a union appropriate to her rank with a son of the house. In her memoirs, she writes:

> The Asseburgs had invited me, and it was as good as settled that in the evening I would become engaged to Axel [the son], so that our relationship would assume the 'socially correct' form. I was getting ready for the occasion and, in an evening dress of grey taffeta, a rose in my belt, preparing to take flight into the security of an existence where the demands of the time were only distantly audible. A melancholy thought. I was not in a very cheerful mood as I stood in front of the dressing mirror and looked myself in the eye.
>
> When there was a knock at the door, I thought Axel had come to take me to the dinner table. But it was my neighbour from the

next room, Kurt Baron von Hammerstein-Equord, General and Chief of Army Command, an old friend of the Asseburgs. He was somewhat ill at ease as he entered (does he want to make an advance?) and intervened in a lifetime decision. He immediately went to the heart of the matter: he would think it a misfortune if Axel and I were to marry. He liked the lad, felt somehow partly responsible for his further fate; I was not the right woman for him. I should think the matter over carefully and also consider that I myself would not be happy in such a tradition- conscious German-national atmosphere. 'You are much too headstrong. A lively, impetuous spirit. I like you, I've taken to you. Excuse me, for meddling in your life, but I considered it my human duty to tell you that.' Then he embraced me, kissed my cheek and went out.

So at midnight no engagement was celebrated with popping champagne corks. Hammerstein winked at me in acknowledgement, and later when we went to our neighbouring rooms I invited him in for a little conversation, which laid the foundation of our later, rather dangerous friendship. We talked about hunting.

Ruth von Mayenburg

A posthumous conversation
with Ruth von Mayenburg (I)

M: Nice of you to visit me. As you see, since my
    second husband departed, I am all alone in
    this old-fashioned apartment. You'll have a
    cup of my ginger tea, won't you? You know, I
    swear by it. The best cure for depression. On
    the Naschmarkt here in Vienna there's a stand
    that always has fresh ginger. You should never
    use powder for it. Chop it small, brew it up
    and let it infuse for five minutes. And now
    tell me, what brings you to me.

E: Your friendship with Kurt von Hammerstein.

M: A wonderful man. I was almost a little in love
    with him. He once saved me from a marriage
    which would have brought me nothing but har-
    mony, security and boredom.

E: You wrote about it in your memoirs. I have
    read every line of your books.

M: You're a writer and you know how much one
    likes to hear that. But how did you get on to
    that subject?

E: It's a very long and a very German story. You
    met Hammerstein at the Asseburgs'.

M: Yes. We were both friends of theirs. Hammer-
    stein had already been a guest at their home as
    a child. Old Asseburg was a passionate hunter.
    When they were still at monastery school, the
    two of them shot their first roebucks on the
    other side of the border in Prussia. Really,
    they were poaching because they were at home
    in Mecklenburg. And, as for me, my father ini-
    tiated me very early into all the secrets of
    the hunt, and anyone who has experienced that
    will never get rid of the passion.

E: And what else did you talk about to Hammerstein?

M: I no longer remember. I think we talked about
    what courage is. He didn't seem much taken by

martial feats. He was more impressed by moral courage. Then we got around to talking about Russia, perhaps because my father and I wanted to go hunting there. I had got it into my head to learn Russian, never suspecting that studying it would later be of great advantage to me. Hammerstein encouraged me. He knew the Soviet Union very well, even if his sympathy for Communism remained well within bounds. Utopias didn't mean anything to him. At the time I was entirely of his opinion.

Finally, he invited me to visit him and his family whenever I was in Berlin. He said I would get on well with his children. They were just as headstrong as I was. When he wished me good night, he stroked my cheek and said 'Pity.'

Last-minute efforts

Kurt von Schleicher, the incumbent Chancellor of the Reich, believed until 26 January 1933 that Hindenburg was sticking to his intention of not appointing Hitler. He was mistaken in that. It was the next three days that decided the future of Germany.

'At home, there was a very nervous mood,' writes Helga von Hammerstein about this moment. 'There was constant conferring with Schleicher, who lived on the other side of the Landwehr canal from the Reichswehr Ministry.'

That day, that is, the 26th, her father made a final attempt to stop Hindenburg entrusting Hitler with the formation of a government. It is, however, not so easy to get a sense of this intervention, because there are at least three versions of what took place, and they are contradictory.

Hammerstein himself writes about it:

On the morning of 26 January, I went to Schleicher and asked him what was true about the rumours of a change of government. Schleicher confirmed that the President of the Reich was more or less certain to withdraw his confidence today or tomorrow and that he, Schleicher, would resign. I went to Permanent Secretary Meissner [head of Hindenburg's office], asked him what was to happen after Schleicher's resignation, and said clearly and plainly that the National Socialists would never enter a Papen–Hugenberg cabinet. Such a cabinet would have the National Socialists as enemies on one side and the Left on the other, and so have a tiny base. The army would then have to defend this 7 per cent base against 93 per cent of the German population. That would be in the highest degree disquieting; could it not still be prevented?

Meissner evidently saw the situation in a similar light and made it possible for me to state my concerns to the President immediately. I did so. Hindenburg was extremely sensitive about any kind of political interference, but then said, apparently to placate me, 'he had no intention whatsoever of making the Austrian corporal defence minister or

Reich chancellor.' (Word for word on 26 January 1933 at 11.30 a.m. in front of a witness.)

In his book about the Nazi seizure of power,
Meissner's son shifts this conversation by two days
and mentions a fourth participant, who was obviously
not there at all.

On the evening of 28 January, Chief of Army
Command, General von Hammerstein, and
the Berlin Army District Commander, General von Stülpnagel, announced themselves
and, as represent-atives of the Reichswehr,
declared to Hindenburg that the removal of
Reich Chancellor and Reichswehr Minister
von Schleicher was 'unacceptable to the army'
and must be prevented. Hindenburg, in some
irritation, interrupted General von Hammerstein before he could make further political
remarks. 'I know myself what is acceptable to
the army and must in this connection reject
any lectures on the part of you gentlemen.'
Herr von Hammerstein and the other generals should concern themselves with the training of the troops and not interfere in politics,
which was the business of himself and the
government of the Reich. With that, the two
generals were fairly ungraciously dismissed.

'That's not at all true,' observed General von dem
Bussche thirty years later. 'The ungraciousness consisted of a handshake and the request not to repeat the
remark about Hitler.' Bussche's version of the conversation in question goes like this:

On the forenoon of Friday, 27 January 1933 [yet another date!], as usual a report to the President of the Reich, by the Chief of Army Personnel Office, General Erich von dem Bussche-Ippenburg, was scheduled. The Chief of Army Command, General Baron von Hammerstein, who did not normally attend these reports, accompanied the Chief of Army Personnel Office to the meeting, in order to express to the Reich President his misgivings about an appointment of Hitler. He knew that the President objected to the presence of non-soldiers at military reports, and wanted to use the opportunity to convey his view to the Reich President uninfluenced by political advisers.

When the two generals entered the Reich President's room, the latter started ranting: 'If the generals aren't prepared to knuckle under, I'll dismiss them all.' Both generals could not avoid getting the impression that there had been a malicious campaign against the army leadership from some quarter. Smiling, General von Hammerstein declared to the Reich President that he could have no grounds whatsoever for disquiet, because the Reichswehr stood absolutely by him, their commander-in-chief.

The Reich President remarked: 'Well, then everything is in order,' and requested that the signatures which had to be presented be dealt with. After this formal business,

General von Hammerstein stated calmly and matter-of-factly his misgivings with respect to a possible appointment of Hitler as Reich Chancellor. He knew that the Reich President did not want to grant Reich Chancellor von Schleicher the dissolution of the Reichstag. He justified his misgivings above all with the extremism of Hitler and his party and expressed fears with respect to a demoralization of the Reichswehr, which could be led astray into gross disobedience. Soon after General von Hammerstein's initial remarks, the President of the Reich declared word for word: 'You will hardly think me capable, gentlemen, of appointing this Austrian corporal chancellor of the Reich.' For their part, the generals were reassured by this quite clear declaration by the Reich President and believed that Hindenburg had understood their reservations and shared them.

In that they were mistaken. They did not know that Hitler had already reached an understanding with Papen and that Hindenburg had nothing against this solution. Nevertheless, Hammerstein is said to have left the Presidential palace seriously worried.

When it became clear that Hindenburg had deceived them, Hammerstein conferred with Schleicher in the Defence Ministry on the morning of the 29th; present were the deputy of the Reich Defence Minister, Ferdinand von Bredow, Eugen Ott of the army department, Erwin Planck and Bussche. Hammerstein said he considered Hindenburg to be no longer of sound mind. They had to declare a state of emergency, arrest Hitler and then reach an understanding with the SPD. For that, it was necessary to put the Potsdam garrison on stand-by.

This was rejected by Schleicher—the men were not willing to follow such a course of action. Hindenburg was revered like a demigod in the populace. For that reason alone the Reichswehr could undertake nothing against him.

The plan was dropped. According to Fabian von Schlabrendorff, Hammerstein 'in later conversations with close friends and associates himself often questioned whether it would not after all have been right to proceed against Hindenburg by force'.

After the conference, Schleicher went to Hindenburg, announced the resignation of his government and recommended the appointment of Hitler as Chancellor of the Reich.

There exist notes in which Hammerstein recorded the further events of that day:

On 29 January there took place in my office a discussion between von Schleicher, who had resigned but was still acting as Reich Chancellor, and myself. It was clear to both of us that only Hitler was possible as future Reich Chancellor. Any other choice must inevitably lead to a general strike if not civil war and so to the extremely undesirable internal deployment of the army against two sides, against the National Socialists and against the Left. We both considered whether we knew any means to influence the situation and avoid such a misfortune. The result of our reflections was negative. We saw no possibilities of still exercising any kind of influence on the Reich President. Finally, I resolved in agreement with Schleicher to seek an exchange of views with Hitler. This took place on Sunday between 3 p.m. and 4 p.m. in Bechstein's house. I explained my concerns to Herr Hitler.

At issue was the question whether Hitler, if appointed Reich Chancellor, would retain General von Schleicher, Hammerstein's friend, as Army Minister. Hitler gave Hammerstein an assurance, although at this point it was already settled that Schleicher would be kicked out and replaced by General von Blomberg.

These discussions make two things clear: Army command was poorly informed about the true situation during those days, and did not see itself in a position to offer serious resistance to Hitler's appointment.

On the evening of the same day, Hindenburg, who a few hours earlier had still been hesitating, finally decided on Hitler as Chancellor. The next morning at quarter past eleven he and his cabinet were already being sworn in.

There were good reasons for General von Hammerstein having had enough of his post.

Third gloss.
On discord.

Straight talking is a much desired quality, above all when it comes to passing judgement on others and not on oneself, an endeavour in which the speaker is invariably too lenient on himself.

As is well known, Hitler's assumption of power met with enthusiastic approval, and not only from his own party. One, first of all, had to become an enemy of the Nazis, one wasn't born that way, is what many said later. 'How grandly it all began,' wrote the poet Gottfried Benn in 1934, 'and how squalid it looks today. But it's far from over.'

Many people who themselves later fell victim to the regime had an ambiguous attitude to the Nazi Party before 1933. That was the case, for example, with Erwin Planck, who as Permanent Secretary and head of the Reich Chancellor's office, supported Schleicher's manoeuvring with respect to Hitler. He very soon recognized, however, that this policy had contributed to the downfall of the Weimar Republic. He became a firm opponent of the National Socialists, was involved in the July 1944 plot to assassinate Hitler and was executed in January 1945. The same is true of Werner von Alvensleben, who knew Schleicher and Hammerstein very well from his time on the General Staff in 1918. He played a very dubious role in the days before Hitler's seizure of power but later joined the resistance. He was arrested in 1934 and only avoided being shot because his brother Ludolf, a senior SS Commander, interceded with Himmler on his behalf. In 1945, he was freed from prison by the Americans.

At first, most officers were unable to withstand the pull of the 'National Revolution'. Among them were men like Claus von Stauffenberg (placed the bomb that was intended to kill Hitler, shot 21 July 1944), Henning von Tresckow (suicide 21 July 1944), Fritz-Dietlof Count von der Schulenburg (executed 1944), Peter Count Yorck von Wartenburg (executed 1944) and Mertz von Quirnheim (shot on 21 July 1944). In 1932, Ludwig Beck (shot on 20 July 1944) was to be dismissed at the request of Defence Minister General Wilhelm Groener because of 'National Socialist tendencies'. Hammerstein had prevented the dismissal. In 1933, Wilhelm Canaris, who had also taken part in the Kapp Putsch, welcomed Hitler's seizure of power; he advanced to head of military intelligence but soon turned against the regime and was hanged in Flossenbürg Concentration Camp in the last days of the war. Wolf Count von Helldorf was a fanatical Nazi, who had become a senior SA officer even before 1933. He, too, later joined the resistance and was executed in 1944. Anyone who holds their political mistakes against people who subsequently paid with their lives is suffering from a kind of wisdom after the event which is difficult to distinguish from *moral insanity*.

No one, however, could accuse General von Hammerstein of harbouring any sympathies for National Socialism. Nevertheless his stance was not free of ambivalences and misjudgements and there is evidence of vacillation on his part.

1930: 'Since the election on 14 Sept., strong national and Comm. wave. The Nazis must be left in no doubt that at any attempt at illegality the most drastic measures will be taken against them.'

September 1930: 'Apart from the pace, Hitler actually wants the same thing as the Reichswehr.'

Spring 1932: 'If the National Socialists come to power legally, then it's all right with me. If not, then I'll shoot.'

15 August 1932: 'I can sleep easily again now, since I now know that, if need be, I can order the troops to fire on the Nazis. In the army, there is at present an extraordinary anger at the Nazis.'

Nonetheless, to the last, National Socialist participation in the government appeared to Hammerstein, as it did to his friend Schleicher, as the 'lesser evil' compared with the risk of a civil war. Again and again, both fell victim to the error that it was possible to 'bind' Hitler and his party through government responsibility, and split and 'tame' them.

Not until 31 January 1933 did such illusions evaporate. Maria Therese remembers the visit of a Swiss friend of the family to Hammerstein's government flat. Inez Wille, a journalist, the granddaughter of a general in the Swiss army, had come to Berlin to hear

Hitler and von Hammerstein at the funeral of Edwin
Bechstein, 1934. This is the only photo in which
Hammerstein is to be seen in the company of Hitler

how the head of the German army assessed the situation. 'Slim, in a grey English suit, sitting opposite my father in an easy chair, deadly serious and almost stern, she asked: "What has happened?" My father's reply was succinct and laconic: "We have taken a leap into Fascism." He held out no comfort to her.' To a younger comrade from the 3rd Guards Regiment, he said: 'Ninety-eight per cent of the German people are simply intoxicated.'

The invisible war

On 1 February 1933, some people from the KPD's military apparatus, camouflaged as a 'literary association', met in the back room of a pub in Taubenstrasse in Berlin. The session was chaired by the leader of the organization, Hans Kippenberger, known as 'Alex', also 'Adam' or 'Wolf'. Leo Roth, who used the cover name 'Rudi', was also present. Hubert von Ranke relates:

> Alex began to speak, commenting on the political situation—he, too, in the manner of Communist functionaries, was unable to elucidate practical questions without first giving a lecture. In his analysis of the situation, he said that Fascism had now moved from a masked stage to an open one. Until now, capitalism had managed to prevent a revolution by splitting the working class

with the help of the Social Democrats. In the
face of the heightening of contradictions, the
immiseration of the masses, unemployment
and social unrest, capitalism had now resorted
to its final instrument—at the risk of itself
being consumed by the forces it had called
on for help. Fascism meant rearmament, war,
smashing of the workers' organizations—
a dangerous path at whose end would
inevitably stand revolution. Alex continued:
'From today, we must regard ourselves as
existing in complete illegality. The coming
period will undoubtedly cause the Party heavy
losses, but also strengthen its fighting spirit.
The tasks are clear: immediate decentraliza-
tion of the Party apparatus. The cells are to be
broken down into five-man groups and at any
time only one comrade must have contact
with the group at the next level—also, always
only with one person. Immediate exclusion of
anyone unreliable, weak, anyone timid. And,
as far as our own circle is concerned, we have
today met for the last time.'

He further said that from now on the
intelligence organization would assume a special significance. All important services and
connections had to be strictly and covertly
separated from the general work of the Party
and, if possible, strengthened by parallel sets
of contacts operating independently of each
other. All illegal material, in so far as it cannot
be destroyed, was to be deposited in safe

places, with persons with no record of activity. Safe accommodation, for every emergency, must urgently be found with sympathizers. All correspondence must be reduced to a minimum, phone calls were only to be made from public telephone booths and while maintaining cover and using secure cover addresses. Information that could not be memorized had to be encoded in accordance with the system specified in the periodical *Oktober* and deposited in a neutral place. 'Caution also within one's family.' The smallest piece of information, swiftly passed on, about the enemy's procedures and intentions, could be of incalculable significance. Alex concluded: 'We find ourselves in a still invisible war and must always be aware, that here, in Lieb-knecht's [actually Eugen Leviné's] words, we are only dead men on leave. Our lives are nothing. The coming weeks and months will be decisive for the fate of the German working class and the revolution.'

We left the pub at intervals of a few minutes. I left with Rudi. From now on I had nothing more to do with the others. I was not allowed to know them any more. After a couple of steps, Rudi also took his leave. I was alone, went home to Olga [his wife, maiden name von Obonyi], told her everything. We were very serious that evening—the future seemed to have grown even darker. We weren't quite able to believe in the bright light of a revolution at the end of the dark tunnel, as Alex had described it.

At this point, exceptionally, it may be permissible to quote from a work of fiction. Arthur Koestler, who was very familiar with the milieu, describes the situation of the KPD after 1933 in his novel *Darkness at Noon* (1940):

> The movement had been defeated, its members were now outlawed and hunted and beaten to death. All over the country existed small groups of people who had survived the catastrophe and continued to conspire underground. They met in cellars, woods, railway stations, museums and sports clubs. They continuously changed their names and their habits. They knew each other only by their Christian names and did not ask for each other's addresses. Each gave his life into the other's hand, and neither trusted the other an inch.

A dinner with Hitler

On 3 February, Hammerstein knew that he had failed. The prospect of the supper with Hitler, which was arranged for 8 p.m. in the dining room of his official apartment, is not likely to have improved his mood. It was an official visit, on which the new chancellor wanted to introduce himself and attempt to win over the generals to the new regime. It was taking place instead of a commanders-in-chief conference which had been fixed for that day. The supper, with which such meetings were concluded, would normally have been hosted by the minister. Blomberg, however, had only just been appointed and Kurt von Schleicher, his predecessor, still occupied the official residence. Consequently, the meal was switched to the apartment of the Chief of Army Command.

At any rate, the dinner with Hitler had been set up by Blomberg, the man who shortly before had booted out Hammerstein's friend Schleicher. He used the sixtieth birthday of Foreign Minister Konstantin von Neurath as a pretext. It could not have escaped the new chancellor that the meeting was taking place in the residence of an acknowledged opponent—that contributed to the tense atmosphere of the evening.

Arrival of the official cars, orderlies, saluting guards. After the meal, Hitler addressed the guests for two and a half hours. General impression: at first, unprepossessing and insignificant. Von dem Bussche, at the time Chief of Army Personnel Office, relates: 'Hammerstein still introduced the Reich Chancellor somewhat "benevolently" and condescendingly, the phalanx of generals was courteous and cool, Hitler made modest, clumsy bows to everyone and remained ill at ease until he had the opportunity after the meal for a longer speech. Hitler's intention of soft-soaping those present was all too evident.'

It doesn't seem to have struck the generals that what he said was in stark contrast to his inaugural statement of policy on 30 January. Then, he had spoken of his sincere wish to maintain and consolidate peace, to limit armaments and contribute to reconciliation inside Germany. General von Becker even asserted that he had 'immediately forgotten again' the content of the speech on 3 February!

Later, Hitler said that he had the feeling that evening of talking to a wall. Nevertheless, the next day the Nazi Party newspaper, the *Völkische Beobachter*, wrote triumphantly: 'The army stands shoulder to shoulder with the new chancellor. Never was the Reichswehr more identified with the tasks of the state than today.'

Attendance list of 3 February 1933

We shall never discover exactly what happened that evening. The reports, the memoirs, indeed even the minutes diverge, as they usually do. Even the details of the guests are contradictory, and so the following attendance list cannot claim to be absolutely accurate:

> Werner von Blomberg, General of Infantry and appointed Army Minister five days previously
>
> Konstantin von Neurath, Foreign Minister since 1932

Kurt von Hammerstein-Equord, Chief of
Army Command

Erich Raeder, Admiral, Chief of Naval
Command

Horst von Mellenthin, adjutant to Kurt von
Hammerstein

Ludwig Beck, General, Chief of Troop Office

Curt Liebmann, Lieutenant-General

Erich von dem Bussche-Ippenburg, Lieutenant General

Hans Heinrich Lammers, head of the Chancellor's Office

Wilhelm Brückner, Hitler's chief adjutant

Walther von Reichenau, Colonel, Chief of
Blomberg's Ministerial Office

Eugen Ott, Colonel, department head in the
Defence Ministry

Were ladies present? Did Frau von Hammerstein
as hostess invite the guests to table and officially
end the meal? Did General von Blomberg, as some
say, bring his daughter? Is that of any importance at
all? And is it possible that Marie Luise and Helga,
Hammerstein's daughters, were behind a curtain and
heard Hitler's speech? Leo Roth later maintained they
had—one of them had officially taken down the speech
and immediately handed the shorthand text to the
adjutants: 'The other daughter made notes, but at first
refused to hand them over, and only did so after two
hours. We got hold of the speech and made three

strictly confidential copies, one for the BB [a section of the Military Organization], one for the Politburo [of the Communist Party] or Th[älmann] personally, and I had one.'

Such a course of events is hardly conceivable, although it's at least true that Marie Luise knew short-hand. The presence of family members was out of the question on such an occasion. And none of the wit-nesses confirms Roth's information. It's no doubt one of those legends in which oral transmission is so rich. What's certain, at any rate, is that at least three tran-scripts of the speech exist which diverge considerably from one another; the most complete of these minutes was only found and published in 2000.

Moscow is listening in

'At that time, the Comintern was in the corner building, which was only three or four storeys high, opposite the "manege",' relates Luise Kraushaar, a German Com-munist who emigrated to the Soviet Union in April 1934 and was employed in the cryptographic section of the intelligence service.

> From my window, I could see the Kremlin towers. The code section was accommodated in a large room in which thirty-five to forty comrades, mostly women, worked. We worked in two shifts until two or three at night. The

radio telegrams were in various languages:
German, English, French and perhaps others.
I think it was German that was mainly used.

That was also true of the following radio message
from Berlin, decoded on 6 February, three days after
the supper in Bendlerstrasse:

92-98-X2-Y-Z2-31-T
Strictly confidential
6/2/33
(HIS)

Concerning: Programme of Fascism.

On 3 February, in the official rooms of General
von Blomberg [properly Hammerstein], Hitler
expounded his programme to the commanders of the
RW [Reichswehr] in a closed meeting. He spoke the
first words calmly, then ever more ecstatically,
leaning across the table, gesticulating. In the
generals' opinion — very logical and good, con-
vincing as far as internal policy problems concerned. Not very clear on foreign policy. In the
manner of his agitational speeches, he repeated
the salient points up to ten times.

Copy of the unofficially prepared
transcript record!

As in the life of individuals the stronger and
better always asserts himself, so in the life of
nations. The strong European race, a small minority, has for centuries subjected millions of
people and built European culture on their backs.
There existed an exchange. Europe gave industrial
products, cultural goods, etc., while the
colonies, the most inferior races, had to give up
their labour, their raw materials, etc. Today, a
reversal has occurred in this normal development.
If one were to fully exploit the total capacity of

the industries in Europe, then the colonies would not be able to offer an equivalent value in return. In addition, industries have come into being, e.g. in East Asia, to a considerable extent in southeast Europe, which produce with cheaper labour and try to supplant the former master race.

To these reasons for the general crisis is added the damage caused by the World War. Why did none of the European powers become healthy in the World War? Because none was sufficiently uncompromising. If England, for example, had imposed only the following condition on Germany — No shipping of any kind, no foreign trade of any kind and no alliances of any kind with other states — then England would be healthy today. England can only become healthy again if it reverts from the standpoint of a world citizen to the standpoint of master race, thanks to which it became great. The same would have been true of Germany in the case of a victory.

Now, what does the situation after the World War really look like? In Germany, in 1918, there was complete autarchy, yet about eight million men were completely excluded from production. In order to be able to fulfil the reparations payments, we began to export. The deliveries in kind called for increased production, the eight million men were gradually re-employed. These developments naturally brought in their train imports. Then rationalization started, men became superfluous, unemployment began.

The third reason is the poisoning of the world by Bolshevism. Poverty and a low standard of living are ideal for Bolshevism. It is the ideology of those who have got used to an absence of needs thanks to long unemployment. It is a fact, after all, that racially inferior people have to be forced to culture. If a recruit is not constantly compelled to wash himself, he doesn't. Hence, these people would like to persist in a state of a voluntary lack of culture. In addition, it is the case that these people feel a greater solidarity with the equally low elements of other nations than with their own national comrades. A culture has been destroyed once before by the ideal of poverty. When Christianity preached voluntary poverty, Antiquity was inevitably ruined.

Now, how can Germany be saved? How can we eliminate unemployment? I have been a prophet for fourteen years and I say, again and again — all these economic plans, the provision of credit to industries, state subsidies are nonsense. We can eliminate unemployment in two ways: 1) through exports at any price and by any means; 2) through a large-scale settlement policy which has as its condition an expansion of the living space of the German people. This last way would be my proposal. Over a period of fifty to sixty years, we would have a completely new healthy state. But the realization of these plans can only be tackled once the conditions for it have been created. This condition is the consolidation of the state. We must return to the outlook upon which the state was founded. One can no longer be a citizen of the world. Democracy and pacifism are impossible. Every person knows that democracy in the army is out of the question. It's also harmful in business — company councils are the same nonsense as soldiers' councils. So why do we think that democracy in the state is possible? In Germany, it is the case that, today, 50 per cent of the people want a state of our kind and have a positive attitude to National Socialism, while 50 per cent reject the state and say it is nothing but an instrument of repression against them. One side abhors treason, the other says treason is their duty. And democracy allows both their free opinion. Only when the one side actually commits treason in accordance with its ideology is it punished. That is contradictory and absurd. Hence, it is our task

to capture political power, to suppress every sub-
versive opinion as harshly as possible and to edu-
cate the nation in morality. Every attempt at
treason must be ruthlessly punished by death. The
suppression of Marxism by every possible means is
my goal.

If, now in Geneva, we plead for equal status
and so limit ourselves to merely enlarging the
armed forces, then in my opinion that's nonsensi-
cal. What use is an army of infected soldiers?
What use is compulsory conscription, if after
their military service the soldiers are exposed to
every kind of propaganda? First of all, Marxism
must be extirpated. Then, thanks to the educa-
tional work of my movement, the army will have
first-class recruit material and there will exist
a guarantee that the recruits will retain the
spirit of morality and of nationalism even after
their period of service. In order to attain this
goal, I aim at total political power. I set myself
the term of six—eight years in order to eradicate
Marxism completely. Then, the army will be capable
of conducting an active foreign policy, and the
goal of the expansion of the living space of the
German people will also be achieved by force of
arms. The goal would presumably be the East. But
a Germanization of the population of the annexed
or conquered land is not possible. We can only
Germanize soil. Like Poland and France after the
war, we must ruthlessly expel several million
people.

The transitional period is very dangerous for
Germany. If France has intelligent statesmen, it
will attack at all costs. It will try to win over
Russia, perhaps even come to an understanding with
it. Consequently, the greatest haste is called
for. With my movement, I have now already created
an alien body in the democratic state. Its whole
structure makes it immediately capable of building
up the new state. It forms a hierarchy with

unquestioned command authority, an image of the new state on a smaller scale.

The development in Germany will be different from that of Italian Fascism. We will crush Marxism just as it did. But our relationship to the army will be a different one. We will stand by the army and work with the army for the army. The glorious German army, in which the same spirit still prevails as during its heroic age in the World War, will fulfil its tasks independently.

I now turn to you, generals, with the plea to fight with me for the great goal, to understand me and to support me, not with weapons but morally. For the internal struggle I have created my own weapon — the army is only there for external policy conflicts. You will not find another man who so commits himself with all his strength for his goal, for the deliverance of Germany, as I. And if anyone says to me: 'The achievement of the goal depends on you!' then I reply: 'Well and good, then let us take advantage of my life!'

A posthumous conversation with Kurt von Hammerstein (II)

H: You again!

E: Yes, I absolutely must talk to you. Herr von Hammerstein, how could a file with such explosive content be made available to Moscow headquarters within a few days? After all, in this secret speech Hitler expressed his aims quite openly: dictatorship at home and the conquest of 'Lebensraum' in the East. He even gives the date of the beginning of the war of aggression as between 1939 and 1941. How was such a failure of all security measures possible?

H: I did not discover it until August 1935.

That's when my daughter Marie Luise was questioned by the Gestapo.

E: But you must have known that your daughters had contacts with Communists, with Werner Scholem and with a certain Leo Roth?

H: I did not know either of these two gentlemen. I did not ever meet either of them.

E: Your daughters not only had access to your office, they evidently also had the opportunity to obtain documents from it. When he was still a schoolboy, your son Kunrat is supposed to have seen them taking papers out of your waste-paper basket which, in one case, were even used by the Opposition in the Reichstag to attack the government. Of much greater significance, however, was the fact that the text of Hitler's secret speech to the generals, undoubtedly taken down in shorthand by one of your adjutants, promptly reached Moscow. One doesn't simply leave such documents lying around — one keeps them in a safe. So how does one explain the fact that one of your daughters, Helga, could get hold of the transcript and, through her boyfriend, pass it on to the Comintern?

H: That's something I don't know.

E: One might suspect, General, that such an occurrence was not possible without your tacit toleration. Could it be that you were pursuing a political aim? Given your good relations with the Russians, that would be plausible. At any rate, Hitler's speech could have served as a warning to the leadership in Moscow.

H: Nonsense. I didn't instigate anything of the kind. And as far as my relationship with my daughters is concerned, I am not accountable to anyone for it. I never said anything about it to the Gestapo either.

E: You retired from your post as Chief of Army Command on 31 January 1934.

Kurt von Hammerstein before his retirement, 1933

H: I wanted to retire even before that — there
was no point in staying any more. The army had
for some time no longer been behind Schleicher
and myself. Blomberg wanted to get rid of
me. In fact, that was already settled on 29
January. Subsequently, I had only nominal
authority. They just didn't yet dare sack me
right away, but I stole a march on them. My
letter of resignation at the end of December
1933 — that was a Christmas present to myself.
I'd had enough of all the palaver.

Fait accompli

The Reichstag, the German parliament, burned on the
night of 27–28 February. 'I wouldn't be surprised if
they set it alight themselves,' said Hammerstein.

The next morning, Hindenburg declared a state of
emergency and thereby annulled basic rights.

With this decree, the right to free expression of
opinion, including freedom of the press, right of association and assembly, was virtually abolished. From
now on, there was no privacy of post, telegrams and
telephone any more. House searches and confisca-
tions without order of a judge were declared legal.
There was, immediately, a wave of arrests not only by
the police but also by the SA, the paramilitary organization of the Nazi Party.

In addition, Hindenburg's decree gave the Reich
government the right to intervene in the powers of the
German states. It put an end to the federal system in

Germany and made possible the centralization and the coordination (*Gleichschaltung*) of the state structure.

That was the real *coup d'état*.

The Reichstag Fire had a legal epilogue—a spectacular trial which began in September 1933 in the Leipzig Reich Court. The indictment was regarded as a state secret. The Nazis had wanted only a show trial to present the Communists as arsonists and insurgents. Consequently, in addition to the loner van der Lubbe, four Communists, of whom the most prominent was Dimitrov, were accused. Whether van der Lubbe, who was sentenced to death, was involved in the arson remains controversial. The Communists, however, had to be acquitted for lack of proof. *The Brown Book on the Reichstag Fire and Hitler Terror* contributed to this victory of the defence. Already published in Paris in the summer by the agitprop genius of the German Communist Party, Willi Münzenberg, it led to an unprecedented international campaign. Translated into seventeen languages, it was distributed in editions of millions of copies.

The essential parts of the secret indictment were printed in *The Brown Book*. An informant from the intelligence apparatus of the KPD, the already mentioned Hermann Dünow, claims to know how it was obtained:

> It turned out that, at the time, General von Hammerstein also possessed a copy of the indictment. It was decided, therefore, to

remove this copy from the general's desk. The whole action also succeeded with the help of the general's daughters. However, we had the indictment at our disposal for only two hours, then it had to be back in place again in the general's desk. I photographed the whole indictment in my flat, page by page, and by the time the original was back in the general's desk, Comrade Roth was already on his way to the airport to take the exposed film to Paris.

Kippenberger's collaborator and lover, on the other hand, heard at the time that it was an elderly gentleman who 'brought the film to Holland, hidden in an umbrella'. The most amusing version of this transport is provided by Helga's friend, Hubert von Ranke:

Alex [Kippenberger] was able to have the Leipzig Reich Court's whole indictment photographed, and it was—as I only later found out—Grete [Helga von Hammerstein] who took the 26 Leica film rolls across the border in a paper bag full of cherries. When the frontier guards came to her compartment she was eating, as if without a care in the world, some of the cherries under which the film rolls were hidden.

On this basis, along with other anti-Fascist texts, Willi Münzenberg published *The Brown Book* which was also smuggled into Nazi Germany in a thin paper edition. I still have a copy in my possession, which is made

132

$\dfrac{A}{203998}:2$

BRAUNBUCH II

[über Reichstagsbrand u. Hitler-Terror.]

DIMITROFF
CONTRA GOERING

ENTHÜLLUNGEN ÜBER DIE
WAHREN BRANDSTIFTER

1934

ÉDITIONS DU CARREFOUR

PARIS

The Brown Book
(Dimitroff contra Goering:
Revelations about the True Arsonists)

up to look like a cheap little paperback and bears the title: Goethe, *Hermann and Dorothea.*

The old working-class movement had a great respect for education, so Schiller had to be included as well—another edition of *The Brown Book* pretended to be bringing his play *Wallenstein* to the people.

But while its propaganda successes made waves abroad, things looked bad for the illegal KPD in Germany itself. One of Kippenberger's agents gives an account of the night of the Reichstag Fire:

> We came out at the Potsdamer Platz exit of the underground and mingled with the people, who were staring with fascination at the flames shooting from the cupola. We stood there for some minutes, fearing the worst, before we agreed that our behaviour probably did not quite correspond to the rules of illegal work we preached and that it would be better if we made ourselves scarce. Kippenberger was undoubtedly high on the wanted list of the new rulers.

The same informant remarks on the position in which the comrades found themselves:

> The collapse of the KPD under the blows of the uncurbed National Socialist terror which now began was evident above all in the fragmentation of the Party. First of all, the shift of the Party organization to illegal activity failed

all along the line—the structure was shattered from top to bottom, the organizational cohesion disappeared entirely. This situation manifested itself in especially drastic form in the isolation of the Party leadership.

The man whose conclusions these were was called Franz Feuchtwanger. His biography is just as remarkable as those of his comrades-in-arms Hubert von Ranke and Helga von Hammerstein and deserves to be recorded in a few lines. Born the son of a well-to-do Jewish lawyer in Munich, he already had contacts with the KPD while at grammar school. He became a Party member in 1928 and soon after, was recruited by Kippenberger into the M-Apparatus.

At the time, his headquarters was in an attic room in the Communist Party's Karl Liebknecht House which could only be reached by a secret stairway. Prominent on the table of the little room, like a ritual object, was an artillery shell, which a little while earlier Kippenberger had presented in the Reichstag as evidence of the illegal rearming of the Reichswehr. He didn't have the disposition of an apparatchik—a Party bureaucrat—and so differed from the bosses of every shade who were increasingly establishing themselves in the party leadership.

At the end of 1930, Feuchtwanger was sentenced to fifteen months' confinement in a fortress for 'preparations for high treason'; he served his time with a group of comrades in Landsberg am Lech, ironically in the same rooms which had once accommodated Hitler and now functioned as a kind of improvised Party academy.

Returning to the central organization in Berlin, he drew the rather modest salary of 300 marks a month as a senior Party official. That was less than half his monthly allowance from his parents, which at first, he says, embarrassed him.

The illegal work, as Feuchtwanger records, ended in disaster: 'All in all, the Apparatus had finally ceased to exist by mid-1935. It was an inglorious expiry. In Prague, the news reached me that I had been expelled "for activities hostile to the Party". I had been unhitched, and, with that, the business was over and done with.'

In 1938, Feuchtwanger emigrated to Paris, was interned in 1939 and in 1940 escaped to Mexico by way of Spain and Portugal. There, he finally turned his back on Hitler, Stalin and the rest and, until his death in 1991, devoted himself to the archaeology of pre-Columbian cultures.

Hindenburg sends his regards

The Reich President
Berlin, 23 December 1933

General,

By instruction issued this day I have granted Your Honour retirement from military service on 31 January 1934 with the rank of Colonel-General, with allowance of the statutory maintenance and with the entitlement to wear the uniform of the General Staff with the insignia of a general.

In honour of your meritorious service in the various command positions, I wish by bestowing the uniform of the General Staff to express for the future also your attachment to the army and its high national tasks.

As outward sign of my appreciation, I shall have my picture with signature sent to you.

With comradely greetings
Your von Hindenburg

A posthumous conversation
with Kurt von Hammerstein (III)

E: You want to be left in peace. I respect that, even if I cannot believe that you are lazy.

H: Who gave you that idea?

E: You don't know? Almost everyone who had anything to do with you says so.

THE SILENCES OF HAMMERSTEIN

H: An impertinence. Only because the never-ending paperwork bored me. You cannot imagine, my friend, what dreary piles of paper end up on the desk of an army commander every day.

E: I certainly can. One needs a large waste-paper basket.

H: Well and good. Let's leave it at that. You are keen, I am lazy. Your cigars were excellent, but now I have no further desire to explain myself to you.

E: Just another couple of minutes, Herr von Hammerstein, then you'll finally be rid of me. On 1 February 1934, there was a farewell parade for you as Chief of Army Command.

H: That could not be avoided.

E: Apparently on this occasion you did not appear at all embittered — it is said that you looked relieved, almost cheerful.

H: It's possible.

E: You apparently tore up the signed photograph Hindenburg sent you and threw it in your big waste-paper basket.

H: You don't say!

E: What did you actually think of him?

H: I knew Hindenburg from the First World War. Politically a nonentity, but he behaved quite decently to me. He was even the godfather of my son Ludwig. And he helped to push through my retirement and made sure that I didn't end up in a concentration camp. Until his death in August 1934, he was able to protect me.

E: You even went to his funeral at Tannenberg in East Prussia.

H: Well . . . May he rest in peace.

E: And after that? A little later, your daughter Marie Luise, later also Maria Therese, was questioned by the Gestapo. Could this be connected with your daughters' conduct?

H: There were enough other reasons for it. My attitude was sufficiently well known to the Hitler government.

E: You had a low opinion of him from the start. As early as 1923, when he wanted to lead a coup in Munich, you declared in front of your battalion: 'A certain Corporal Hitler has gone crazy in Munich.' And then, shortly before he took power . . .

H: Yes, at the last minute I called on Hindenburg once again, to warn him against a Hitler chancellorship. I explained to him that the army unconditionally stood by him as commander-in-chief. Hitler's goals, however, were quite boundless. If the Reichswehr were subject to his influence then it could be led into disobedience. Hindenburg was as always very testy, precisely because he himself was at his wits' end. He refused to consider any political advice. Just to calm me down, he assured me in the end that he would not appoint 'this Austrian corporal' as chancellor.

E: Did you believe him?

H: If you really want to know: I have never believed a politician. Just think what it was like in Germany at the time! A political shambles! Party politics in the muck! Criminality and stupidity! If it had been up to me, I would already have fired on the Nazis in August 1932.

E: But you didn't.

H: I wasn't sure if the army would follow me. Apart from that, virtually everyone was conspiring behind my back — Papen, Blomberg, Reichenau, the whole gang, even my friend and comrade Schleicher. I never understood more than half of his machinations and calculations. They all went disastrously wrong anyway.

E: From autumn 1929 you were Chief of the . . .

H: . . . of the Troop Office.

Farewell parade with Kurt von Hammerstein, 1934

E: But that was only a cover name. In that capacity, you knew in detail about the secret cooperation between the Reichswehr and the Red Army.

H: What does secret mean? Even before I was appointed, Scheidemann had revealed the whole story in parliament.

E: That didn't stop the Reichswehr from continuing. In 1927—28, the number of officers sent to Russia was even increased. Tank experts were trained in Kazan and about a hundred military pilots in Lipezk. Near Saratov, chemical weapons were developed with Soviet help. The inventor of poison gas, Fritz Haber, helped set up the Moscow Institute of Chemical Warfare. German experts were involved in the construction of armaments factories in Leningrad, Perm and Sverdlovsk.

H: You're well informed.

E: All violations of the Versailles Treaty.

H: So? What were we supposed to do? An army of 100,000 — the French had 800,000 under arms — without conscription, without a General Staff, without tanks, without an air force. An intolerable state of affairs!

E: From 1928/29, you yourself travelled to Russia several times, attended manoeuvres and negotiated with the leadership of the Red Army.

H: Part of my duties.

E: What about?

H: That I no longer remember — and if I did, I wouldn't tell you.

E: At any rate, your relationship with General Tukhachevsky is described as very warm.

H: Comradely. Like me, he had been in the Third Guards Regiment, only on the other side. In Berlin, we always talked in German.

E: And Marshal Voroshilov?

Mikhail Nikolayevich Tukhachevsky, Semyon Mikhailovich
Budyonny and Kliment Yefremovich Voroshilov, 1935

H: At the time he was not yet Marshal, but People's Commissar for Defence. Decent fellow, then at least. Until 1933, he always sent me two big tins of caviar at Bendlerstrasse.

E: And Georgi Zhukov, who later conquered Berlin, is said to have trained with you during your time as Chief of the Armed Forces Department, so in 1929 or 1930.

H: I don't remember the young man.

E: In 1941, at the beginning of the war, he became Chief of Staff.

H: I'm sure his training with us will not have done him any harm then.

E: In spring 1931, you are supposed to have said to officers of the Group Command in Kassel: 'German foreign policy seeks the support of Russia as long as the West is not prepared to offer something like equality of status.'

H: And how do you know what I said at such confidential discussions?

E: There are files. The bureaucrats don't lose anything.

H: Well and good. But I did add: '[The] relationship with Moscow is a deal with the Devil. But we have no choice. Fear is no philosophy of life.'

E: Your children also adopted that motto.

H: In that they didn't disappoint me.

A posthumous conversation with Werner Scholem

E: Herr Scholem, I've come to see you because your name still means something in Germany.

S: That must be a mistake. You're probably confusing me with my brother Gershom. He was cleverer than me and emigrated in good time. I can well imagine that he made something of himself in Palestine.

E: A great scholar. There are many anecdotes about him.

S: Is that why you're here?

E: Not at all. I'm interested in your story.

S: All the worse.

E: How did you actually come to join the KPD? Your father was a wealthy entrepreneur of altogether German nationalist views.

S: Exactly.

E: So there were conflicts with your parents from an early age?

S: You can say that again. When I began to take an interest in Zionism, my father sent me into exile in Hanover. He didn't want to know anything about his Jewishness.

E: At the school in Hanover, the Gildemeister Institut, you had a classmate called Ernst Jünger. He says your relationship was marked by ironic sympathy.

S: Even then I didn't have very much in common with him. Then, at eighteen, I joined the SPD. That was an altogether worthy association in those days, but, to my father, it was the proverbial red rag. The final break came when I married my girlfriend Emmy without telling him. Because she was from a working-class background and had an illegitimate child. In his eyes, those were two unforgivable sins. And so on.

E: Is it true that you were already tried for treason once before in 1917?

S: It was quite petty. After the SPD split, I opted for the Left and I joined the comrades on a demonstration against the war wearing my uniform. A couple of months in prison — that was all. Not worth talking about.

E: And after 1918 you became, if I may say so, a professional revolutionary. A founder member of the KPD, an editor at the *Rote Fahne* (Red Flag), on the wanted list after taking part in the March Insurrection of 1921 in central Germany, in prison for a couple of months, elected to the Reichstag in 1924, then a member of the Politburo along with Ruth Fischer and Arkadi Maslow.

S: Yes, yes, yes. The whole litany. You're boring me.

E: Your brother Gershom, who became a Zionist, didn't like it at all. Even Walter Benjamin responded very harshly to your political activity, although he himself sympathized with Communism.

S: So?

E: He talked of the terrible impression which the record of the Reichstag debates, which he came across from time to time, made on him. 'The Germans,' he wrote, 'in full view of their country and of the world have now happily handed over the rostrum to the scum of their nation. A band of soldiery on the one side and opposite them rascals like "Scholem MP", whom I know. One would have to be quite a Kabbalist to cleanse oneself of the fraternal relationship with that character.'

S: Benjamin was intelligent, but a pure bookworm. And as for my brother, Gershom — even as seventeen-year-olds we argued like mad about politics. I probably also insulted him sometimes. That was fairly normal for us. But, when it really came to it, we always stuck up for each other. You probably don't understand that.

E: I do. I have brothers myself, Herr Scholem. But back to your political career. When Stalin finally imposed his line, you joined the ultra-Left opposition. Like Ruth Fischer and Arkadi Maslow, you were mercilessly slandered and in 1926 expelled from the Party.

THE SILENCES OF HAMMERSTEIN

S: Stop it!

E: But *you* didn't stop. When the Nazis celebrated their first successes, were there not some attempts at a rapprochement with the KPD?

S: Of course there were. We were all caught between the millstones. Karl Korsch — do you even know who that is?

E: The intellectual mentor of the Left opposition.

S: Yes. He advised us to act in accordance with the maxim 'If they'll take you, join the Party again. Without an organization nothing is possible.' Ruth Fischer and Arkadi Maslow did as he said and applied to join.

E: They could not imagine a life outside the Party.

S: I could.

E: In 1929, you wrote to your brother Gershom: 'Either the revolution comes . . . or the rule of barbarism.'

S: I quite quickly realized that it would be the latter. That's why I prepared to emigrate.

E: Then it was already too late.

S: I was arrested the day after the Reichstag Fire. A couple of weeks later, proceedings against me for high treason were initiated.

E: The court files have survived. Perhaps you're interested in what's in them?

S: Presumably nothing but lies.

E: You and your wife Emmy were accused of 'continuously having prepared the treasonable undertaking of changing by force the Constitution of the German Reich, in particular the intention of making the Reichswehr and the police incapable of fulfilling their duty of protecting the German Reich and its states against assault on its internal or external status'.

S: What fabulous prose!

E: The evidence was rather meagre. Witnesses said they had encountered you in a 'pub frequented by Communists' with the nice name *Dreckige Schürze* (Dirty Apron). The Hansa Cell met there, which allegedly wanted to subvert the Reichswehr.

S: In the pub. The Hansa Cell wasn't up to much. And that's supposedly why I was arrested? It was only a pretext!

E: At any rate, you were already picked up on the night of the Reichstag Fire but released again.

S: Yes. The Nazis were drunk with victory. Parades and pogroms, chaos and capriciousness, fear and routine — an indescribable confusion. So it was that the police didn't hammer on the door of our apartment in Klopstockstrasse until 23 April. They probably thought I had cleared off abroad long ago, and so came to arrest my wife instead. The officers wanted to persuade her that I was involved in the Reichstag Fire. They would leave her and the children in peace, they said, if she was prepared to cooperate with the Gestapo.

E: You were in the bedroom and came out in order to protect your wife.

S: They took us both away. She was released in November, I stayed in Moabit Prison. Fortunately, Emmy was able to get away to London with the children via Prague, with the help, incidentally, of a senior SA commander whom she knew. Things like that happened too. This Herr Hackebeil then evidently also did a lot to make sure they were taken care of in London.

S: Emmy did everything she could to exonerate you. I have here copies of letters she wrote from London to the examining judge. In them, she goes in particular into your relationship with Marie Luise von Hammerstein, who worked for the military organization of the KPD. Did you know that, as a result, you too were suspected of spying for the Comintern? It was even suggested that you had induced your girlfriend Marie Luise to do so.

S: What kind of nonsense is this? Are you trying to provoke me?

E: Not at all. I'm trying to clear up the whole story, in so far as that's possible. Do you want to hear what your wife wrote?

S: If it's necessary.

E: 'After my release I had to establish *why* I was arrested and also *why* my husband was arrested: because there was nothing against us except for a statement by Marie Luise, daughter of the General of the Reichswehr, Baron von Hammerstein-Equord, from which it emerged that she claimed she had come into contact with the Communist Party through my husband and myself. Because we were not told about the statement, presumably to protect the general and his daughter, but were nevertheless to be kept in custody, the necessary 'witnesses' were then found.

'As for the Hammerstein case itself, I inform you that this provides no reason whatsoever to proceed against my husband and myself. In my statements I have never ever mentioned the daughter of Baron von Hammerstein, so as not to cause her any inconvenience. But since, however, I have learned that she was a member of the Hansa Cell, I request that you question her as a witness.

'As a supplement, I state the following:

'My husband made the acquaintance of Fräulein Marie Luise von Hammerstein in 1927–28 as a law student. She was also studying law in Berlin at the time. As a result, I too made her acquaintance. Already, she often went to Communist meetings. She, therefore, had this interest long before she met us. In the course of 1928, she expressed the wish to become a member of the KPD. I advised her against this, but she was not to be dissuaded. Personal contact between Fräulein von Hammerstein and my husband and myself ceased completely in July—August 1931.'

S: That's all true. Well done!

E: 'Since then, neither of us has had anything to do with her. By this time, my husband had long ago been expelled from the KPD and my membership was limited to paying my dues.

'My husband and I were extremely and very unpleasantly surprised when the well-known publications of documents of General von Hammerstein took place. Were proper open proceedings to be initiated because of this document theft, it would immediately become obvious that we have nothing to do with it.'

S: That was the only right line of defence. Only, unfortunately, it didn't do any good.

E: At any rate, such legal proceedings never took place. Can you explain that? A spy scandal like that would have suited the Nazis down to the ground.

S: But that's quite simple. They wanted to protect General von Hammerstein for political reasons. It's true he had lost backing in the Reichswehr, but there were still enough influential officers who supported him. At that point in time, Hitler could not afford any conflict with the senior commanders. Originally, the Nazis put me in a concentration camp as a hostage, in order to be able to blackmail the general should he risk breaking cover. Later, such justifications were no longer necessary. As far as the business with the Hansa Cell was concerned, the court had to acquit me for lack of evidence, but it was soon clear that they were never going to release me again. After 1938, I still had the chance to emigrate to Shanghai, but my application was

Werner Scholem, around 1930

rejected without explanation. Presumably you know how things ended.

E: You should not believe that you are forgotten, Herr Scholem. Posterity knows all about what the Nazis did to you, right up to 17 July 1940, your last day in Buchenwald. The name of the SS guard who shot you is in the files.

S: That surprises me. But you will understand that my satisfaction remains limited. Incidentally, if you are interested in my biography, then you'll know that, as a Communist without a party, I had broken off all contacts with the organization loyal to Moscow. Even in the concentration camp, the Stalinist kapos persecuted me as an 'enemy of the Party and a renegade'.

E: Perhaps you'll be pleased to hear that your girlfriend Marie Luise survived.

S: I warned her in time. But, obstinate as she was, it was impossible to talk her out of her faith in the Party. I don't know what the Gestapo tried to pin on her. It could even be that she fell victim, if one wants to call it that, to a confusion with her sister. I don't have to tell you who the real victim was.

A born intelligence man

The case of Helga, the younger sister, is a clearer and more obvious one, because while there is proof that from 1930 at the latest her friend Leo Roth was an agent of the illegal M-Apparatus of the KPD, this can with good reason be doubted when it comes to Scholem. Essentially, the M-Apparatus was an intelligence and espionage service with the following tasks:

screening Party members and monitoring functionar-
ies, observation of SPD and NSDAP, subversion of
the Reichswehr and the police, commercial espionage,
in addition forging passports, procuring arms and
hiding places. Roth was primarily responsible for 'top
contacts'—informants in government, military and
business circles, the diplomatic service and the press.

But he also passed on information to journalists
like Margret Boveri and to foreign newspapers whenever it appeared politically opportune to the Party
leadership. From May to October 1931, he attended a
course at the Military Academy of the Communist
International in Moscow, which was intended to train
cadres for civil war-like conflicts. Of course, there was
the usual indoctrination as well, and the students were
plagued with both dialectical and historical materialism and the official history of the Party.

Following his return to Germany, Roth lived illegally. In 1933, he rose to one of the most important
positions in the secret organization. He used a large
number of Party or cover names: Viktor, Ernst Hess,
Rudi, Stefan, Berndt, Friedrich Kotzner, Albert.

The information he provided went via the Soviet
Embassy in Berlin or to Moscow headquarters by way
of the Comintern's own mobile radio connection
which was installed on a boat.

Herbert Wehner, Technical Secretary of the Politburo of the German party at the time, worked with
him from 1932. In his *Notes* of 1946, he describes Roth

as one of the most competent organizers he had ever got to know:

> He created and maintained contacts on a scale I never again came across either before or after. The Kippenberger organization had roped him in when he had been threatened with expulsion—in the Berlin Youth Association he had belonged to the most extreme 'Left'. He placed all of his youthful energy, his enormous thirst for revolutionary activity, his exceptional intellectual grasp of political nuances at the service of this work, which absorbed him completely. It was evidently his ambition to prove that he, whom they had been going to expel because of his political views, was able to achieve more than the professional 'politicians' of whose weak sides he, more than others, got a better view in his new work.
>
> The alternative role he had chosen for himself, in a parasitic relation with these debased braggarts, was that of a man who is never mentioned in public, but who through the contacts he organized and maintained got the satisfying feeling of 'actually' being the one who was able to do everything. Viktor wanted to serve the Party and he evidently thought that he did it best in his own way. He didn't believe in the ability of the politicians who stood in the foreground. Ultimately, and deep down in his views of the official Party, he

was a completely disillusioned man who saw squalor and corruption on all sides and knew no other way out than to rise above dismal reality through outstanding performance in his special field. But with what perspective? He believed that in his 'apparatus' there was a crystallizing of the revolutionary 'elite', which in the appropriate situation would act as the core of a kind of military organization, more exactly, 'the real Party'. He did not want to give up these potential possibilities which lived in his imagination. Thus, he resisted the repeated attempts to take him into the service of specialized Russian apparatuses. He probably knew more about these apparatuses than anyone else. He dreaded the existence of a completely rootless agent.

When I said goodbye to Viktor, I had the impression I was saying goodbye to a man who no longer hoped for or expected anything for himself. We had often met in the years after 1932 and had various things to do together. Our views were very much in conflict—I disagreed with his basic positions in almost every respect. But I had found the man to be personally decent and a sincere, cooperative comrade who, furthermore, distinguished himself through great personal courage. I knew that he and his wife (a daughter of General von Hammerstein-Equord), whom I had also got to know and who had sometimes and reliably helped us in Berlin, and who was studying in Germany, inevitably suffered greatly from the uncertainty he faced.

Luise Kraushaar, the woman who later decoded radio messages in Moscow for the Comintern, also met Leo Roth during her time in Berlin. A famous name, which one hardly expects to find in the context of conspiratorial activity, turns up in her unpublished memoirs.

The first secret office, where I worked from spring 1931 until about the middle of 1933, was in Berlin-Friedenau, in a quiet, peaceful street which was easy to oversee and where we would have spotted any observer loafing about outside. I worked in a room in a large apartment, in which the secretary of Albert Einstein and her sister lived. Both of them went out to work every day and I was usually alone there. I think they knew that what I was doing was illegal, but, of course, they didn't know anything about its character and content.

Leo Roth had presumably discovered this quiet apartment and arranged to use it. He must have had a key, too, because now and then he was there without me. After one such visit, there was once a wonderful big apple on my typing desk. With it a couple of lines: '*Bon appétit*, Viktor'.

In 1931, Viktor will have been about twenty-three. Despite the great seriousness of his tasks he was always cheerful and optimistic, personally always very charming. His girlfriend was the daughter of General Hammerstein-Equord, a pretty girl with long blonde curly hair, at that time about twenty years old. Since she passed interesting notes on to us about conversations with guests in the parental home I from time to time met her alone. I was always pleased to meet the two of them together.

Kippenberger's wife Lore was less taken with the couple. About Helga she said: 'She was a plain, pale, slight girl, whose "noble" origin was not obvious to look at. After the Röhm business I asked her, when I met her in Holland, whether she had not been anxious about her father. She replied that she didn't care about him at all.'

Leo Roth 'was handsome, had a good figure, dark eyes, dark hair', but she didn't like that he was well-dressed and that, although a Jew, he moved fairly unselfconsciously and freely around Germany. She thought him adroit and flexible, but also conceited. The judgement of other comrades who were involved with Roth in the secret M-Apparatus of the KPD, was not much more favourable. His principal responsibility, as specialist for what were called top contacts, was to collect information about the Nazi Party, the army, the bourgeois political parties and business. Among these contacts, according to Franz Feuchtwanger in his memoirs, 'were for example the legendary daughters of General von Hammerstein. Alex [Kippenberger] treated him with friendly, sometimes also slightly mocking condescension; studiously devoted to his boss, Stefan's [Leo Roth] behaviour to his colleagues was both arrogant and full of enigmatic self-importance.'

On the one hand, Roth was considered a 'born intelligence man', but on the other, as high-handed and wily. 'Tendency to order people around', 'phoney', 'shady money dealings', 'pushy', 'touch of the dandy', 'by type the political con-man', 'very full of himself', 'dishonest' and 'politically unreliable'—that's what the comrades said. He had acted very impudently, liked to live well, wore only made-to-measure clothes and expensive hats, always travelled with very elegant travelling things and often went on extensive holiday trips. Apart from this, he is supposed to have claimed to speak fluent Arabic and be able to handle machine guns . . . and so on and so on. Soon, the fact that he had moved in 'absolutely bourgeois circles', as was his assignment, was turned against him. All of it can be read in the cadre files, which in this milieu were always kept meticulously, even underground and in exile, not least because they could at any time serve as material to blackmail and incriminate.

All such judgements must, of course, be regarded with the greatest caution; they were, at least in part, probably made under pressure—there will always be some who expresses themselves thus about their companions, in a session of the investigating committee or under interrogation, in order to save their own necks.

Two very different weddings

The Hammerstein children had become very attached to the apartment in the Bendler Block and leaving it was hard for them. In March 1933, the family held one more big party there—a month after Hitler took power. The Reichstag had burned five days before and now it seemed as if, all at once, Marie Luise had left her political adventures behind.

Because, exactly five days after her former lover, Werner Scholem, had been arrested, she married Mogens von Harbou, the son of an old colleague of Hammerstein from the General Staff during the First World War. His father, Bodo von Harbou, had been one of those 'three majors', who had so much influence in the first days of the new Weimar Republic. He, however, had already retired in 1919. He went into industry and became a successful, very wealthy manager.

There is a striking photograph of this wedding which was celebrated at 14 Bendlerstrasse. The scene is arranged as in a comparable picture from 1907. Then Kurt von Hammerstein had married Maria von Lüttwitz, and, just as on that occasion, the ladies appear in pale dresses and the gentlemen in tails or dress uniform. Apart from the army bishop with his splendid order clasp, there is hardly a guest to be seen who hasn't got an aristocratic title, eleven persons of the Hammerstein clan, four of the Lüttwitzes and eight members of the bridegroom's family. Kurt von

Schleicher, the former Reich Chancellor and the bride's godfather, is also among the guests, as he was before the First World War. Now accompanied by his wife Elisabeth, he is the most prominent person there.

And yet the similarity to the photo from the days of the Wilhelmine Empire is misleading. There is a touch of melancholy to the scene, as if those present sensed that the world from which they came was near its end. Only Harbou, who, although he had already completed his law studies, looks very boyish, seems to be enjoying himself, whereas Marie Luise, the bride, appears serious and composed, even gloomy. Her mother smiles bravely, her father assumes a mulish expression and consoles himself with a cigar. Franz and Kunrat, the little brothers, are bored, and Helga, who has for a long time devoted herself to illegal activities, stares at the floor as if she wanted to avoid being recognized. On the night of the Reichstag Fire, she had found a safe hiding place for Klaus Gysi to save him from imminent arrest. (Much later, Gysi would be Minister of Culture in East Germany.) Conspiratorial behaviour had already become second nature to her.

Resplendent at the wedding dinner, incidentally, was a carved block of ice with caviar, a rare extravagance, presumably a gift from the Soviet People's Commissar Voroshilov. It was placed in the middle of the same table at which, a month earlier, Hitler had introduced himself to the generals and announced his war plans.

The marriage which was celebrated there was an ill-starred one. Although Marie Luise was soon pregnant, it only lasted two years. Harbou did not have the least interest in Communism, while Marie Luise, although she had left the Party, could not deny her sympathies. In spring 1934, the Gestapo came and conducted a house search. Marie Luise was interrogated for several days. During the questioning, the proceedings which in 1930 had been quashed at the general's intervention were also brought up. Primarily, however, the Gestapo was concerned with Hitler's notorious speech of February 1933. She was asked if she had talked to anyone about it. She successfully denied it and was then left in peace.

No one in the family, however, believes that any of that was the grounds for the 'terrible divorce business'. There were private reasons for that. After the parents' separation, the Hammersteins' first grandchild remained with the Harbous, whose family history later took a sad turn: Bodo von Harbou committed suicide in 1943 and his son Mogens did so two years later.

In 1937, after the divorce from Harbou, Marie Luise married a second time, a Herr von Münchhausen, who owned an estate, Herrengosserstedt, near Weimar. There, loyal to family tradition, she had three more children. In those years, she kept quiet about her political views.

Maria Therese, like her older sister Marie Luise, also took a new direction after the end of the Weimar

Republic. At the grammar school in Nürnberger-strasse, she had already got to know many Jewish fellow pupils. In 1933, she fell in love with a young medical student called Werner Noble, nicknamed 'Naphta', the son of a rabbi. She became pregnant but did not want to keep the child. In these times, she said, Germany is not the place where one should give birth to a child. Shortly afterwards, her lover had to flee to Prague; she met him there once more but, under the circumstances, a marriage was out of the question. Naphta then emigrated to the United States by way of Strasbourg. The two saw each other again after the war.

In October 1933, Maria Therese rode on her motorbike to a party by the Müggelsee Lake in Berlin at the house of Klaus Mehnert, a young editor and Russian expert. There she met Joachim Paasche, a law student who was impressed by her 'archaic amazonian strength'. 'I would not like to be emotionally dependent on her,' he is supposed to have said. 'She is unique, and I shall probably be deeply wounded if I lose her. So it's better not to be tied to her at all.'

Soon after, there occurred an episode which was to have curious consequences. In January 1934, General Reichenau, head of the Ministerial Office in the Reichs- wehr, offered Maria Therese a post as secretary to General Kühlenthal, military attaché, German embassy, Paris. She travelled to Paris.

The next morning, however, when I woke up in my hotel, a call came from Berlin with the instruction to return immediately. There was a new regulation, which said that all applicants had to be checked by the Gestapo before they took up a post abroad. Waiting for me, when I arrived at the Anhalt Station, were my mother and Joachim Paasche, who proposed to me while we were still in the taxi. The next day, I was summoned to an office at the Defence Ministry, in the same building where we were living. [A section of military intelligence in the Bendler Block.] There, for the first time in my life, I was exposed to an atmosphere of pure hate.

Although only one of his grandfathers was Jewish, under Nazi racial legislation Joachim Paasche was excluded from studying law. He felt threatened and was very worried about Maria Therese. Only later did he say: 'It was the best thing that could have happened to me'—because his true passion was Japanese culture. He enrolled at the East Asia Institute, learned the language and became absorbed in Buddhism.

Joachim and Maria Therese decided to go ahead and marry. Ironically, each of them hoped by this decision to protect the other from the dangers they faced. At the registry office, Maria Therese refused to give the prescribed Hitler salute, while Paasche, who believed he could not risk such a gesture, reluctantly did so. The wedding party, in March 1934—that is, after Hammerstein's retirement—was very modest 'with only close friends' present. It took place in the apartment of Russian émigrés in Keith Strasse. To avoid attracting any attention, not only the father of the bride but also her brothers and sisters stayed away from the party. Klaus Mehnert was one of the witnesses. The bride's mother brought the food: no caviar this time but 'a bucket of trout in gelatine' which the bridegroom interpreted as a good sign. Asked what she wanted as a wedding present, Maria Therese replied: 'A large suitcase.'

The legal expert Carl Schmitt, who knew her because he frequented Schleicher's circle, had warned her against the marriage. Paasche's father Hans was half-Jewish. He had been a naval officer who, during the First World War, had become a pacifist, a vegetarian and a feminist. In May 1920, a sixty-strong Freikorps gang surrounded his house on Waldfrieden estate in the Neumark of Brandenburg and murdered him while he was swimming in the lake. They carried his body into the house and Joachim and his siblings heard them singing: 'Black—white—red ribbon, swastika on helmet/ the Ehrhardt Brigade is what we're called.' (The murderers were never called to account.)

Naturally Maria Therese paid no attention to Schmitt's advice. She admired her late father-in-law.

Through her schoolfriend Wera Lewin, Maria Therese had, long before her marriage, got to know people from Palestine who were keen to recruit young Jews to Zionism and prepare them for hard physical work. 'That gave me the idea of interrupting my studies and working as an apprentice gardener. Then I was employed in an institute of food research for a while. I sat in a potato field with a microscope and counted chromosomes.' That didn't please her father; he pleaded with her 'not to turn farmer'.

'I cannot explain,' says her son Gottfried, 'what drew my mother and also her sister Helga to Jews. Probably the girls were fascinated by the very different, highly intellectual society they found among them. Most of her friends and professors were Jews. The aristocratic self-confidence of the Hammersteins allowed the girls never to bother about aiming for a good match.'

After 1933, her father used his position to protect people under threat from the Gestapo. Gottfried Paasche says that Hammerstein obtained secret service reports in order to find out who was to be arrested. He used his children as messengers to warn those at risk. 'Over breakfast he would mention names, and the children, who were familiar with bohemian and academic circles, knew what they had to do.' Maria Therese took some of them to Prague on her motorbike. Once, she brought a warning to the famous architect Bruno Taut, whom the Nazis regarded as a 'cultural Bolshevist'. He left Germany the same night, went first to Switzerland and later worked in Japan and Turkey.

The newlyweds decided to emigrate—they were to have an adventurous life in exile. Maria Therese was not much interested in the Communist ideas of her sisters. More interested in Zionism, she suggested to her husband that they emigrate to Palestine. In October 1934, they arrived in Kibbutz Givat Brenner, situated between Tel Aviv and the port of Ashdod. The arrival of a general's daughter in the Zionist milieu caused a certain stir. Maria Therese enjoyed the pioneer work, and would probably have liked to stay. Her husband, however, didn't care for agriculture and feared the conflicts between Jews and Arabs and the British Mandate government. Even then there were watchtowers on the kibbutz as protection against Arab intruders. Their friends advised the Paasches to come home; they thought the two of them could be more useful to their cause in Germany. That, of course, was a serious misjudgement. After only a couple of months, a typhus epidemic settled matters and the couple returned to Berlin. Saying goodbye to her friend Wera Lewin, who had emigrated to Jerusalem, was especially hard for Maria Therese; they did not meet again until 1971.

Shortly afterwards, Maria Therese, who was pregnant, was questioned by the Gestapo. 'I could not understand the cautious people around me who were always trying to get by one way or another, without taking the least risk,' she says. 'I didn't want my child to be born in Nazi Germany.' At the end of 1935 the couple fled to Japan. When she took leave of her father, she was thinking of returning in two years; she would never see him again.

Hammerstein gave his son-in-law a visiting card to take with him, addressed to his friend Eugen Ott, whose political career had ended abruptly when Hitler took power. Hammerstein and Ott had known each other ever since both had served on the General Staff in the First World War. In 1932, Ott, as a close confidant of Schleicher, had worked out plans for a *coup d'état*, which, of course, were never realized. 'I saved Ott,' said Hammerstein, 'and had him transferred very far away—to Tokyo, as military attaché.'

There, the major-general (retd) protected the Paasches, especially after he was appointed ambassador in 1938. That was very necessary; after all, Japan was allied to Nazi Germany. 'After two years, we would rather have left the country if that had been possible. We had the feeling we would never understand the Japanese, and they wouldn't understand us either,' writes Maria Therese. The Japanese were very suspicious of all foreigners, and the German colony, the overwhelming majority of which supported Hitler, wanted to have nothing to do with the Paasches. The family lived in great poverty. Maria Therese had four children to look after. 'I had to wash, cook and clean like a slave.' Although there was much that she appreciated in Japanese culture she would have preferred not to stay. 'Simply because of the children it would be much better to go to America. They have suffered poverty and hardship for years, and I would gladly

Eugen Ott, 1934

offer them another life.' There was no hope of that, of course, before the end of the war.

As for Eugen Ott, who became ambassador in 1938, Ruth Mayenburg, who got to know him at the Hammersteins', relates that he became an involuntary informant of Dr Richard Sorge. Like Ruth von Mayenburg, this master spy worked for the Fourth Section of the General Staff of the Red Army. The brilliant charmer and skilled agent soon became a close friend of the German ambassador; the latter's family simply called him 'Uncle Richard', and he had access to all rooms of the embassy and of the residence. He even embarked on an affair with Ott's wife Helma. He supplied his Moscow principals with valuable information, not only about German rearmament but also about the imminent attack on the Soviet Union. Once, at a birthday party in Ott's apartment, the Paasches sat next to Sorge; he impressed them both greatly.

Ruth von Mayenburg is not the only one to think that Eugen Ott lacked the necessary caution when it came to official secrets—they also thought so in Berlin. He was recalled in 1942 and lived as a private person in Beijing until the end of the war.

The Paasches at any rate survived the war years in Japan with his help. Not until 1948 were they able to leave the country.

Maria Therese with Joan and Gottfried, 1940

A Prussian lifestyle

After he retired, Hammerstein moved to 19 Breisacher
Strasse in the suburb of Dahlem with his family, to a
housing development built for civil servants, and at
that time surrounded by cornfields. (The house is still
standing; in the 1980s, a plaque commemorating
the general was placed on it.) An estate in Steinhorst
near Celle, which belonged to a cousin, Wilhelm von
Hammerstein-Loxten, had already become a family
meeting-place for him and his children in the 1920s.
From then on, it served as a place of refuge from the
impertinences of the regime.

A thrifty way of life was the rule. Money was always
short.

'In the last century,' wrote his daughter Helga,
when he no longer wanted to take an active
part in affairs, a grand seigneur withdrew to
his estates, and there he had his income.
Papus was a grand seigneur but without
money. In March 1933, I had to talk to him
about financing my studies. 'At the moment,'
he said, 'I can pay for you to study but as soon
as I'm away from here, it won't be possible
any more.' Then, after he retired, I worked
and paid for it myself. His pension was not
very large, and he had to go without many
things. He was offered plenty of jobs in
industry, but he would have had to make
political compromises wherever he went and
he didn't want to do that. So he was virtually

imprisoned in our house, with all the noise of a big family and Ama's [her mother] inspired disorder. That must have been hard for him. And, of course, there were also constant frictions. I remember a walk with him, I was perhaps twenty-two or twenty-three, on which I tried to reason with him about Ama. But he was terribly bitter, and I was shocked because I didn't achieve anything. It became clear to me that he was in a horrible situation, which in general, however, he overcame with generosity and calm.

At this time, invitations to go hunting were the only possibility of getting away. He couldn't afford other trips.

People from the resistance, like General Ludwig Beck and the SPD politician Carl Goerdeler, met in the Hammersteins' house. Martin Niemöller was minister at the nearby Dahlem Protestant Church until his arrest in 1937, when he was succeeded by Helmut Gollwitzer. The three youngest children, Ludwig, Franz and Hildur, were confirmed there. They were more or less aware of political considerations; it was clear to them that nothing of what was said at home could be spoken outside.

The massacre

Within one year, from January 1933 to spring 1934, the SA, originally a private army of the Nazi Party, had swollen to a strength of 400,000. Ernst Röhm, its Chief of Staff, a former army captain from Bavaria, on first name terms with Hitler, demanded a 'second revolution' and wanted to submerge the much smaller Reichswehr in the 'brown flood'; the generals were to be neutralized and replaced by SA cadres.

Röhm thought that he and his people had been betrayed by Hitler. He organized big parades of his troops and armed them with heavy infantry weapons. Tensions between the army and the SA increased; there were attacks on army officers. The minister of defence warned Hitler that the army would defend its monopoly of force; he would have to expect civil war if he allowed Röhm to have his way. Hindenburg would then declare a state of emergency and transfer executive power to the Reichswehr. That would have deprived Hitler of power. Furthermore, there were rumours that Röhm was conspiring with General von Schleicher, who had never come to terms with the loss of his position, although there was no truth to that.

From 30 June to 2 July, and in the days that followed, Hitler had Röhm and the entire leadership of the SA killed by SS units. The exact number of victims remains unknown, but in three days at least two hundred people are said to have been murdered.

Reactions abroad were devastating. The massacre also opened the eyes of many Germans—not, however, of Dr Carl Schmitt, President of the Union of National Socialist Jurists: his essay in the *Deutsche Juristen-Zeitung* (German Jurists Times) bore the title 'The Führer Protects the Law'. He wrote: 'In truth, the Führer's act was genuine jurisdiction. It is not subject to justice, but was itself supreme justice.'

A settling of accounts of quite a different kind

Hitler and Himmler, however, also took advantage of the so-called Röhm Putsch to settle old scores. On 30 June, they had the last Chancellor of the Weimar Republic, Kurt von Schleicher, and his wife, Elisabeth, shot by an SS squad. One day later, Schleicher's deputy and head of military intelligence, Major-General Ferdinand von Bredow, was murdered in Lichterfelde, Berlin, by men of the Adolf Hitler Leibstandarte of the SS. Papen was spared only at the explicit request of Hindenburg and shuffled off to the diplomatic service. As for Erwin Planck, he was later told that he had 'simply been forgotten'.

After the seizure of power, the Schleichers had retired from the capital. As late as February 1934, Eugen Ott, by then in Tokyo, tried to persuade the general to flee to Japan. Schleicher refused—he did not want to emigrate voluntarily. He moved into a villa by

Griebnitzsee lake in Babelsberg, Potsdam, which Otto Wolff, a friend with interests in heavy industry, had provided for him, and which, incidentally, was very close to the home of Konrad Adenauer, later the first Chancellor of West Germany. According to Ludwig von Hammerstein, 'Schleicher often visited us even after Hitler came to power and we visited him in Babelsberg. He made jokes about Hitler and made no secret of what he thought. He also still remained on friendly terms with foreign ambassadors, in particular François-Poncet.' The report of an agent in the Reich Defence Ministry, which was intended for Moscow, also states that Schleicher, but especially his wife, always criticized the regime very incautiously at parties in Babelsberg; they had often been warned, but in vain. A servant who had not been in their house for long was suspected of being a Nazi informer.

What happened there on 30 June is described by the Schleichers' housekeeper, Marie Güntel:

Present in the room was the general, who was seated at his desk, and Frau von Schleicher, who was sitting in the easy chair beside the desk with some needlework. At that moment, the bell of the garden door rang noticeably loud and vigorously. There appeared five men, one of whom also asked where the general was. This man—I estimated him to be thirty years old—was wearing a dark suit. The other men appeared to me to be considerably younger, and were all wearing lighter-coloured suits. I replied at first, 'Herr General is not at home,' then, 'he has gone walking.' At that, the man in the dark suit pushed past me and snapped at me in a rough voice that I shouldn't lie to him but immediately tell the truth about where the general was. At that moment, all five men had one hand behind their backs. That they were already holding revolvers I was able to ascertain a few seconds later. As I realized that I could not, after all, prevent any further intrusion into the house by the men, I said: 'I shall go and see.'

Before I could say anything more, I heard a voice immediately behind me: 'Are you the general?' Herr General, still sitting at his desk, turned half way round to the door and said, 'Yes, indeed'. In that fraction of a second, three shots were fired almost simultaneously. I know with great certainty that, before the shots, were fired Herr General made no further movement apart from the half-turn of the upper half of his body, in particular did not with one hand reach into his pocket, to the desk or anywhere else. There was no question whatsoever of any kind of resistance on the general's part. In all of this, I was standing in the middle of the room. At the moment of the shots, Frau von Schleicher was sitting beside the desk just as calmly as her husband. As I, scared to death, ran out of the room screaming, I also heard Frau von Schleicher screaming and further shots fired.

Marie Güntel made her statement in front of a notary two days later. She was unable, as she says, to get over the death of her master. In July 1935, she committed suicide in the Heiligensee lake in Potsdam.

The new leadership of the Reichswehr was at first quite well disposed to Hitler's break with legality, because they regarded Röhm and his gang as plebeian competitors. It is remarkable, however, that most of the generals also accepted the murder of their former defence minister without protest. They thereby made themselves accomplices to the massacre. They did not grasp that in the SS, the true winner in these events, a much more dangerous rival than the SA had emerged. At the time, Erwin Planck told Werner von Fritsch, Hammerstein's successor as Chief of Army Command: 'If you look on without doing anything, then sooner or later you will suffer the same fate.'

The agent's report to Moscow already mentioned states:

> Gentlemen from the Defence Ministry say that the point in time for the Reichswehr to intervene has once again passed. A state of emergency should have been proclaimed on Monday, 2 June. At the same time, or at latest at the cabinet meeting on Tuesday, the ministers Neurath, Blomberg, Papen, Seldte would *have* to have resisted. They *should not* have approved the course of events, instead they had all knuckled under in fear of their lives. The bourgeoisie is dominated by a

general state of paralysis, by a fatalistic wait-
and-see attitude—everyone whispers in his
neighbour's ear, full of fear of exposing themselves, all feel that 'something else is still to
come.'

In business circles, there were worries about
increasing indebtedness and the raw materials crisis.
What would happen when there was no more work, but
no dismissals were allowed? 'Then there'll be hell to
pay.' Parallels were being drawn with Russia: National
Socialism was turning into German Bolshevism. In
that case, what happens to the Reichswehr? Another
way out was war, but that would mean an end to
Germany's existence. So much for the worry lines of
capitalism.

The anonymous correspondent also commented
on Kurt von Hammerstein's role. During the days of
the Röhm crisis, he had been the centre of attention
of Berlin officers' circles; comrades from the ministry
had protected him, as it had been feared that he might
be arrested at any moment.

What is certain is that in a memorandum which
opposition groups in the army addressed to Hindenburg, in July 1934, it was proposed to replace the
Hitler government by a directorate led by Hindenburg. Kurt von Hammerstein's name turns up in this
document as well; he was supposedly designated as
minister for the army.

The Blue Book, as it was called, which published
the memorandum, runs to only a few pages and was

printed in 1934 under the title *Englische Grammatik* (English Grammar), giving Leipzig as the fictitious place of publication. This camouflaged text included, in small print and on special paper, a *White Book About the Shootings of 30 June*. The unnamed publisher was the illegal KPD. The original had previously appeared in Münzenberg's Paris publishing house.

For Hammerstein, the killing of his old friend Schleicher, to whom, irrespective of all political differences, he had always remained loyal, and of Schleicher's collaborator, Ferdinand von Bredow, was more than he could bear. 'These people,' he said, 'have turned an old soldier like me into an anti-militarist.' In defiance of an order from his nominal superior, Werner von Blomberg, he was the only general to attend Schleicher's funeral in the Park Cemetery in Berlin-Lichterfelde. He was accompanied by his wife and his daughter Maria Therese, who was a godchild of Schleicher and very fond of him. In the face of the terror exercised by the regime, this was an altogether hazardous gesture. Erwin Planck, to whom Hammerstein was to remain close, also turned up.

The few mourners, however, waited in vain for the coffins. In order to cover all traces of the murder, the Gestapo had had the corpses burned. Not until after the sham burial were the urns with the ashes handed over to members of the family.

Sidelined (I)

Following his retirement, Hammerstein apparently lived very quietly and outwardly at least refrained from taking up any political position. In April 1934, shortly before Schleicher's murder, Jacob Wuest, the American military attaché, reports to Washington that the general and his family have moved to a modest home in Dahlem.

> He leads a very active life, however, and is perhaps busier than he was in the Reichswehr, where he was well-known for taking his duties lightly. He remains close to Schleicher and von Alvensleben, who formerly, as Chairman of the Herrenclub [Gentleman's Club], pulled the strings in German politics. Hammerstein, like Schleicher, cultivates a certain predilection for Russia, which he knows well; he was on good terms with Khinchuk, the Soviet ambassador in Berlin, who has just been relieved of his post.

> The meetings at the Hammersteins' house are made up of various circles. At the moment, an evening is planned which is intended to bring together industrialists and other experts, in order, as it's said, 'to discuss the political situation'. Three days ago, there took place a private meeting with three English generals, of whom only one spoke German, and, in mid-April, the German military attaché in Paris, General von Kühlenthal

paid Hammerstein a discreet visit. In recent weeks, I had the privilege of frequently calling on him and his family on quite informal occasions: a car tour, a picnic, a bathing excursion, an invitation to tea or a supper with the family.

Under the conditions prevailing in Germany, it seems to me that General von Hammerstein has got involved in a risky, not to say dangerous game, which I believe has to do with the possibility of a political crisis in the unstable situation of the country.

A posthumous conversation with Ruth von Mayenburg (II)

E: Am I intruding?

M: Not at all. I find your eagerness amusing. You've evidently taken a liking to my tea.

E: Indeed, but that isn't what brings me here. I have, if you like, set my heart on your friend Hammerstein. You, after all, met him a number of times after his retirement. You were by that time, I believe, a convinced Communist.

M: Naturally.

E: Nevertheless, a fairly unusual choice for someone like you, born into an aristocratic family.

M: Well, I wasn't the only one. Just think of the general's two daughters! Apart from which, it's perhaps easier for people like us than for the bourgeoisie to get on with the working class. I was living in Vienna. I got to know my husband Ernst Fischer there. We married in 1932. You probably don't know that there was a workers' uprising two years later.

E: Oh yes. Dollfuss, Social Democratic Schutzbund against right-wing Heimwehr, army and police.

M: Sixteen hundred dead and wounded. I took part with Ernst.

E: A dangerous business.

M: Yes. Our friend Elias Canetti hid us after the uprising was suppressed.

E: That's when you joined the Austrian Communist Party (KPÖ).

M: What else!

E: And your family, what did they have to say about all of that?

M: Oh, my family! They were afraid, of course. In their eyes I was an outcast. We had to flee abroad. With my husband I went first to Prague and then to Moscow.

E: You are supposed to have worked for the Comintern as a courier and as an agent under the cover names Lena and Ruth Wieden.

M: Oh no. I made a much more exciting choice. I belonged to the Fourth Section in the General Staff of the Red Army.

E: Espionage, therefore.

M: That ugly word didn't exist in our vocabulary. I saw myself as an ambassador, also, if you like, as a scout. As an extended arm of the Red Army, in which I reached the rank of major.

E: But Madame, how on earth were you able to reconcile that with your lifestyle? Always the best hotels, the champagne breakfast, the sleeping cars, the hunting parties, the casinos, the good addresses in Berlin's west end, the elegant yellow spring costume in your suitcase . . . Here a big party at the Hungarian embassy, there an excursion in the silver Steyr

Ruth von Mayenburg.
Portrait by Rudolf Hausner, 1951

cabriolet or in the Tatra limousine . . . and the signet ring . . .

M: . . . with the cyanide capsule under the gold lid. Let's leave it at that!

E: And at the same time the workers' bars, the smoky back rooms in the safe houses.

M (laughs): Such a double life was absolutely necessary — and I greatly enjoyed it. You have no idea how much the fashionable appearance that you make fun of helped me in my work. It gained me access to circles that would have been quite out of reach of the comrades. Apart from which, the glamour functioned like a cloak of invisibility! The Nazis and their accomplices were mostly very, very ordinary people, full of inferiority complexes.

E: And it was in your capacity as major in the intelligence service that you called on Hammerstein again.

M: Already on my first visit to Berlin.

E: Did you seriously imagine that he would be willing to enter into relations with the Red Army?

M: Why not? That would really have been nothing new for him. He had told me about his Soviet expeditions often enough. He had nothing against the Russians. The only problem was that such contacts could now cost him his head. It's in any case something like a miracle that Hammerstein survived the slaughter of 30 June. When we got the first news of it in Moscow, I thought of him at once. Yes, I was really very worried about him, believe me.

E: You called him Hako?

M: An inconspicuous name to call him by, which could also be used on more formal public occasions.

E: Thirty-five years later, in your book *Blaues Blut und Rote Fahnen* (Blue Blood and Red

Flags), you wrote down in detail your conversations with him. I admire your memory!

M: Yes, then it was still all right. Today, not much of it is left. I don't know where it came from, but for a long time I was able to repeat long conversations, overheard remarks, information of some kind, which seemed important to me — and in those days everything seemed important to me — with the precision of a gramophone recording. Read for yourself! You'll be surprised at what I was capable of.

A posthumous conversation
with Leo Roth

R: I'm afraid I can't even offer you a chair. You can sit on the bed if you like. Well?

E: What I always wanted to ask you, Herr Roth: Did you see it coming?

R: What?

E: The Stalinist purges. You knew the Party and its apparatus from your own experience.

R: You can leave out the Herr Roth. Just call me Viktor. We weren't fussy, not in Germany and not in Moscow. Everyone who joined the Communists knew very well that there would be setbacks, mistakes and victims. I myself was already expelled from the club in 1926. Left deviation, suspicion of Trotskyism and so on. And that there had been countless dead since 1917, we knew that too. In October, in the civil war, in Kronstadt, in the campaign against the kulaks, in the first trials of the saboteurs . . . You know, or you don't, what happens when you make an omelette.

E: Did you never feel threatened by your own comrades?

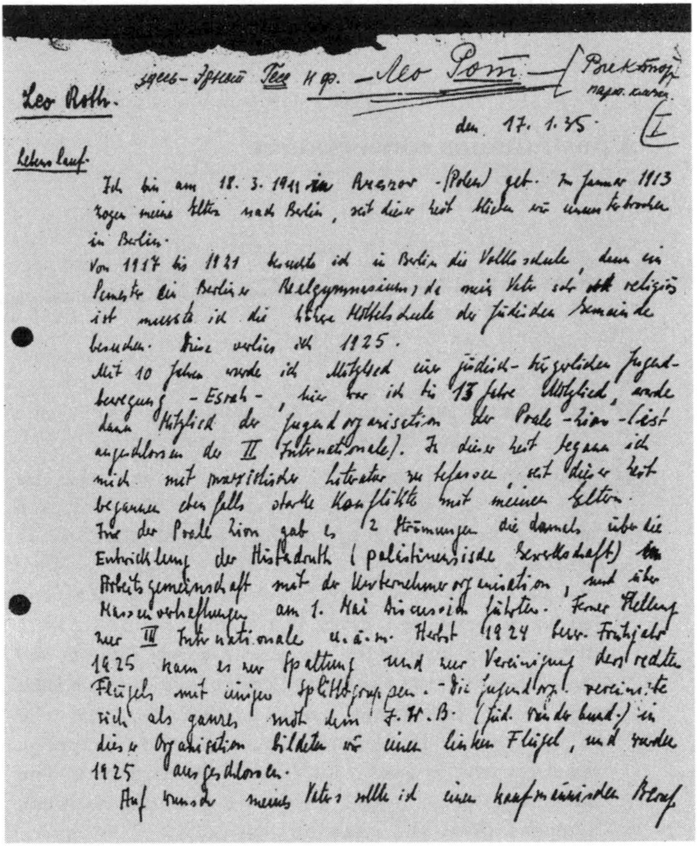

Leo Roth.

den 17. 1. 35.

Lebenslauf.

Ich bin am 18. 3. 1911 in Rzeszow (Polen) geb. Im Januar 1913 zogen meine Eltern nach Berlin, seit dieser Zeit blieben wir ununterbrochen in Berlin.

Von 1917 bis 1921 besuchte ich in Berlin die Volksschule, dann ein Semester ein Berliner Realgymnasium; da mein Vater sehr religiös ist musste ich die höhere Mittelschule der jüdischen Gemeinde besuchen. Diese verliess ich 1925.

Mit 10 Jahren wurde ich Mitglied einer jüdisch-bürgerlichen Jugendbewegung – Esra –, hier war ich bis 13 Jahre Mitglied, wurde dann Mitglied der Jugendorganisation der Poale-Zion-Linke angeschlossen der II Internationale). In dieser Zeit begann ich mich mit marxistischer Literatur zu befassen, seit dieser Zeit begannen ebenfalls starke Konflikte mit meinen Eltern.

In der Poale Zion gab es 2 Strömungen die damals über die Entwicklung der Histadruth (palästinensische Gewerkschaft) Arbeitsgemeinschaft mit der Unternehmerorganisation, und über Massenverhaftungen am 1. Mai Diskussion führten. Ferner Stellung zur III Internationale u.ä.m. Herbst 1924 bzw. Frühjahr 1925 kam es zur Spaltung und zur Vereinigung des rechten Flügels mit einigen Splittergruppen. – Die Jugendorg. vereinigte sich als ganzes mit dem J.W.B. (Jüd. Wanderbund) in dieser Organisation bildeten wir einen linken Flügel, und wurden 1925 ausgeschlossen.

Auf Wunsch meines Vaters sollte ich einen kaufmännischen Beruf

Leo Roth, handwritten curriculum vitae, 1935

THE SILENCES OF HAMMERSTEIN

R: There were enough other enemies.

E: I'm surprised that you were so unsuspecting. Hans Kippenberger, your boss, had already realized in 1934 where things were going. At the time your colleague Franz Feuchtwanger — I'm sure you remember him — found him 'disheartened as never before. Emigration didn't appear to suit him,' he said, 'but above all he was very bitter about developments in the Party leadership, where Ulbricht was more and more emerging as the strong man. And he, not without reason, regarded the M—Apparatus as a hindrance which could only be smashed by means of political slander and starving it of funds.'

R: Yes, Alex knew the score. He was right, of course. But just like me he suffered the consequences.

E: Herbert Wehner relates that you met in 1935. You were to receive instructions for your trip to Prague.

R: Oh, Wehner. He always knew it all. Did you know him?

E: No.

R: Pity. I would like to know what became of him. I bet he saved his neck.

E: You're right. He says that shortly before you went to the Soviet Union, you entrusted something to him.

R: Really? I'm surprised.

E: On behalf of the organization you are supposed, to have maintained contacts with the British, French and Czech military attachés, general staffs and intelligence services. Allegedly, you also had conversations with André François-Poncet, who as French ambassador in Berlin was a person of some consequence.

R: Naturally. That was all part of the business. Without my contacts with the embassies and with foreign journalists, I would never have been of any use to the Party. As a result, I was able to report on the Reichstag Fire, the indictment of Dimitrov, the map-exercises of the German General Staff and the progress of German rearmament.

E: Wehner says that, in May 1936, you asked him for advice as to what was better: to talk about these contacts or to withhold them. It had been clear to him that the matter would make your personal position that much more difficult. That's the way he put it.

R: Ah! So he was worried about me! How considerate of him! And what does he say he advised me to do?

E: Tell it all. He thought you should tell Comrades Pieck and Ulbricht, but also the Comintern, the truth.

R: Sounds just like him.

E: Did you not feel uneasy?

R: In the work I was involved in, one constantly felt uneasy.

E: But you knew your Lenin.

R: I know what you're getting at. But, given the choice, I preferred to be a useful idiot instead of a useless one. One can't be a Communist with impunity. There's nothing more to say. And now if you'll excuse me. I'm tired, very tired.

Soundings

In the course of 1935, Ruth von Mayenburg, already in Soviet service, reduced her links to the German party, above all to German émigré circles, because penetration by Gestapo informers was suspected there, and returned to Germany with forged documents.

My first call in Berlin was on Colonel-General Kurt Baron von Hammerstein-Equord. The general, now in civilian clothes, was somewhat surprised to see the small person again after several years. 'What does she want here?' I thought I could read from a sidelong glance. Yes, I did want something. But first of all he had to be quite clear about my political position and I had to be clear whether there were now limits to his opposition to Hitler which he would not cross. I said to him: 'In Austria, we went to the barricades against Dollfuss. I was there. Here, in Germany, why did the Reichswehr at least not undertake something against the fellow?'

'It would have meant civil war.'

'And?'

'I'm against civil war. Coups? Never. But you're a bold one.'

What Hammerstein thought about the Nazi dictatorship, about its deeds and misdeeds and the calamity which was still to come of it for Germany and Europe, 'if the fellows don't do each other in first, which one might hope for . . .', was expressed with laconic brevity—nothing was left unsaid. But—and this was the crucial question for me (and no doubt also for the Gestapo)—was this most important thinker of the old Reichswehr working on a military and political General Staff plan against the regime? Did he have allies? Or was he content with the role of someone who is resigned, who only takes part in events as a hostile observer, and otherwise goes hunting?

That first visit was followed by more to the house out in Dahlem, not far from the church of Pastor Niemöller of the Confessing Church. At first, they were only occasional, fitted in between trips through half of Germany, then they became ever more frequent. When I came back from abroad, I reported immediately. I studied him with a purpose in mind.

'What do you think of the stab in the back legend, Herr von Hammerstein?'

'Nothing at all.'

'But others think differently. Quite a few million in fact.'

'Millions don't think—they're only talked into it.'

'And the humiliating Versailles Treaty? The best card in the Nazis' hand?'

'It's a marked card.'

'Well, it's done pretty well so far.'

'It'll ruin us all.'

When we talked about the Nazis, he never minced words. Otherwise, he rested—'as in a hammock', I mocked—calmly and discreetly in his intelligence. No event, no matter how stormy, capsized him, caused him to look for something to hold on to. His ability to characterize people in only a few words, to sum up the essence of a matter, compressed substantial conversations into a minimum period of time. One had to watch like a hawk to grasp the significance of remarks made in passing.

In summer 1935:

I tried to reflect calmly and clearly on whom I'd been with recently and what had been talked about. For example, there were Hako's two daughters, Esi [Maria Therese] and Helga Hammerstein-Equord. Helga worked at the Kaiser Wilhelm Research Institute, in a kind of secret department. They want to make sugar out of wood—that would be a militarily important discovery. There are also Japanese working there. She is good friends with one of them. I picked up Helga two or three times from the Institute. Esi is learning Japanese, isn't she? With Helga, Esi, two Japanese men and a German we went first to the Esplanade hotel, later to a disreputable private apartment. Talked politics half the night—all as opponents of the Nazis. All? Were the Japanese not a little reticent? The girls are said to be Communists. Do they still have a link to the Party, a fresh one? The apartment and the German looked like it to me. But Esi

allayed my mistrust. The Hammersteins'
house? It's undoubtedly watched. It's a likely
point of penetration at any rate.

There were further meetings. Once, as Mayenburg
relates,

we travelled on the same train. Hammerstein,
the old cigar-puffer, in a non-smoking compartment, I in a smoking compartment. He
had very sensitive eyes and constant inflam-
mations of the eyelids which dotted his stubby
pale lashes. We turned it into an undercover
expedition, didn't know one another, went to
different hotels in a spa. I think it was Bad
Homburg. A completely unpolitical atmosphere. No smell of the cesspit.

'Just watch out to see if they're shadowing
me. I'm meeting someone here, it could be
unpleasant for him, if they found out.' It was
the only occasion I discovered him behaving
in a conspiratorial way. At the time I suspected he had contacts with the British.
Hammerstein, who could presumably also
rely on internal information, which still
flowed to him as before, saw through the
deceits of the Nazi leadership, believed
neither in their 'desire for peace' nor in the
protestations of 'non-intervention and equality of rights of nations'. Several times he
expressed his disapproval of the appeasement
policies of the British government. Hammerstein said: 'The gentlemen should change tack

before it's too late.' It seemed to me likely, therefore, that he got his warnings to the Foreign Office through certain channels. High time to let him know who his true friends are.

How and when—that required careful consideration. Also consultation with Moscow. The opportunity to talk to Hammerstein alone and not in the family circle or in the presence of guests was also found in Berlin. Despite the protests of his wife, who didn't like him going out into the street alone at night and feared SS gangsters could waylay him, he always insisted on accompanying me to the last underground or to the bus. His revolver in his coat pocket, he said scornfully: 'Shot while attempting to escape—not with me!' It was on this walk across the deserted, barely illuminated terrain that began behind the garden, across the fields to the main road, that we had our tentative and finally very open conversations.

A posthumous conversation
with Helga von Hammerstein (I)

E: Frau von Hammerstein . . .

H: My name is Helga Rossow.

E: Forgive me, I'm talking about the time before your marriage. Did you not fear at the time that through your actions you were putting your parents and your brothers and sisters at risk?

HANS MAGNUS ENZENSBERGER

H: I see no reason why I should talk to you. I would like you to leave me in peace. It's all so long ago.

E: That's exactly why. Forgetfulness is not a virtue. Apart from that, I admire the bravado and the determination with which you proceeded.

H: I don't care. If you absolutely must know: I saw no grounds for showing consideration for my father. I found his hesitation in those days, when Hitler was just around the corner, simply insufferable. Presumably, my brothers and sisters still hold it against me that I behaved the way I did and not otherwise. They say: 'But he always stood by you, he protected you all those years.' That's true. But what business is all that of yours? It's not something you can understand.

E: But I would like to try to understand.

H: But you haven't got a clue. I don't mean that as a reproach. It's not your fault that you live in more comfortable times. Perhaps I should even congratulate you on not having experienced anything out of the ordinary. But don't be pleased too soon! Who knows what's still in store for you and your people. Then we'll see whether you get through it all scot-free.

E: One more reason to study your story. Although I very much doubt whether we can take you as a model.

H: You will make your own mistakes.

E: That's certain.

H: Well, why don't you at last come out with what you want?

E: Your meeting with Leo Roth was not chance. He was assigned to you, in order to get access to your father's papers. I have here a document from Moscow which proves that. It bears the date 16 December 1936.

H: Leo was on trial then.

E: Yes, criminal case No. 6222. Do you want to hear what is in the files of the examining judge? It concerns the statement of a certain Gustav Burg.

H: That was his Party name. In reality, he was called Gustav König. Yes, Leo knew him. Probably they blackmailed him. He no doubt wanted to save his skin, as did most.

E: If that was his intention, then it didn't help him. In 1937, he too was sentenced to death.

H: And you know what was in the statement? How?

E: After 1989, the Moscow archives were accessible for a couple of years, at any rate to people who knew how to negotiate with the responsible officials.

H: I see. I can hardly believe it. But, assuming it's true, what did this man Burg say about Leo and myself?

On criminal case no. 6222

On 16 December 1936, Burg, a former member of the M-Apparatus, made the following statement to the examining judge in Moscow:

It was in 1929 that Comrade Hess [that is Leo Roth], who then was working in the intelligence apparatus of the German Communist Youth League, informed me that he was acquainted with the daughter of General von Hammerstein. She was studying at Berlin University and was the eldest daughter, by name Marie-Luise. He proposed to me that we make use of this girl for our work and I was

Leo Roth, 'Viktor' cadre file of the
Executive Committee of the Comintern, 1936/37

in agreement and immediately gave Com. Leo concrete assignments which he was to give the daughter.

After a couple of days, Com. Leo communicated various pieces of information to me. If I remember rightly, these were pieces of information about the then political situation, Hammerstein discussed it with his father-in-law, General von Lüttwitz. These communications were quite interesting.

Through Com. Leo, I gave the daughter the instruction to go and look at her father's desk, to see what was to be found there. The girl informed us that there were very many documents there. She could not, however, tell us a great deal about their contents, and instead suggested that the next day we ourselves come to her house, which was on Hardenbergstrasse near Zoo Station, because that day her parents were not at home.

Taking all due precautions, Com. Leo and I went to the apartment. There was no one else present apart from the daughter. We looked through all documents and took a number away with us in order to photograph these; we had two days, because her father was on a tour of inspection. We photographed all the material, I gave Com. Alex [Kippenberger] a copy, Com. Thälmann got a copy and Com. Seelmann.

Hammerstein then became head of the Reichswehr. We noticed, when we took up the work again, that the girl now gave us only few and uninteresting communications. It appeared as if she didn't want to work for us any more. Com. Leo spoke to her about it. She told him she now had to devote herself to her studies and suggested we work together with her younger sister, who had more time and who wanted to work [with us]. There was yet another sister but she was not reliable [Maria Therese]. Com. Leo then worked with the younger sister [Helga]. I no longer remember her name. She brought us interesting communications, because at this time General Hammerstein travelled to the Soviet Union.

Shortly before Hammerstein travelled to the Soviet Union, we made an impression of the key to the safe, in order, at a suitable opportunity, to see what documents are to be found there. From the Berlin intelligence apparatus we requested a good locksmith for safes—to make a good impression of the key and then make a second key from this impression.

One day, Com. Leo came and informed me that, while trying it out, the younger sister had broken off a bit of the key. We discussed the matter and came to the conclusion to try everything possible to remove the broken-off bit from the lock. Hammerstein himself was not present in Berlin. One night, therefore,

Com. Adolf went into the apartment with the younger daughter. I think her mother was not in the house at the time. Com. Adolf worked for a very long time and managed to break apart the bit inside the lock.

Then, after a certain time, Hammerstein came back. The next day he wanted to open the safe, but the original key no longer fitted—it only went halfway into the lock. Hammerstein made a big fuss and then informed the counter-intelligence section of the Army Ministry, which then soon sent a couple of officers.

The younger daughter later told us the following: all the family members were questioned about whether they had been at the safe, all denied it.

We then broke off the contact entirely, in order to prevent the daughters possibly falling under any suspicion.

A posthumous conversation with Helga von Hammerstein (II)

E: What do you say to that, Helga? Forgive me if I insist.

H: About what?

E: About the Moscow sources from the years 1936 and 1937.

H: No doubt they all kept their mouths shut, including Leo.

E: All? I can hardly believe that. One thing at least emerges from the document — you were instrumentalized. First Leo Roth tried, as it says here, to 'make use' of your sister, Marie Luise. Only when she refused was he put on to you.

H: I was already a committed Communist when I got to know Leo and I did nothing, then at least, which I would not stand up for.

E: You lived with Roth from 1930/31, underground.

H: You will hardly expect me to provide you with information about my love life.

E: In Moscow, he always maintained you were his wife.

H: We didn't believe in registry offices. Leo was my husband — that's all.

E: Then, under the cover name Grete Pelgert you worked for the Department for Special Contacts in the military policy section of the KPD. Authorized to give instructions there was Hans Kippenberger.

H: You're well informed. Perhaps you yourself are working for some principal or other.

E: I fear you overestimate the interest of today's secret services in these old stories.

H: Then why are you spying on me?

E: Listen! I am interested in the history of your family because it says a great deal about how one could survive Hitler's rule without capitulating to it. If you call that spying, you're doing me an injustice. I have talked to your siblings Franz and Hildur. They, too, ask themselves how it came about that you worked for the Comintern, how long you remained true to your Communist convictions and when you broke with the Party.

H: What business is it of my family? Tell them they shouldn't bother me. It's been hard enough for me. And now will you just go! I don't want to talk about it.

A birthday and its consequences

On 26 September 1936, Kurt von Hammerstein was
fifty-eight. Ruth von Mayenburg took part in the cele-
brations at his home.

> I brought a couple of dozen crayfish with me,
> freshly caught with my own hands [in the
> River Havel]. Red crayfish added a touch of
> elegance to the Hammersteins' truly Prussian
> feast: cured spare rib of pork, overcooked
> potato dumplings and sweet prune sauce with
> it. I feel ill even today when I think about it.
> Lots of people I didn't know. Lots of dishes to
> be rinsed.

> Hako steered me to his side without inter-
> rupting his noticeably intense, half-whispered
> conversation with a guest. I had not seen him
> so animated for a long time. The guest, a
> senior serving officer [Eugen Ott] in civilian
> evening dress, must just have returned from
> Japan after a long absence. Apparently, he
> was German military attaché in Tokyo. He
> seemed alarmed by what Hammerstein threw
> at him in terms of political analyses of the
> world situation, of internal German events
> from the point of view of an enemy of Hitler.
> The guest, on the other hand, visibly agitated,
> expounded on the necessary struggle against
> world Bolshevism and, related to that, shared
> German–Japanese interests: 'Over there,
> we're working on a close alliance between
> ourselves and the Japanese . . .' Hako: 'Pact

against the Russians?' After a quick glance at me, the guest avoided the question. They could continue the conversation later, just the two of them.

Then I picked up the words 'heavy artillery'. Hako said them with such astonishment that I threw all caution to the winds. 'You must be mistaken—*heavy* artillery, we don't have that yet!'—'Yes, yes . . .' The guest looked through his wallet and from a scrap of paper read out the name of the place, somewhere in Schleswig-Holstein, a tiny place he had been unable to find on the map. Hako repeated the name, thought for a moment: 'Don't know it! Must be a completely new facility . . .' He appeared honestly surprised.

Mayenburg's contact man with the Red Army was surprised too: 'Four weeks later, this courier meaningfully handed me a sealed letter. In it—to my almost startled astonishment—was a flattering personal letter from Marshal Voroshilov.'

Hammerstein also talked to Mayenburg about his appraisal of the situation:

Hammerstein considered the idea of a coup, a seizure of power by parts of the Wehrmacht leadership, to be crackbrained. He and General Schleicher had knowingly missed what had possibly been the right moment, when the government crisis was at its height before the appointment of Hitler as Reich Chancellor. Since then, he had often asked himself whether they should not have acted then. But he had underestimated Hitler and overestimated Schleicher. He himself had been concerned to keep the Reichswehr out of the political power struggles, out of the Party's political intrigues.

He told me a number of dramatic details from the days around 30 January 1933, about the behaviour of Hindenburg and his son Oscar, about Franz von Papen and others, all of whom he described as 'scoundrels' and 'crooks'. I encouraged him to put it down in writing, and I offered to get a report of such political, indeed historical, importance safely out of the country. 'So that you lot can publish it, when it suits you—no!' Naturally, I protested. Hako tapped my hand: 'Rest assured, little one, if I do put something on paper—then it won't be lost. That's for certain!' [Hammerstein made sure that his account, written in 1935, of the last days before Hitler took power, promptly found its way into an English safe. After the war, his son Kunrat tracked it down and published it.]

'Should another crisis situation like that of 30 June 1934 arise, and the Wehrmacht become involved in it, then it would be altogether possible'—Hammerstein conceded—'that certain people among the commanding officers would advocate the army taking power, indeed perhaps even attempt it.' It was much more likely, however, that the few who thought politically, would rather take retirement than want to be responsible for the 'pigsty'. 'Like me, for example,' said Hammerstein word for word. 'If the German herd voted for such a leader—then they should also take the consequences.' They should not be spared that bitter experience, otherwise they'll never learn. 'You're ducking out, you're retreating to the position of an aristocrat!' I said to his face. Hammerstein smiled: 'That's the only intelligent thing a gentleman can do now. I'm not a "hero"—there, you're mistaken in me. I stand my ground, if I have to. But I don't shove my way to the wheel of history as your lot do!' And then he said something completely disarming: 'I'm too lazy for that!'

The explanation that followed, that laziness was a good character attribute, that it allowed human beings to develop their reason, to act with circumspection, culminated in the sentence: 'One has time to think. Diligence is only an intrusion.'

A quite different life as an agent

The following is known about Leo Roth's movements after Hitler's seizure of power:

In 1933, he was in Paris several times. He handed the indictment in the Reichstag Fire trial to Münzenberg there.

In December of the same year, he went to Switzerland, because the Berlin organization had been smashed by the Gestapo. At Christmas, he talked to Wehner at a meeting in Spindlermühle just across the border in Czechoslovakia.

In January 1934, he returned to Berlin where he stayed in a safe house until May.

He then travelled to Moscow where he lectured at the military policy school of the Comintern. The Party ordered him not return to Germany where he appeared to be at risk.

In June, and until August, 1934, he was assigned to 'planning work' in Paris. That consisted of bombastic reflections on how uprisings could be instigated in the Saarland and in Hitler's Germany.

In September, he made contact with colleagues in Geneva, Vienna, Prague and Zürich.

At the end of September, he was detailed to Saarbrücken to direct the Party's political agitation in the run-up to the Saar Plebiscite. There, he obtained a journalist's identity card for Herbert Wehner and arranged for his accommodation. With the help of French Communists, he also began to organize armed groups which, however, never went into action.

After the victory of the supporters of the Saar's return to Germany, he had to flee to Amsterdam at the end of 1935. Based there, he was, for one year, head of counter-intelligence and responsible instructor for western Germany.

The underground activity necessitated numerous journeys with forged passports. He stayed illegally in Düsseldorf, went to Paris and to Prague where he met Pieck and Ulbricht.

At the end of July, together with Helga von Hammerstein, he was in Amsterdam again where he lived in a 'smart neighbourhood'; Herbert Wehner also stayed there for a while.

In October 1935, the first conflicts with the Party leadership took place. At the Brussels conference, the Politburo decided to replace Hans Kippenberger, Leo Roth and others. It was the beginning of the end of the secret M-Apparatus, which was then entirely liquidated in the course of the Moscow Purges.

Herbert Wehner had to inform Comrade Viktor that he had been relieved of his functions and ordered to Moscow. First, Roth treated himself to a twelve-day winter holiday in the Tyrol, accompanied by Helga. The Party had also put a forged passport at her disposal. Before they took leave of one another at Zürich central station, the couple agreed that Helga should try to emigrate to the Soviet Union where Leo Roth intended to stay. He arrived in Moscow in January 1936.

While she waited for news from him, Helga von Hammerstein went to Prague where she once again handed a KPD official, presumably Herbert Wehner, documents from the Army Ministry.

The mole in the Bendler Block

In June 1936, however, Leo Roth had to disappoint his superiors:

> *Regarding General Staff War Game 1936*
>
> At the beginning of April, I received a letter informing me that at this year's General Staff Game von Hammerstein would have a *leading* role.
>
> To an inquiry on my part on 23 April, I received the information that von H. will take part in the game and there is a possibility of obtaining it.
>
> At the beginning of May (6th), I received the information that von H. is *not in charge* of the game and that there are differences, and it is doubtful whether the game can be obtained.
>
> On 6 June I received a letter [from Helga]:
>
> 'I have now got the brochures for the trip after all! I believe I understand your reasons and so will *for the time being* let them be. (This refers to my negative letter on the basis of the discussion *here*.) But please write to me *immediately* whether you really consider it right. Because I don't rightly know whether I can take the responsibility.'

The involved turns of phrase can be explained by the years of conspiratorial training on the part of the author. 'Travel brochures' presumably refers to secret documents about the General Staff Game.

Leo Roth, handwritten note for the cadre section
(*Regarding General Staff War Game 1936*)

Helga evidently had scruples whether it was right to pass them on. It is also possible, however, that she acted as courier. If that is true, then it was most likely the last service she carried out for the Party.

The 'game' to which Roth refers, is what was called the Leader Journey of the commanding generals of the Wehrmacht, which took place annually in May. In it, the army's plans for mobilization were drawn up anew each year and rehearsed. It's obvious that precise details about these proceedings were of the greatest interest to the Soviet side.

At this point, however, the Moscow leadership had for some time not been dependent on Helga von Hammerstein's collaboration alone—it had other sources available to it. The same mole in the Army Ministry, who in 1934 had reported on Schleicher's murder and provided detailed reports about the mood inside the army, presented, in July 1936, an astonishingly thorough analysis of the secret war game. Like all his reports, it reached the 'Central European Countries Secretariat', an office attached to the Executive Committee of the Comintern and headed by Palmiro Togliatti under the cover name Ercoli. His later assistant, Kurt Funk, was a familiar figure: Herbert Wehner. Presumably, the Foreign Section of the NKVD and the Fourth Section of the Red Army also saw these reports.

This unknown person evidently had access not only to all documents of the operational command but also to the political considerations underlying them. It may be assumed, therefore, that he had good contacts in the ministry, perhaps also in counter-intelligence and the staff of Admiral Canaris.

Strategic planning provided for an attack on Czechoslovakia without a preliminary declaration of war, leading to the enemy's capitulation within a few days. After that—a pincer movement in the west against the French army. The extensive dossier contains not only a detailed disposition of units down to battalion level, but also a list of all the participants, among whom, surprisingly, Kurt von Hammerstein also appears, although he had retired some time before. It is unclear how he was able to gain access to the secret war game; Fritsch, his successor as Chief of Army Command was just as suspicious of him as Blomberg, Hitler's Defence Minister. Older loyalties, which every department head has to take into account, may have played a part. Perhaps they just wanted to make use of his expertise. At any rate his influence was still sufficient to allow him an insight into the plans of the regime. As emerges from her letter, it seems doubtful that it was his daughter Helga alone who copied and got them to Moscow through intermediaries.

The agent's report is supplemented by information about the state of rearmament, raw materials supply and logistics. The foreign policy implications are also discussed at length. Further, there is information about rivalries between Army Command and Luftwaffe and about corruption in the arms industry.

Finally, the mole comments on the political attitude of the senior members of the officer corps to the Nazis: 'There is almost no one among the younger officers who does not unconditionally acknowledge Hitler as leader and National Socialism as ideology. The army of the Reich is increasingly ceasing to be an independent political factor. The old Schleicher clique has been broken up.' About the senior officer corps he writes:

> They grumble, criticize and are 'reactionaries' in the Nazis' sense. But there is no evident *active* political current of any description among the leading officers. They are also completely passive in their attitude to the regime. Nowhere does one hear anything about what would replace the Nazis or Hitler in particular. Insubordination of any kind against the Supreme Commander is very improbable given the psychology of the German officer. There is no discussion whatsoever in these circles about what could come after Hitler. They try as best they can not to think so far ahead, because then everything becomes unimaginable.

Such information goes far beyond what Helga von Hammerstein could come by in her father's safe. Nevertheless, as late as 1941, the Soviet foreign intelligence service remembered her again. It asked Dimitrov about her, who passed the inquiry on to Ulbricht. Here is the latter's reply:

Confidential!

12.5.41/2Ex/Bi

Concerning the inquiry about the daughter
of General *Hammerstein*: A daughter of General Hammerstein — I do not know her first
name — was the wife of Viktor, the head of
the intelligence service of the KPD in
Kippenberger's time. Viktor was dismissed,
he came to the Soviet Union and was
arrested here. Viktor had contacts with
the English espionage service. At the end
of 1936 or the beginning of 1937, his wife
requested to talk to the head of our
counter-intelligence apparatus. This talk
took place on the Czech border with Comrade Nuding. As far as I can remember the
information of the time, the woman
declared herself prepared to maintain contact with one of our comrades even after
her husband's dismissal. She asked about
the possibility of emigration to the
Soviet Union. We rejected that and
instructed the head of the apparatus to
break off the contact. Since then nothing
more is known about the woman.

Ulbricht.

The Soviet secret service did not let itself be dis-
couraged by this scanty information. Also in 1941 it
asked Herbert Wehner, then in Sweden, if he saw a
possibility of recruiting her to the 'Red Orchestra' spy
ring. They could have saved themselves the effort.

Yet another double life

What was the identity of the mole who was so well informed about what occurred in the Bendlerstrasse between 1933 and 1936? That remains uncertain. Much of the evidence, however, suggests that the man involved in this espionage activity died in Dresden in 1990, long after the Second World War, as an honoured artist of the people.

His biography, like that of many of his contemporaries, is ambiguous, febrile, torn apart by the maelstrom of history. Gerd Kaden, born in Berlin in 1891, was the son of a Saxon officer, who later reached the rank of lieutenant-general in the Wehrmacht. He, too, joined the army young, at the age of fifteen, graduated from cadet school and was sent to the front in the First World War. But he liked the drill as little as he liked the attitude of his 'ultra-conservative and strictly religious family', and, after 1918, he decided to dedicate himself to painting. In the 1920s, he adopted the artist's name Caden, presumably to distance himself from his family, and had great success as a set designer. In his autobiographical notes, he mentions the two most important Berlin variety theatres, the Admiralspalast and the Grosses Schauspielhaus: 'In the summer of 1925, the Admiralspalast puts on the first big Negro musical show, *Chocolate Kiddies*, with a Negro troupe from New York,' and that same year the Schauspielhaus shows a spectacular revue, 'an epoch-making, then entirely new programme in the American Broadway style'.

But that was only the first step to another life that soon took on hazardous and radical forms. Caden found himself at a performance by the 'Rote Sprachrohr' (Red Megaphone), a left-wing agitprop group, and was so impressed that he read the works of Marx, Engels, Mehring and Stalin and, in November 1930, became a member of the KPD.

One year later, Hans Kippenberger was able to recruit him for work in the Party's illegal apparatus. From then on, Caden used 'Cello' or 'Schellow' as a cover name. 'At first we met only rarely,' he writes,

> since contact with me was maintained solely through Comrade Leo Roth under conditions of the strictest secrecy. He was 'Alex's' closest collaborator. When I got to know him, he was very reserved towards me at first, which changed immediately when he learned that my wife, with whom I got on very well, was Jewish. We soon became friends. He was always punctual to the second, very cautious, very smart, very well informed. It was also 'Rudi' who told me triumphantly that he was close friends with the daughter of General von Hammerstein.

Caden's assignment was to infiltrate German nationalist circles, in particular the 'Stahlhelm' (Steel Helmet, an influential right-wing organization, part veterans' association, part militia) and the Reichswehr. He accomplished that task with gusto. In summer 1931, he installed himself as subtenant in the apartment of Lieutenant-Colonel, later General, Rinck von

Baldenstein in Pariser Strasse. The master of the house 'asked me whether I was the son of General Kaden in Dresden, which I confirmed. As a result, social, indeed familial relations were immediately established. My life as a painter was accepted with a friendly smile, a bit crazy, but well . . .' The role even proved to be an advantage, since in the circles in which he mixed, 'it was considered smart to take an interest in the arts, and to include artists who, furthermore, wore a tie, had clean fingernails and good manners, among one's acquaintances and friends.'

On top of that, Frau von Rinck, née von der Decken, had already known Caden when he was at cadet school in Dresden. 'This woman,' writes Caden,

was extremely supportive of my work (whether consciously or unconsciously I never found out). My close social ties with the von Rinck family served me as excellent camouflage throughout my work from 1931 until June 1938.

Lieutenant Colonel von Rinck worked in the personnel department of the Defence Ministry and was well informed about many details of army activity. He was very hospitable and was an old military academy comrade of General von Hammerstein, of Herr von Papen and Major Pabst. [Waldemar Pabst was the Freikorps officer who had Rosa Luxemburg and Karl Liebknecht murdered in 1919 and a year after that took part in the Kapp Putsch. He got away with it all and died in Düsseldorf in 1970 as a wealthy arms-dealer.]

But as if that were not enough, Caden declared himself willing, after consultation with the KPD, to become a member of the 'Stahlhelm'. 'With raised hand, I had to swear a kind of oath, to be always absolutely loyal to the Stahlhelm and to be a fierce opponent of the "Commune." ' Next, he joined the 'Society for the Study of Fascism' which was run by Pabst. It met in the Kaiserhof hotel and served as a meeting point for people of influence in business and the army and professors and bankers who sympathized with Hitler. A further source presented itself, when General von Cochenhausen accepted Caden in his 'German Society for Military Policy and Military Sciences', a circle to which senior officers and big industrialists belonged and which had access to the plans of the Defence Ministry.

For seven years, Caden led an extremely precarious double, if not triple, life. That is an astonishing achievement which says a lot for his talent, his tenacity and his nerve. On the one hand, he continued his career as a painter and sculptor and frequented Berlin's artistic and theatrical circles. In Herr von Rinck's home he lived 'almost as a member of the family' and pumped the guests. As a former officer, he had an effortless command of the language of the officers' mess and so won the confidence of the gentlemen in the 'business'.

At these meetings, extremely illuminating conversations, often lasting into the early morning, were carried on over a glass of wine and a cigar. I got a very clear insight into the conflicts between army command at the time (General von Fritsch) and the progressive expansion of the power of the SS (Himmler). As a member of the Military Science Society, I received permission to attend the test firing of artillery and exercises with the new anti-aircraft batteries and dive-bombers.

And third, Caden moved quite easily in the secret service apparatus of the KPD. In the nights after the Reichstag Fire, he sheltered Kippenberger in his studio, likewise the following autumn, when his superior was put on the wanted list and had to flee. From 1935, his 'liaison man' was Helga von Hammerstein 'who was then very active and courageous in the cause of the anti-Fascist struggle'.

Leo Roth notes at one point that Caden was probably already 'unhitched' in 1936—that is, lost a part of his contacts; that too suggests that he was the nameless mole. Nevertheless, he continued his triple existence until spring 1938, when he noticed first signs of suspicion on the part of an involuntary informant and decided that the time had come to emigrate inconspicuously. He managed to do so legally, since he had in any case often travelled to exhibitions in Brussels and Paris and hence had a valid passport.

He lived in France until the outbreak of war, first in Paris and then in Sanary-sur-Mer, where Franz Werfel and the Mann family had also found refuge for a while. In 1939/40, as a German citizen, he was interned in Les Milles camp. In 1942, he was able to obtain an English transit visa (to cross Spain) and reached a ship sailing to Cuba where he was admitted. There, too, he was not only active as a painter but also politically—he set up the 'Comité Antifascista de Cuba' and supported the 'Freies Deutschland' (Free Germany), a Communist inspired broad front organization. He returned to Germany in 1948 and immediately joined the SED: the Socialist Unity Party, the official name of the Communist Party in East Germany.

A pity that in 1954 the old conspirator allowed himself to be recruited once more, this time by the Ministry of State Security of the GDR. In the 'operative preliminary to recruitment' it is stated: 'The candidate expressed no misgivings of any kind and signed the binding undertaking. He was acquainted with the password, the control meeting place was also fixed and he was carefully instructed in the obligation of secrecy.'

From Leo's cadre file

To the cadre section,
Concerning the entry of the wife of
Comrade Viktor.

20 April 1936

Viktor has made an application for the entry of his wife, since in the near future he will be used for work in the Soviet Union.

Here the following:

The woman is the youngest [actually third] daughter of General von Hammerstein—Hitler's closest collaborator. [!]

In 1929, by way of the Socialist School Students' League and the Student Organization, she joined the Communist Youth Union under another name and was at this time active in the School Students' League.

In 1930 [actually 1928], she first of all got to know Comrade Viktor, who, with the agreement of the Apparatus, enlisted her for other tasks of a confidential nature. She carried out all assignments conscientiously and is described by all comrades (not only by Viktor) who know her from [Party] work as trustworthy and devoted to the Party.

Her entry is to be recommended from several points of view:

The 'Hammerstein business' was probably quashed by Hitler himself, since it involved his confidant [!], although the

Gestapo already had quite an amount of material that led them to the daughters of Hammerstein. Presumably, they simply do not know yet which of the three daughters was at the time responsible. Consequently she is very much in danger.

It is not expedient to leave persons familiar with the 'business' in the country. At the moment, although she is living in Berlin with her parents, working as a chemist at the Kaiser Wilhelm Institute, she is constantly in danger.

Her entry with other documents is possible since she possesses another passport, made available to her by the Party, with which she can travel abroad and come here.

In Moscow itself she has no acquaintances. Despite that, one would have to send them together to a city in the provinces, to avoid any possible encounter with Gestapo agents and embassy people. In Germany, she is known only to pronouncedly Reichswehr circles.

Mertens

(Com. Pieck approves entry.)

Without Helga

In Moscow, Roth first lives in the Hotel Soyuznaya. In his entry application for Helga, he asserts that he has been married to her since 1930. The reply is long in coming. First, he goes to a holiday home in Suuksu in the Crimea. Then, in July, the German mission at the Comintern writes to the director of the Nati metal plant in Moscow: 'In accordance with a resolution of the Central Committee of the German Party, Comrade [Roth] is to start work in a Soviet factory.' It's a bad sign. The experienced intelligence man rightly interprets this instruction as a demotion.

In September, the German Party leadership decides that Roth's admission to the Communist Party of the Soviet Union does not appear 'appropriate'. At the same time, Leo states that Helga is 'still in Germany'. So her entry to the Soviet Union has not been approved. That was her good fortune—she would not have survived exile in Moscow any more than her friend did.

Roth could have no inkling of the grounds that led to the rejection of his request. Basically his fate had already been sealed in June 1936, when the following denunciation was received by Dimitrov and other cadres of the Comintern:

Strictly confidential, 5 copies

Me/Lüch
8 June 1936

Dear Comrades!

It is expedient to make a principled decision in the following matter:

Viktor [Leo Roth]: From mid-1933 to the end of 1935, he maintained regular contact with the English and French embassies, which led to important material being supplied to both places and for which money was paid. There was also contact with the Agent Service [!].

The decision on this matter is one in principle, but depends directly on the further employment of the comrade.

This communication was signed by Grete Wild, cover name Erna Mertens, who had already been entrusted in 1935 with investigating the M-Apparatus and 'exposing' and 'unmasking' those in whose files there was anything that could be used against them in such a purge. With this denunciation began the interrogations that led to the arrest and sentencing of Leo Roth.

His Jewish friend Nathan Steinberger, who had been living in Moscow since 1932, had already become a member of the Communist Youth League as a sixteen-year-old in Berlin. He got to know all three Hammerstein daughters: first Maria Therese, then Marie Luise and finally Helga. Not until 1929, when he

Grete Wild, alias Mertens, informer. Moscow, about 1934

became a KPD member, did he learn of their espionage activities for the Comintern. In 1936, his name
turns up in a list of the Cadre Section concerning
'Trotskyist and hostile elements in the strength of the
emigration in the KPD', which was handed to the
NKVD. Steinberger was arrested in May 1937, expelled
from the KPD and sentenced to five-years' camp
imprisonment, later to 'eternal exile'.

> In the course of the interrogations I was also
> asked about other persons, about whom I had
> little or no knowledge. Yet, to my surprise,
> one name was never mentioned: Leo Roth, to
> whom indeed I had been personally close
> since my childhood. Roth had been arrested
> several months before me, and I expected to
> be questioned about my relations with him.
> Leo was arrested on 4 November, on 20
> November he was shot in the Lubyanka. At the
> time I asked myself: given that occurrence,
> how will my examining judge assess my rela-
> tionship with Leo Roth? Because it was known
> to the NKVD as it was to KPD headquarters.
> And it was also known that Leo's correspon-
> dence, when he was summoned to Moscow,
> went by way of my address. There were, after
> all, any number of ugly examples of the equa-
> tion of personal and criminal links. Why was
> this pattern not followed in my case? The
> reason, in my opinion, is this: Roth had func-
> tioned as liaison man between the military
> apparatus of the KPD and senior officers in the

Reichswehr. His companion was the daughter of one of the highest-ranking officers of the Reichswehr, General von Hammerstein. The examining judge was not allowed to know about such a delicate matter.

From the thicket of deviations

Throughout their history, the Communist parties displayed virtuoso skills in discovering and punishing real or fictitious failings of their members. There follows here a list of possible deviations which shows that, simply on grounds of logic alone there, could have been no one above ideological suspicion:

Adventurism	Capitulationism
Anarchism (petty bourgeois)	Cosmopolitanism
Anti-Bolshevism	Liberalism (lazy)
Avant-gardism	Left deviationism
Blanquism	Left opportunism
Block formation	Liquidationism
Bonapartism	Economism
Defeatism	Personality cult
Entryism	Lack of principles
Formalism	Putschism
Factionalism	Right deviationism
Levelling	Right opportunism
Individualism (bourgeois)	Right Trotskyism
Social democratism	Revisionism

Social fascism

Social patriotism

Trotskyism

Reconciliationism

Centrism

ary

Zionism

Forming circles

Brandlerian

Titoist

Bundist

Diversionary

Enemy of the people

Renegade

Two-faced

Element (hostile)

Class enemy

Counter-revolution-

Menshevik

Party parasite

Provocateur

Saboteur

Informer

Ultra-leftist

A message from Moscow

In late autumn 1936, Ruth von Mayenburg's head-quarters, the Fourth Section of the General Staff of the Red Army, ordered her to Paris, and from there she was summoned to Moscow by a coded command. Using different passports every day, she travelled on the Orient Express via Vienna to Istanbul, where she had to wait for days in the Pera Palace hotel because she had no contact address and was forbidden under any circumstances to approach the Soviet Embassy. Finally, she was fetched at night and brought to a Soviet freighter sailing to Odessa. From there she took the train to Moscow.

On her arrival, her husband, Ernst Fischer, member of the Politburo of the Austrian Communist Party in exile, was not at the station. The officer in civilian clothes who was waiting for her explained: 'It's nothing to do with us . . . He has another woman. She's even expecting a child by him.'

'The blow hit me hard,' writes Mayenburg in her memoirs. She tried to make sense of the fix she found herself in, and it became clear to her, for the first time, that the political climate in Moscow had changed radically:

> They had always wanted to separate me from Ernst. The apparatus was supposed to be my only commitment. The period of the great political trials and persecutions had begun. The GPU was emerging as an opponent of the leadership cadre of the Red Army. A horrible business!
>
> [. . .]
>
> My reports were apparently informative enough for Voroshilov, the People's Commissar for Defence, to ask to speak to me in person. The meeting, with only a very small number of people present, took place in a private apartment of the kind that were assigned to senior officials, in the 'house by the river' opposite the Kremlin.
>
> The main topic of the conversation was Hammerstein. Voroshilov spoke of him with great appreciation, indeed warmth.

He related anecdotes from manoeuvres and inquired in detail about how he was, in material respects as well. Anticipated as a vague possibility was what then finally took place, though only after the devastation of Europe and millions of dead: the revolt of the generals on 20 July 1944, which then ended so badly. A major role was planned for Hammerstein in such a venture. After my return to Hitler's Germany to work for the Apparatus, I was to break my incognito to Hammerstein, communicate Voroshilov's personal greetings and find out what position he then took up. An alternative was also considered: to invite Hammerstein to emigrate to the Soviet Union with his whole family. 'He can go hunting here too,' said Voroshilov. To expect a Prussian officer of Hammerstein's calibre, however much he rejected the Hitler regime, to leave his fatherland, to get out of harm's way or even assist the Red Army in word and deed, that seemed to me, to put it mildly, dumb. 'He would rather let the Nazis bump him off than do anything like that.'—'Then the general isn't such an enemy of Hitler as you say?' A logic I did not understand. Finally, the suggestion was dropped.

Instead, it was decided to attempt to win over Hammerstein for a revolt by those generals in the Wehrmacht, who were prepared to take action against Hitler. Entrusted with this mission, in the company of

the writer Lion Feuchtwanger, who was being celebrated in the Soviet Union at the time, Mayenburg
travelled from Moscow, through Poland to Prague,
and from there on to Berlin.

The inquisition

On 1 September 1936, Dimitrov signed a highly secret
memorandum of the Cadre Section 'On Trotkyists and
other hostile elements' in the exile KPD. In March
1938, 70 per cent of the German Communists in the
Soviet Union were arrested. Hundreds were sentenced
to death, thousands to imprisonment in the Gulag.

Leo Roth was arrested on 4 November 1936, but
his former boss, Hans Kippenberger, was also caught
in the 'Moscow mantrap' (Reinhard Müller). As his
long-time companion 'Lore' recounts, one evening he
came home [to the Hotel Soyuznaya] 'in a quite hysterical state and said that the contacts Rudi [Leo Roth]
had maintained were being presented as pure espionage contacts and it looked as if his, Alex's, utter
destruction was the aim.' He was first of all sent to
a Moscow factory which produced typesetting or
printing machines. 'He could no longer bear sitting
around doing nothing. After one month, he was a
Stakhanovite worker and earning 300 roubles. He had
lost a lot of weight and said: "It's hard filing iron all
day by hand." '

The informer Mertens, alias Grete Wild, was soon also on a list of comrades with 'Trotskyist and right deviations'; she was put in prison one year after her victim Leo Roth. Her reward was eight years' imprisonment in the camps which she did not survive. Walter Ulbricht, Wilhelm Pieck, Franz Dahlem, Paul Merker and Herbert Wehner were among the few who survived the terror unscathed.

How the inquisition proceeded in detail can be seen from Kippenberger's example. In 1935, he had already been replaced by Herbert Wehner, who knew the milieu inside out and wrote the following about the Party's internal informer system:

> The surveillance which was carried out by the functionaries on each other was the 'substitute' for the democracy which had been suffocated in the Party organization. With the help of this surveillance, the so-called intelligence service (which felt itself to be the soul of the organization) collected material which served partly to create and round out an archive, partly for the ongoing information of the most senior officials in the districts and in the Politburo.

A true flood of interrogation transcripts relating to Kippenberger's case has been preserved in the Russian archives—it makes for harrowing reading. Anyone who wants to understand the methodical paranoia that guided such procedures cannot avoid a couple of samples from these texts. Their prose is calculated to wear the reader down—it is packed with repetitions, making abbreviations unavoidable—and the Russian interpreter was not fully in command of German grammar. For that reason, the reader is spared a precise diplomatic version.

On 25 March 1937, after sixteen months' custody, torture and countless interrogations Kippenberger stated:

> In the years 1932–33, during the Schleicher government, it became known to the Party leadership that the counter-intelligence section of the Reichswehr is very well informed about the resolutions and intentions of the Party leadership, and that through an agent very close to the Party leadership. I was entrusted with the investigation of these facts. My suspicion immediately fell on Werner Hirsch, who through his mother had relatives in aristocratic and Reichswehr circles.

Hirsch, a former chief editor of the Party newspaper *Rote Fahne*, speechwriter for Ernst Thälmann and ghostwriter for Wilhelm Pieck, arrested in Berlin in 1933, tortured and put in a concentration camp, was released a year later and was able to flee via Prague to Moscow. An investigation against him was initiated even before his arrival, and he was incriminated by Wehner, Wild and Kippenberger. For his part Hirsch suspected Kippenberger of being a 'Reichswehr informer'. As Hannah Arendt writes, there arose in

Moscow 'an atmosphere in which knowingly or unknowingly everyone spies on everyone else, everyone can present himself as an agent, everyone must constantly feel himself threatened.'

'In mid-February 1933,' Kippenberger continues, 'I received the transcript of Hitler's speech which Hitler gave at the conference of the Reichswehr generals. After a few days my assistant Hess [Leo Roth] informed me that the counter-intelligence section of the Reichswehr knows that the Party is in possession of this speech. Again my suspicion fell on Werner Hirsch.'

Then Kippenberger and Hirsch were brought face to face.

QUESTION TO HIRSCH: Do you confirm these statements by Kippenberger?

ANSWER: No, I deny them categorically. Kippenberger told me in considerable detail about the taking of the documents from General Hammerstein's apartment. He told me about the involvement of General Hammerstein's daughters in the apparatus of the Party intelligence service.

QUESTION TO KIPPENBERGER: Why do you continually mislead the investigation? What aims are you pursuing?

ANSWER: I cannot give any answer to that question.

The confrontation is interrupted.

The interrogation continues on 25 April. Kippenberger's statements point to only one conclusion, that

Transcript of an NKVD interrogation of
Hans Kippenberger, 1936

in the meantime he has been tortured. He now no longer dares to contradict and confesses everything that the investigating judge wants to hear from him, in accordance with a carefully prepared script.

QUESTION: To all questions, principal questions, which the investigation put to you, you were forced to admit that your answers were incorrect.

ANSWER: My behaviour is to be explained by the fact that since 1929 I have been employed by the Counter-Intelligence Section of the Reichswehr. I was in direct contact with [Ferdinand] von Bredow, the head of the Counter-Intelligence Service of the Reichswehr and closest confidant of General Schleicher. Intelligence that there was an authoritative provocateur in circles close to the Party leadership found its way into the Party for the first time in 1931. This information disquieted me considerably, because I understood that my work on behalf of the Counter-Intelligence Section of the Reichswehr can be exposed if I [don't] throw suspicion onto another person. I gradually made a series of accusations against Hirsch which were false but difficult to check.

QUESTION: What were your motives in working for the German intelligence service?

ANSWER: I carried out this work proceeding from my nationalist convictions.

QUESTION: The prisoner Hess has alleged that he made contact with the English intelligence service in summer 1933, because of your approval and because of your direct instruction. Do you confirm that?

ANSWER: Yes, Hess made contact with the English intelligence service in accordance with my instruction.

QUESTION: With what aim did you enlist the Party intelligence apparatus led by you for military espionage on behalf of the English?

ANSWER: I was given the assignment by Bredow, the head of German counter-intelligence. Bredow explained that he belonged to those Reichswehr circles which regarded the Hitler regime as inadmissible and see the salvation of Germany in the establishment of a military dictatorship. For that, said Bredow, the aim justifies the means.

The interrogation is interrupted.

I have read this record, it was prepared from my words.

Hans Kippenberger.

Werner Hirsch, arrested long before being brought face to face with Kippenberger, died in 1941 as a result of his years of imprisonment in Moscow's Butyrski Prison. Hans Kippenberger was sentenced to death on 3 October 1937 and shot. Five weeks later, on 10 November, his former friend and comrade Leo Roth followed him down to the execution cellar of the Lubyanka.

Nor was 'Lore', Kippenberger's companion, spared—she was brought before an investigating judge who presented her with a lengthy interrogation transcript. In it Kippenberger described how he had come into contact with Ferdinand von Bredow, Hammerstein's head of counter-intelligence. One day, in summer 1932, as he had been eating lunch in the Reichstag restaurant, an attendant had approached him and said that Herr von Bredow wished to speak

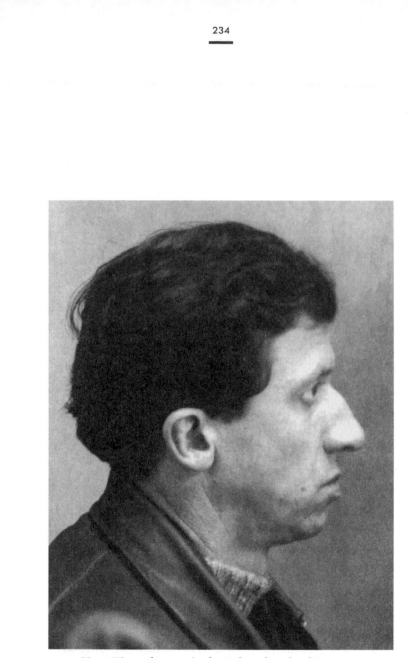

Hans Kippenberger, in the Lubyanka after his arrest,
November 1936

to him. He had gone over, and Bredow had asked him why he, who had himself been an officer in the World War, always expressed himself so dismissively about the Reichswehr. It was surely much more sensible to meet from time to time and to aim at a business-like exchange of opinion.

Lore comments on this statement in her memoirs: 'At the time, I was very perplexed by this "confession" and angry at Kippenberger that he had put it on record, because that was more than enough to have a comrade put up against the wall. He could simply have said nothing about the contact.'

During another interrogation, the investigating judge asks her what objections she might have to Leo Roth.

I replied that politically I considered him to be immature, but not a traitor. Then he said: 'How could Kippenberger enlist the services of such a man for confidential work? Do you know what your Rudi is? A collar seller in a little, dirty Jewish shop.' Like a schoolboy he raises his finger and says: 'I know something else! He pulls out everything that is somehow evidence against Kippenberger.' I asked the investigating judge why he was alluding to Rudi's Jewish origin; he was Jewish himself, and asked him to tell me one clear example of treachery so that I could be convinced that Kippenberger was a traitor. He remained silent at my question, so evidently nothing of the kind existed. I added: 'Then you'll no doubt have him shot!'—'No,' he said, 'he won't be shot.' He said it out of pity for me, because he asked: 'Have you always loved him?' I merely nodded. Suddenly, I was overcome by such tiredness, that I folded my arms on the table and laid my head on my arms.

After a few days, I was led to an official in a small room. He placed a scrap of paper in front of me and said: 'Sign that!' On the scrap of paper I read: 'Because of counter-revolutionary activity Christina Brunner is sentenced to eight years in correction and labour camp.' That was all: indictment, trial and sentence in one. For days I was as in a daze. How was something like that possible?

Anna Kerff, also called Lore or Christina Brunner, was not released until 1946. She went to the GDR and finally emigrated to Bulgaria. She wrote her memoirs in 1972.

The third daughter in the espionage web

Leo Roth was brought before the investigating judge on 23 February 1937, more than three months after his arrest. During this interrogation he not only seriously incriminated his boss, Kippenberger, but he also commented on his relationship to the Hammerstein daughters:

THE SILENCES OF HAMMERSTEIN

Interrogation transcript
of the accused HESS Ernst

I had seen Kippenberger's errors for a long time.
I considered him unfit to be in charge of the
Party intelligence service but did not inform the
Comintern about it so as not to cause his politi-
cal and personal destruction. I shall now however
make full statements about it.

1. At the end of 1931 or the beginning of 1932, a
commander of the Red Army, who worked officially
as a chauffeur in the accredited diplomatic mission of the USSR in Berlin, asked Maria Therese
von Hammerstein, a daughter of the general, who
was an informant of our intelligence service,
regarding the information about the Reichswehr,
which she occasionally passed on to us. He only
spoke allusively about it and not in a form which
was in any way binding.

 After this conversation, the Defence Ministry
requested our Berlin mission to recall the commander concerned. Kippenberger knew about this conversation with Maria Therese. As I later found out
from my wife Helga von Hammerstein, the head of the
Counter-Intelligence Section of the Reichswehr,
Major-General von Bredow, informed her father of
the incident. When I asked Kippenberger, how
Counter-Intelligence (Abwehr) got wind of the
matter, he replied that the Reichswehr probably
had an agent in the Soviet mission.

2. In January 1931 and in February 1932, Maria
Therese worked in the Rolland Bureau. Rolland has
since 1914 been one of the most important agents
of German intelligence and counter-intelligence.
He worked closely with General von Bredow and for
cover purposes maintained an office at Lützowplatz
which officially appeared as the representation of
a Spanish company dealing in oranges. As I found
out from my wife, Rolland was at this time also
carrying out espionage against the Soviet Union.

At the beginning of 1932, my wife Helga, who knew that I was working in the intelligence apparatus, gave me material from the Rolland Bureau. She had it from her sister Maria Therese who worked there as a secretary. There were at least 200 pages. About two weeks later, I got the same material once again from Kippenberger but in a distorted form and with a trivial overall content. Kippenberger did not know that through my wife I already knew the originals.

3. In February 1933 [in fact January 1934], General Reichenau offered Maria Therese a secretarial post with the German military attaché in Paris. At this time, Maria Therese was in contact, even if not all the time, with our intelligence apparatus. I informed Kippenberger, who was then in Paris, of this course of events and suggested that the loose connection with her be maintained. She went to Paris, but the same day received a telegram requiring her to return to Berlin immediately. Her recall took place, as we discovered soon after, at the request of the Abwehr, in fact of Canaris personally. Only Kippenberger and I knew of the intention of using Maria Therese in Paris for our purposes.

Bredow was also in Paris at this time. We also knew that the German military attaché, General Kühlenthal, a close friend of Bredow, was very well informed about the activity of leading German Communists in France, about their contacts and their undercover journeys.

The interrogation was interrupted.

Was written down according to my words, read by me.

Ernst Hess.

These statements by Leo Roth throw up a number of questions, above all as to his motives. It is extremely ea-3.

СОВ. СЕКРЕТНО.
ЛИЧНО.

И К К И

тов. ДИМИТРОВУ

По имеющимся у нас данным ГАММЕРШТЕЙН Мария-
Тереза, дочь германского генерала ГАММЕРШТЕЙНА-
ЭКУОРД Курта, якобы в прошлом стояла очень близко
к коммунистической партии Германии.

В 1933 году ГАММЕРШТЕЙН Мария-Тереза выехала
в Париж на работу в немецкое посольство.

Просим сообщить известна ли Вам ГАММЕРШТЕЙН
Мария-Тереза и не располагаете ли Вы данными, указы-
вающими ее местонахождение в настоящее время и харак
теризующими ее.

(Ф И Т И Н)

" мая 1941 года.-
№ 2/1/4529.

Inquiry to Dimitrov about
Maria Therese von Hammerstein, 1941

unlikely that Maria Therese ever intentionally worked for the Communists. Against it is not only the fact that she was considered 'unreliable' by her sister's comrades but also her frequently attested aversion to all materialist doctrines. Her employment in the Rolland Bureau probably did not go any further than simple secretarial tasks. It's possible that Maria Therese spoke to her sisters Marie Luise and Helga about matters relating to the Reichswehr and was used by them as a source. It's also conceivable that Roth attempted to shift possible grounds for suspicion from his wife to her sister, because he knew that she had emigrated long ago and could not be called to account by either the Germans or the Russians. As late as May 1941, the Soviet Secret Service inquired of Dimitrov, the General Secretary of the Comintern, whether anything was known there of her whereabouts. That, too, suggests that in Moscow they had never quite been able to tell the daughters of the general apart. The Stalinist bureaucracy was not infallible.

Fourth gloss.
The Russian seesaw.

Although it's not long ago, no more than a couple of decades since it came to a standstill, 'we', the Germans, have already almost forgotten the feeling of dizziness that the Russian seesaw caused in our heads over many generations. Strange!

Because the fluctuating relation with our sometimes close, sometimes remote, vast neighbour to the
east was full of promise and fateful for both sides. Perhaps easiest to grasp is the beginning of this obsessive
relationship in the era of the French Revolution. The
seed of a German–Russian brotherhood in arms was
sown in 1793 by a Russian–Prussian secret treaty
which was directed against Poland 'in order to oppose
the spirit of rebellion and of dangerous innovation'.
But then came the 'arch enemy' from the west. That's
the way the old monarchies saw it and also, given the
Napoleonic occupation, most Germans. The Prussians
were forced to march with Napoleon against the
Russians. At the end of 1812, after his devastating
defeat, this unstable alliance was reversed. An initial
armistice between Prussia and Russia was signed at
Tauroggen, where those present included a lieutenant-
colonel in Russian service called Clausewitz and a
Prussian major-general called Yorck. The results were
not so slow in coming: Napoleon defeated, Prussia
saved, wars of liberation, Battle of the Nations at
Leipzig, Vienna Congress, 'Holy Alliance' with the
Tsar, Poland partitioned, peace and quiet all round.

All of that still took place in the context of classic
diplomacy. But the nations were no longer willing to
unquestioningly subordinate themselves. The Poles
were particularly active disturbers of the peace, but in
western Europe too there were problems for the rulers
by God's grace. Despite all the revolts and revolutions,
however, the Russian–German friendship held for

almost eighty years. It was based on quite rational political calculations. Balance counted as the guiding principle of foreign policy.

Under the surface of power politics, however, other, very deep-seated ambivalences, rivalries, hopes and resentments had long been proliferating. Educated men and women read Tolstoy and Dostoyevsky; Rilke made a pilgrimage to Russia. Many Germans saw the Third Rome as a panacea against the cold, soulless, capitalist West, a pinch of anti-Semitism included. But Russia also served as a projection screen for the utopias of the Left; they sympathized with the Narodniks and with the 1905 Revolution.

When in 1890 the German government terminated the Re-insurance Treaty which Bismarck had negotiated, the seesaw was set in motion once more. In 1914, Russia was again transformed into a dangerous enemy and the forces' postcards bore the message: 'A bullet for every Russky!' The subhumans in the east were not an invention of the National Socialists.

There were soon signs, however, of another reversal. In order to weaken its enemies, the German imperial government supported the Bolsheviks and, in 1917, at the suggestion of the General Staff, allowed Lenin to travel across Germany to Petrograd. In return, at the end of 1917, after the October Revolution, the new Soviet government agreed an armistice with Germany. Less than three months later, the apparent harmony was overturned—the German army attacked and advanced into the Crimea, to the Caucasus and into

Finland. Lenin was forced to conclude a separate peace with Germany.

Germany's defeat and the Treaty of Versailles created a new situation. Both powers, the Germans and the Russians, now found themselves isolated, even if for different reasons. Tactically at least, pariah states always have common interests. A new alliance of convenience came into being at last in Rapallo in 1922. The anti-Polish aspect was also important; the Germans had not given up their claims on territories lost to Poland at Versailles, and the Poles for their part responded with a mixture of fear and anger to every attempt at rapprochement between their two neighbours.

The seesaw did not come to rest for ideological reasons as well. Anti-Western feeling in Germany found its classic formulation in 1918 in Thomas Mann's *Reflections of an Unpolitical Man*, and, eleven years later, Ludwig Klages published a fat book with the title *Der Geist als Widersacher der Seele* (The Spirit as Adversary of the Soul). German 'Kultur' was enlisted against Anglo-Saxon and French 'civilization'—a dispute in which the famous Russian soul was a very welcome auxiliary. Oswald Spengler saw in Russia 'the promise of a coming culture, as the evening shadows grow longer over the West', and advocated an alliance with the Soviet Union.

For the German Left, which was less enthusiastic about speculations in the philosophy of history than about the dictatorship of the proletariat, the star of revolution had risen in the east. Without the model of the October Putsch, Spartakus and the KPD would have seen no prospects for the future in the Weimar Republic. 'Hands off Soviet Russia'—that was a slogan around which the Left could unite. In the 1920s, a particularly curious part was played by what have been called 'left-wing people on the Right'. Although these National Bolsheviks wanted to act independently of Moscow, they shared the KPD's aversion to Western civilization. Ernst Niekisch, their most important ideologist, wrote in 1926: 'To be a Westerner means: to set out to deceive with the word freedom, to initiate crimes with a declaration of belief in humanity, to destroy peoples while calling for reconciliation between peoples.'

As far as the 'German spirit' goes, in those years it never quite knew where its place was. Pulled back and forth between fascination and fear, distrust and hope, it staggered between East and West, Right and Left. While some feared the Bolshevik devil, others saw the Soviet Union as their salvation. Artists, theatre people, and writers were not only enthusiastic about the Russian avant-garde, they also believed in a new New World in the east. Even the Nazis were not immune to the Russian temptation. In 1924, Goebbels wrote in his diary: 'Russia, when will you awaken? The Old World longs for your redeeming deed! Russia, you hope of a dying world! *Ex oriente lux*! In spirit, in the state, in business and in high politics. Russian men, send the Jew rabble to the Devil and give Germany your hand.'

A couple of days after taking power, Hitler announced his plans—much more serious in character and the exact opposite. Marxism had to be eradicated, living space for Germans created in the east through subjection of the Slavs. The war of aggression was only a matter of time.

The next turnabout was not long in coming: in 1939, the Hitler–Stalin Pact was signed and Poland divided once more. The seesaw was tipping up and down ever more violently, ever more senselessly; two years later German forces attacked the Soviet Union, and the war of extermination in the east turned the Russians into 'subhumans' again.

'In the relationship between Russians and Germans,' says historian Karl Schlögel, 'war is the most important common experience—a kind of negative common capital.' That is true at least of the military on both sides.

> But there's something else involved here, that adds a macabre and tragic aspect to the general misfortune which war represents. It's the fact that in the war groups of commanders encountered one another, who knew each other well and who now that matters had got serious were supposed to practise what before the war they had taught each other on joint manoeuvres.

At any rate, Hitler's war against the Soviet Union also sealed the end of a common interest. In the barbarism of the war of extermination, the old military class which had once been the bearer of German–Russian cooperation was destroyed.

After the victory of the Red Army, after the expulsion of the Germans from eastern central Europe, the old, neurotically charged, ambivalence assumed fixed form in the cold war and in the division of Germany into two states. Good and evil were now clearly defined. The seesaw was screwed down by international law, even if old emotions continued to rumble quietly below the surface. The new *Ostpolitik* of the Brandt years in West Germany put an initial damper on them, but not until 1989 did Germany's 'long path to the West' come to an irreversible end. Even the deluded efforts which a German government undertook at the time of the Second Iraq war could do nothing to change that result. The 'Paris–Berlin–Moscow axis' was no more than an eerie reminiscence of centuries of giddiness from which the Germans had at last freed themselves. They had come to terms with the loss of their old areas of settlement in Silesia and East Prussia, and, even if the Poles found it hard to do without their old enemy, they would in the long term have to get by without an arch-enemy in the west.

Granted: such an outline as the one above has nothing new to say to anyone with a degree of historical knowledge. It may nevertheless be useful to those who would like to understand Hammerstein and his contemporaries.

The marshal's greetings

Ruth von Mayenburg remembers:

> The most important assignment, which I car-
> ried around with me for weeks like a time
> bomb, without being able to get rid of it, I dis-
> charged not in Fascist Germany but in Fascist
> Italy. In Berlin, there was no opportunity to
> talk to Hammerstein in peace. That the cru-
> cial conversation would take place in the
> South Tyrol, where my ancestors had once
> lived, I took as a good omen; Hammerstein
> travelled to Bozen and Meran. To have a good
> rest, as he said, which I didn't quite believe.
> On a walk through the blossoming landscape,
> lightly and as if by the way, as if it were a
> handkerchief, I dropped the bomb: 'Marshal
> Voroshilov greets you warmly. A major of the
> Red Army has the honour of personally bring-
> ing Colonel General von Hammerstein the
> greetings of the People's Commissar for
> Defence.'
>
> For a while, we walked silently beside one
> another. The Prussian officer's face, seen from
> the side, showed no movement. Everything in
> it was familiar to me: the broad, pale fore-
> head, flattening out at a sharp angle at the
> temples; the thin-lipped mouth, pushed back
> by the short and vigorously jutting chin; the
> delicate small nose between the red-flecked
> cheeks; and then the curious growth in front
> of the left ear which stretched down to the

neck. If I hadn't seen him for a while, then I found it had grown larger each time. But when I teased him, saying he should get a serious examination of the 'thing', then he became impatient: 'Stop it. It's harmless— swollen glands.' [In 1943, Hammerstein died from the cancerous tumour which his doctor, Ferdinand Sauerbruch, considered no longer operable. The homeopathic family doctor, whom Hammerstein trusted, had been put in prison by the Nazis.]

Hammerstein was the first to break the silence: 'Were you over there?'

'Yes.'

'The Russians think I could do something, don't they?'

'Yes.'

'Are you going back again?'

'Yes.'

'What I say to you doesn't go via the Berlin embassy?'

'No.'

Hammerstein had some solid pieces of advice ready for the Russians: They should do everything to improve their relations with the British— the pact with France would be of no benefit to them; a more thorough training of the lower and middle ranks of the Red Army would be worth every effort; 'get everything on wheels'—without maximum motorization, 'the whole of Clausewitz would not be much help'.

Aside from that, he would have to disappoint his old friends. (Hako read more than disappointment in my face.) 'What else can I tell you . . . Say to them: Hammerstein-Equord returns the greetings of Marshal Voroshilov. I think no differently now than at the time we were on good terms and worked together. I would not take part in a war against the Russians.'

I waited in case he had anything more to say, because it seemed to be suggested by a reflective pause. 'Tell them—no, that's all. I cannot promise more than that.'

When we parted, he embraced me and asked: 'Are you coming back to Berlin?' I felt his heart beating, his hand clumsily stroking my hair. His voice brought me up out of the abyss of melancholy into which everything sank that was going on around us—the noise of the station, the hurrying people, even the man who was standing so close to me. Accompanied by a couple of pounding heartbeats, a warning: 'Be on your guard against Tukhachevsky!'

The beheaded army

There can be only one explanation for this ominous sentence: Hammerstein, who still had good connections, must have heard of rumours circulating in

German intelligence circles in autumn of 1936 concerning Mikhail Tukhachevsky, Marshal of the Red Army.

Tukhachevsky was born into an aristocratic Russian family. In the First World War, he had served against the Germans as a lieutenant, was taken prisoner and, in 1916, spent several months in a POW camp in Ingolstadt. (There, incidentally, he met Charles de Gaulle, with whose help he was able to escape to France.) By way of London he reached Petersburg in 1917, joined the Red Army and, before long, was a general in the war against Poland. Even then he came into conflict with Stalin whom he held responsible for the defeat inflicted by the Poles.

He rose rapidly, became deputy to Voroshilov, the People's Commissar for Defence. From the beginning, he advocated a modernization of the army and called for it to be ready to develop aerial and tank warfare. In order to achieve these goals, he made contact with the leadership of the Reichswehr. He also got to know Hammerstein with whom he talked in German and whom he accompanied during several military exercises.

To what extent he was a committed Communist is not quite clear. The first (illegal) air force general of the Weimar Republic, Major-General Hilmar von Mittelberger, who met him in 1928, claimed at the time: 'It's generally known that he only became a Communist for opportunistic reasons. He is also credited

Tukhachevsky as a young Red Army officer

with the personal courage to dare abandon Communism, if in the course of further developments that should appear expedient'—an assessment whose soundness one may doubt. It's certain, however, that to the last and for too long he stuck to cooperation with the Germans. As late as October 1933, he declared: 'The German Reichswehr was the teacher of the Red Army. Don't forget, it is politics that separates us, not our feelings, the feelings of friendship of the Red Army for the Reichswehr.'

In late autumn 1936, there was apparently an elaborate German plot against Tukhachevsky. Dubious émigré circles in Paris had spread the rumour that a group of conspirators in the Red Army was planning a coup. The aim was the assassination of Stalin and a military dictatorship. The intelligence service of the Nazi Party, led by Reinhard Heydrich, seized on these quite unfounded claims and produced forged documents which appeared to substantiate them. Documents dating from the period of cooperation with the Reichswehr were used which bore Tukhachevsky's original signature. Among them were also letters to Hammerstein from the 1920s dealing with purely routine matters. Only the signature was used for the forgeries. The material was then leaked to President Beneš in Prague through a Czech agent in Berlin. Hammerstein must have heard about these documents and believed them to be authentic; he guessed what was going to happen, and wanted to warn Ruth von Mayenburg against the consequences it could have for her.

Tukhachevsky
shortly before his execution, 1937

Heydrich's provocation did indeed prove to be effective. Beneš, who thought the forged documents to be credible, handed them to the Soviet ambassador in Prague on 7 May 1937. The latter immediately forwarded them to Stalin. The Politburo concluded from the forged papers that the alleged conspirators planned a close cooperation with Hitler's Germany. The first arrests took place in Moscow shortly afterwards. On 26 May, it was Tukhachevsky's turn. The trial before a military court concluded with death sentences for the Marshal and his co-defendants; they were shot in the courtyard of the Lubyanka on 11 June.

Three of five marshals and thirteen of fifteen generals fell victim to the purge that followed. Six thousand officers up to the rank of colonel were arrested and 1,500 of them executed. In total, more than 30,000 cadres of the Red Army are believed to have been murdered. Most of Tukhachevsky's judges did not survive the trial for long either; they too were likewise liquidated.

The Red Army had not yet recovered from this 'beheading' by the time the Second World War broke out.

Helga or loneliness

Leo Roth's death must have hit Helga von Hammerstein very hard. She never said a word about this period. Later, she also absolutely refused to see Herbert Wehner again, whom she had last met in Prague in 1936; and when Nathan Sternberger, who was a friend of Leo Roth, wanted to tell her of his death, she declined to listen to him. 'We knew nothing at all about it,' say her brothers and sisters. Her father, of whom that is not true, protected her until his death and passed over her Russian martyrdom in silence.

She was never inactive. Already after breaking off school she had attended a private science academy and worked in a laboratory for six months. When she realized that she could not acquire any adequate qualification by this route, she went to the Technical University as an auditor and sought out a school in Neukölln, a working-class district, in order to make up her leaving certificate; she was already able to take her exams in 1934 and 1935. Then, as Ruth von Mayenburg reports, she first worked for a year at the Kaiser Wilhelm Institute of Chemistry, then in industry until 1938, and in 1939 took her doctorate at the Technical-Chemical Institute of Berlin's Technical University with *Beiträgen zur Kenntnis von Kunstharzen als Zusatz zu Viskosespinnlösungen* (Contributions to the Understanding of Synthetic Resins as Supplement to Viscose Fibre Solutions).

Not until that year did she enter into a new relationship; through a common friend, the Berlin painter, Oskar Huth, she had got to know a young man who was more than two heads taller than her and

Helga von Hammerstein, around 1932/33

whom she liked. Politically they matched. Before 1933 they had been at home on the militant Left, but they had both, each in their own way, after 1936 at the latest, definitely turned away from Communism; they subscribed rather to an anthroposophically inclined Socialism. Opposition to the National Socialist regime was something both took for granted.

Walter Rossow came from a lower-middle-class family and had trained as a gardener. They married in 1939, just before the war. Helga let Hubert von Ranke know she would visit him in Paris for the Fourteenth of July.

> I went to the big parade with her, and we had very serious political conversations, also discussed how we could remain in touch, whatever might happen. Her father, Colonel General Kurt von Hammerstein-Equord, had been removed from his high active post soon after the Nazi seizure of power, but with his fellow generals kept a close eye on events and was deeply mistrustful of Hitler's war plans. These were exciting aspects. When Grete [Helga] said goodbye, we both suspected that it would be for a long time, if we survived the coming epoch at all.

Helga's husband was classified unfit for active service because of a lung complaint; he avoided call-up. That allowed him to establish a market-garden on a bio- dynamic basis in Stahnsdorf just outside Berlin.

It was a niche in which they could survive and which proved beneficial to the whole Hammerstein family and their friends—the Rossows were able to supply them with fruit and vegetables.

Fifth gloss.
On the scandal of synchronicity.

> Among the most shocking and at the same time most important experiences in working one's way into a time, strange to us as a later generation, is that of the synchronicity of the non- synchronous, of the coexistence of terror and normality, of the everyday and the sensational, of headline and small print, of political lead article and advertising prose, of retouched propaganda photo and trivial advert, that one encounters when reading newspapers,

writes the historian Karl Schlögel. He continues:

> Here next to the proclamation of death sentences the announcement of a piano competition; items on the expansion of the number of hairdressing salons and dry cleaners next to reports on the growing threat of war. Playing in the cinema are Hollywood-style comedies, while the apartments in the 'House of the Government' next door are emptying because of arrests. The prisons are within

sight of newly built schools and everyone knows what the black vans are transporting.

Schlögel is quoting from *Pravda* and from the Moscow evening paper *Vyechernaya Moskva* of 1936. but what it describes is also true of the *Münchener Abendzeitung* (Munich Evening Times) of 1938. In one and the same edition of the paper, one can read the following:

Bonbonniere: Non-stop success! Every day at 8 *The Humour Jab* . . . The Old Synagogue and the last prayer hall of the Jews in Munich has been removed . . . We brood over problems and overlook what's close at hand. Just try *Black and White* and suddenly you'll realize just how incredibly well and reasonably it's possible to smoke . . . All offers with this asterisk are processed with the well-known Eversmooth support . . . To market my top-class corselet-girdle, etc., I am looking for capable female representatives. Kleeberg Corsets, a pure Aryan business since 1933 . . . Gauleiter Wagner settles the score with the Jews . . . Late performance *You Can Count on my Discretion* . . . The Jew shops are not shut for the time being, but permanently . . . Which older woman, feeling lonely, would like to spend a sunny old age with me. Am cheerful by nature and looking for happiness . . . Big St Hubert's Day celebration of Upper Bavaria Hunting District . . . With the recent transfer of Felsenthal & Co, Cigars and Tobacco

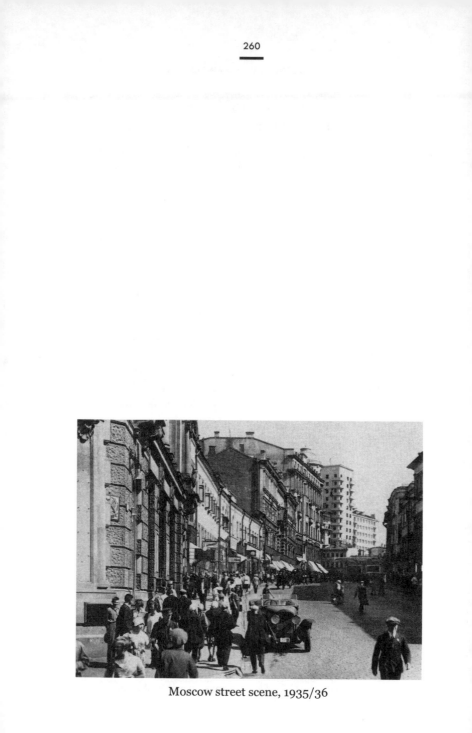

Moscow street scene, 1935/36

Products, to German ownership the Aryaniza-
tion process in the German cigar industry may
be regarded as by and large complete . . .
Sparkling wine is cheap, Haus Trimborn
Cabinet, carbonated, ½ l. bottle 1.50 . . . So far,
about a thousand Jews have been arrested in
Munich, so that there are pledges in hand for
all eventualities. It has proven that every one
of them already has something to answer for.

Nevertheless, the very visible pogroms of November 1938 are more the exception than the rule. Unlike
the Stalinists the Nazis did not usually openly display
their crimes but camouflaged them as 'confidential
Reich business'. Common to both regimes, however,
are the non-synchronicities Schlögel talks about. They
have to do with the invincible tenacity of everyday life.
When it comes to overcrowding, love affairs, money
worries, lunch and the washing of nappies, then at
some point ideology and propaganda come up against
their limits. Consequently it's only possible to talk of
totalitarian societies, not total ones. Even under the
most extreme conditions of the concentration camps,
the guards never managed to completely extinguish the
everyday; even there people still bartered, whispered,
argued and helped.

That's even more true of the remnants of civil
society in Hitler's Reich. Numerous niches survived
there until the final years of the war. In the summer,
the beaches were crowded, bee-keepers devoted themselves to bee-keeping, football was played, postage

stamps collected, amateur sailors went sailing. The *Volksgemeinschaft*—the 'Community of the Nation'—remained a fiction. While some cultivated their allotments after work, others went to the thé dansant at the Adlon or met at the Jockey Club.

There was of course no lack of attempts to control and instrumentalize even these residual worlds. Mass entertainment was a top priority. While the Nürnberg Race Laws were being proclaimed, the UFA studios were producing films like *Whenever I'm Happy* and *Two times Two in a Four Poster Bed*. As rearmament proceeded apace, holiday trips and cruises were organized for 'workers by hand and brain' under a slogan, 'Strength Through Joy', that would make any present-day advertisers turn pale with envy. Aside from that, in the 1930s and 1940s, total rule came up against technical limits. The possibilities of surveillance as they exist today even in democratic societies were still inconceivable. It explains, perhaps, how astonishingly frank and unguarded many diaries and letters of those years appear and why the widespread 'grumbling' usually had no repercussions. The principal weapon of the Gestapo was not an omnipresent bugging and surveillance apparatus but the rampant denunciation.

It is, however, no comfort that under the conditions of such a regime there existed zones of apparent normality; on the contrary, it appears sinister. It is inevitably difficult for later generations to understand how, in the face of the terror, 'unpolitical' worlds could overwinter and be so unmoved. The scandal of synchronicity is not, however, to be addressed by swiftly pronounced moral judgements; because it can't simply be relegated to the past. Its virulence has not faded under contemporary, much more comfortable historical conditions.

Visits to the country

Exercising due caution, Hammerstein always maintained his contacts with people of the same mind. Among them was the family of the Count zu Lynar, who had an estate in the Spreewald, southwest of Berlin. (During the war, the count was adjutant to Field Marshal Erwin von Witzleben who was executed after 20 July 1944.)

In his diary, Ulrich von Hassell notes what struck him on a visit in December 1937: 'At Kurt Hammerstein's. He is about the most negative one can imagine when it comes to the regime of "criminals and fools", also places little hope in the beheaded and castrated army.'

In an account of his experiences, that Carl-Hans Count von Hardenberg wrote down on New Year's Eve 1945, one can likewise read something about the views of his friend:

> The very intelligent Colonel General Baron von Hammerstein, who, despite his serious illness—he died before 20 July 1944—worked

closely together with Colonel General Beck, took the view that an assassination must absolutely be avoided, since the Germans did not have much political talent in that respect, that they would *never* see the necessity, if they had not drunk the bitter cup to the dregs. They would always maintain that sheer ambition had killed the genius Hitler. We seriously examined this view and could not deny its truth. If finally we did not follow it, then it was because we considered that it was the duty of those who see clearly, not to let German youth go on dying senselessly.

Reinhild Countess von Hardenberg remembers many meetings in those years. During Hammerstein's time as Chief of Army Command, he and his family had often been guests for the summer or over the weekend at Neuhardenberg estate where the knight commander's house was put at their disposal. They drove there in the official car, went hunting and enjoyed the idyllic surroundings.

The respect which my father [Carl-Hans Count von Hardenberg] felt for Kurt Hammerstein was based on the conspicuous courage with which he faced the orders of the National Socialist regime. Hammerstein was all his life as loyal to people as he was to his principles.

The friendship between Kurt and Maria Hammerstein and my parents was also passed on to me and to their children. This was true above all of Hildur and Ludwig Hammerstein.

Carl-Hans Count von Hardenberg

Tall and gangling with a thick pair of glasses in front of short-sighted eyes, Ludwig always seemed a little undernourished. He was a frequent visitor at Neuhardenberg and with his engaging impudence contributed a great deal to our entertainment. All his life, Ludwig was distinguished by a great tolerance for those of dissenting opinions. Sometimes, however, it occurred to me that this tolerance was more a result of a fear of conflict, because in fact he avoided arguments wherever he possibly could. It's all the more remarkable then that he placed himself at the service of the resistance without the least hesitation.

There was a stream of visitors to Neuhardenberg in those years. Above all, there were friends of the count, who discussed the political and military situation with him: apart from Hammerstein there were in particular Kurt von Plettenberg, Ulrich von Hassell, the Counts von der Schulenburg, General Ludwig Beck, Heinrich Count von Lehndorff, Fabian von Schlabrendorff and Nikolaus von Halem.

As occasion there were the hunting parties, which were part of the rituals of aristocratic society. Hammerstein's son Ludwig, with whom Count Hardenberg got on well, usually took part.

At daybreak, on hunt days, a forester blew the prince's greeting on his horn at every corner of the house as a wake-up call. After breakfast, my father made his way to the wood with the hunt guests. There, Forest Superintendent Ristow directed the hunters to their places, and the hunting horns signalled the first drive. Now the beaters, already in position, began to 'press' the game until the end of the drive was sounded. At midday, there was a thick soup and mulled wine in the wood. In autumn, ducks were shot and in winter, wild pigs, hare, red and roe deer. In Tempelberg there were also bustards, big, shy steppe birds, which, however, rarely showed themselves.

The hunt ended as darkness fell, and the whole gang returned to the castle. In front of the steps of the house the bag, grouped by species, was laid out on the ground on a bed of fir branches. Once again, the hunting horns sounded, the kill was 'blown' by the foresters. There was a special short signal for each variety of game, finally 'hunt over'. Then the guests disappeared to their rooms in order to change for the formal dinner, at which the hunters and their ladies appeared in the conservatory again.

A farewell

In October 1937, Ruth von Mayenburg came to Berlin once again, as usual with excellently forged documents. But her dreams of work as an agent were already over, although she didn't realize it yet.

I first called Hammerstein. Maria Hammerstein answered, a little cool and unfriendly: 'My husband is away hunting. I don't know when he's coming back. Are you staying in the country for long?'—'No, I'm not staying long, but I would have liked to see your husband, the whole family again.'—'One can never say what will happen . . .' As she didn't invite me to visit her, I never looked up the house in Dahlem or any of the Hammersteins again— except in my head and heart. Only Hako's voice reached me once more in Lietzenburger Strasse, from a public telephone: 'Can you hear me, little one?'—'You're so far away—so terribly far!'—'I'm not calling from home—be careful, little one!' He was going to get in touch as soon as he was back from his hunt visits again. 'Good luck, Hako! I'm going hunting too . . .' It was a brief huntsman's conversation, incomprehensible to a stranger's ears, and at the end the promise on both sides: 'See you soon!'

We didn't keep it.

A posthumous conversation

THE SILENCES OF HAMMERSTEIN

with Ruth von Mayenburg (III)

E: I fear I'm getting on your nerves with my never-ending questions.

M: Nonsense. I've been expecting you. Don't feel you have to be so polite.

E: I've been reading your book, which appeared in 1969 with the nice title *Blaues Blut und Rote Fahnen* (Blue Blood and Red Flags), and in it I noticed how enthusiastic your remarks about the Soviet Union are.

M: And?

E: For example, where you write about your meetings with Marshal Voroshilov who, as you yourself say, was one of those closest to Stalin: 'To feel the grip of his hand, to look in his bright eyes, that was as if one were looking straight in the face of the great Bolshevik Party of Lenin, which led the Revolution to victory, created the Red Army and built Socialism.' And so on.

M: Oh yes, that's right. I had quite forgotten it.

E: The great purge and the Terror are mentioned only in passing, as if they were regrettable slips.

M: Now that's really not very charming of you, my dear, to confront me with such quotations. By the way, you're welcome to smoke if you like. I gave up long ago, but I love the smell of tobacco. A remembrance of old times. Have I told you that Hammerstein always had a good cigar in his pocket?

E: You're changing the subject, Madame!

M: Of course, if you ask me such unpleasant questions. But I'm happy to answer you, as long as you don't get it into your head to interrogate me.

E: I would never dare do that.

M: Well. It was only the purges at the very top of the Red Army that directly affected me. It began with the secret court martial of Marshal Tukhachevsky and his co-defendants. The army was virtually beheaded and the heads of my superiors fell too.

E: They were all accused of treason.

M: It was a well-aimed and very successful German disinformation campaign. Even my friend Hammerstein was brought into it, with forged documents, which he had never seen, never mind signed. Of course, I wasn't involved in these events. I had no explanation for the smashing of the army leadership.

E: You got through unscathed?

M: More or less. After the arrests there was first of all silence. There were no signs of life from my section. Dimitrov personally ensured that I was released from my obligations to the military apparatus, so that I was able to live with my husband in Moscow.

E: Ernst Fischer, of course.

M: Yes, he was a leading figure in the Austrian Communist Party.

E: And so you were both guests in the well-known and notorious Hotel Lux . . .

M: . . . which I had never set foot in before. Because as long as I was working as an agent, I had nothing to do with the Comintern. That was excluded simply for security reasons. I was working for the Red Army. That was something quite different.

E: Something better?

M: At any rate they weren't just office bodies.

E: Perhaps that's also why in the Moscow archives there are none of the usual cadre files on you.

M: The Red Army looked after its own secrets.

Vyacheslav Mikhailovich Molotov, Jossif Vissarionovich
Djugashvili (Stalin), Kliment Yefremovich Voroshilov, 1938

E: It struck me that your second book, which appeared in 1978, has quite a different tone from your memoirs. There's not much trace of enthusiasm any more. You describe your colleagues in the Soviet 'organs' as bloodhounds. Your assessment of Voroshilov is also noticeably cooler. You now call him 'simple-minded, so not dangerous'.

M: You live and learn.

E: In a film about the Hotel Lux that Heinrich Breloer made in the early 1990s, you appeared as a contemporary witness. It's very impressive the way you remember so well the nightmare of the purges, the reciprocal denunciations, in which, as you say, Herbert Wehner was also involved.

M: We were living next door to each other. Every night we were expecting the NKVD to knock and take us away. 'It's better to go back to Germany,' I said to the émigrés. 'It's better to die among enemies than among friends.'

E: But you stayed to the last.

M: Yes, until the victory over Hitler.

E: And after that. Until your return to Vienna.

M: If you want to know exactly: I left the Party in 1966. And Ernst Fischer, my husband, was expelled a year after the Prague Spring. For him it was very difficult, but as for me there had been no pleasure in it for a long time.

E: Pleasure?

M: Well, my dear, have you never had anything to do with drugs? I don't mean your cigarettes, but more refined, stronger and much more dangerous ones. Substances which you hope will give your fairly useless existence a meaning. The promise of a game with high stakes. A risky drug which goes to your head and frees you from boredom. That's what Communism was for me. As you can tell, I'm not talking like

Ruth von Mayenburg, about 1955

Herbert Wehner, personal file, Moscow 1937

a good comrade. But neither of us is young any more and there's no need to pretend.

E: And how did you cure your addiction?

M: There's no clinic for it. It was very hard for some. But in my case it was no drama. I don't have much time for conversions. It was a very gradual estrangement, I could almost say that, in a way, it took place behind my back. One day, after the death of my husband, Communism had simply disappeared from my life.

E: And you didn't miss it?

M: I managed without it. As you can see. Have another cup of tea with me, my dear, before it gets too late.

War

In September 1938, during the Sudeten Crisis, the Wehrmacht Oberkommando wanted to make use of Hammerstein again. In the context of an operation plan with the code name 'Case Red-Green' aimed at France and Czechoslovakia he was earmarked as Commander in Chief of Army Command 4.

On the 26th of the same month, he celebrated his sixtieth birthday in Berlin. Among the well-wishers was Chief of the General Staff of the army, Franz Halder, Ludwig Beck's successor. The latter had resigned in August in protest at Hitler's emasculation of the Wehr-macht leadership; he had recognized that he could neither rely on the generals nor convince Hitler, who had already assumed supreme command of the Reichswehr in 1934 and put it under oath to himself; from then on, he only accepted generals in the military leadership who didn't contradict him.

Halder assured Hammerstein that he and his friends Beck and Adam would act if Hitler went to war. Both Halder and his predecessor Beck were part of a group of conspirators who had planned to remove Hitler from office in the event of a military response by Britain to the Sudeten Crisis. Under the command of General von Witzleben, a unit was put together which was supposed to detain Hitler at the moment of a declaration of war. The Munich Agreement, however, with the concessions made to Hitler by Chamberlain, Daladier and Mussolini removed, so they believed, their moral and political justification.

Hitler, in fact, was by no means overjoyed at his triumph but, instead, felt annoyed. He regarded the agreement as a defeat; he had seen the Sudeten Crisis as an opportunity to begin his war in the east, which he had been planning since 1933, without the intervention of the Western powers. Right up to his final monologues in the bunker, he argued that 1938 would have been the ideal moment for the beginning of the war. In the lead-up to the attack on Poland he was still haunted by the shadow of Munich: 'My greatest worry is that at the last minute some louse comes up with a mediation plan again,' he said to his generals. He left open whom he meant—probably he was alluding to Mussolini, who had intervened in favour of a peaceful solution to the Sudeten Crisis.

Generals Beck and Adam thereupon retired from active service, because they were no longer willing to accept Hitler's policies. Adam said after the war:

Hammerstein was a man of great farsightedness, indeed with a gift for political prophecy. He always kept the coolest of heads and betrayed no visible passion. He never disguised the fact that he wasn't greatly interested in purely military affairs. In truth, he was a pacifist and a citizen of the world. In December 1939, when I moved from Berlin to Garmisch, and we took leave of one another, he predicted the terrible end of the war.

At about the same time, Hammerstein's wife wrote to her son Ludwig: 'Papus considers the war quite hopeless, it should be broken off immediately. I can't write any more than that, tear this up in any case.'

After taking his school-leaving certificate, Ludwig considered becoming a regular officer. That fell through because of his short-sightedness and he began to study mining. When war broke out, his parents advised him on no account to volunteer. That did not save him from being called up. Ludwig phoned Count Hardenberg, who commanded a grenadier battalion at Potsdam and who promptly made a request for him—a step which was to have certain consequences later on. Just like his brother Kunrat, Ludwig was immediately sent to the front and wounded early on; he suffered a permanent hearing impairment as a result. In addition, he caught TB while Kunrat suffered from multiple sclerosis. This proved to be a blessing in disguise—from then on, both were exempt from active service.

It is hard to explain why Kurt von Hammerstein was reactivated once more before the attack on Poland, even if only for a few weeks. On 31 August, he wrote to his wife from Breslau: 'For the time being, I'm called Commander in Chief Silesia. But have no more to do than a deputy commanding general and so don't use the highfalutin title.'

Shortly after that, he was appointed Commander in Chief Army Group A in the West. He quartered in Cologne in the house of the arms industrialist Otto Wolff, whom he knew well and who, admittedly very late, had become an enemy of Hitler. In this post, too, the enthusiasm of the general remained within bounds: 'The longer things remain boring here in the West, the better,' he wrote home. After the end of the Polish campaign, he was even once again earmarked as "Commander in Chief East' but then, on 24 September, he was finally put on the retired list. Possibly, the rumour that he planned to arrest Hitler should he visit his sphere of command played its part here.

It's a matter of dispute among historians whether such a plan ever existed. Hammerstein himself never said anything about it. There is, however, one witness, Fabian von Schlabrendorff, who later undertook a failed attempt to kill Hitler with a bomb and worked closely with the 20th July conspirators. He describes Hammerstein's intentions like this:

A lucky circumstance had ordained, that Colonel General von Hammerstein re-emerged from obscurity and was placed in command of an army on the Rhine. A far-reaching plan was linked to this fact. Hitler was to be induced to make a visit to the army, so as to demonstrate during the Polish campaign the military strength of the Third Reich on the Rhine in the face of the expected relief attack by France. Colonel General von Hammerstein was determined to use this visit to detain Hitler and overthrow him. When, despite all Sir Nevile Henderson's efforts, hostilities had broken out between England and Germany at 11.15 a.m. on 3 September 1939, I was given the task of informing the English of Hammerstein's imminent plan. The English embassy in Berlin had already been evacuated. But between 1 and 2 in the afternoon I was able to reach Sir George Ogilvie Forbes in the Adlon Hotel on Unter den Linden and discharge my assignment.

Hammerstein's plan was not carried out. Hitler, who had what seemed like an almost uncanny nose for personal danger, cancelled the planned visit to Hammerstein's army. Shortly after, he decreed a change in the army leadership. So Hammerstein went into retirement once again.

Sidelined (II)

Even after his final departure from service, the general only appeared to withdraw to a quiet private life. Until shortly before his death, he continued to be involved in preparations for the 1944 revolt, as emerges from a report that the Chief of the Security Police and of the Security Service (SD) made to Reichsleiter Martin Bormann:

Confidential Reich Matter

Berlin, 29 July 1944

Concerning: 20th July 1944

Instigators of the Attempt

In the investigations, it proves repeatedly that the *intellectual preparations of the attempt* go back a considerable way. Werner von Alvensleben mentions, for example, a gentlemen's evening which took place in February 1942 at the home of General von Hammerstein who has meanwhile died. Present were Beck, Goerdeler, Gessler and the editor Dr Pechel (arrested some time ago for his hostile activity). Already at that time the position of the Reich was described as so hopeless, because of the anticipated [*sic*] entry of the United States into the war, that a *conclusion of peace* was considered to be an *absolute necessity*. Gessler was given the task (which he thus far denies) of travelling to *Switzerland* at some point *to sound out the enemy side*. As an old acquaintance of Admiral Canaris, Gessler worked for counter-intelligence and on its behalf undertook several journeys to Switzerland. In summer/autumn 1942, he returned with the answer (statement by von Alvensleben) that *Churchill was not prepared to negotiate with a National Socialist government*.

[In the Weimar Republic, Otto Gessler had been
Minister of Defence from 1920 to 1928 and had to
resign because of the secret rearmament of the Reichswehr. He was arrested after 20 July and interned in
Ravensbrück Concentration Camp until the end of the
war. The journalist Rudolf Pechel was under constant
surveillance by the Gestapo; he maintained contacts
with Goerdeler and Hammerstein and functioned as a
courier for the resistance. He was arrested in 1942
and taken to Sachsenhausen and Ravensbrück concentration camps; but he escaped with his life and,
after 1945, was one of the founders of the Christian
Democratic Union.]

Later generations may wonder why the genocide of the Jews evidently did not play a part in the
discussions of such resistance groups. The notorious
Wannsee Conference, at which the organizational cul-
mination of the 'Final Solution' was decided on, had
taken place in January 1942. It has to be remembered
that these plans were subject to strict secrecy. The officers were dependent on eyewitness reports from the
occupied eastern territories and on rumours. As far as
Hammerstein is concerned, in spring 1942 he had
already talked to his immediate family about 'organized mass murder'. In December of that year, he
learned from his Steinhorst cousin, who was working
for the Red Cross in Lvov, that the Jews were being
killed with gas. In general, however, such pieces of
information only hardened into certainty after his
death in April 1943.

Significant in this context is a discussion which his son Kunrat had three months later with his mentor Carl Goerdeler, who was urging the military to strike as soon as possible. Kunrat thought about the objections of his father, who had said that armed action against Hitler was in principle naturally correct, but the difficulties should not be underestimated, which was what most people tended to do; it was better to leave the thing alone because the harm consequent on failure would be tremendous. The Nazis would immediately use the opportunity to eliminate all their internal opponents and so destroy any further possibility of resistance.

If someone should dare kill Hitler [wrote Kunrat in his notebook] before it has become clear to every last German, into what an abyss we have fallen because of him, then after the war he will still benefit from the stab in the back lie. 'Only our dead miracle man could have prevented [defeat, but for] a second stab in the back!' is what a large number of people would say and spread the old poison anew.

To Goerdeler he said: 'Why should we risk anything for these national comrades? As long as Hitler keeps on winning victories for them, they don't care about the Jews.' Goerdeler contradicted him forcefully. But on one point at least Kunrat was right: it was very late before the murder of the Jews gained significance as motivation for the military resistance

From Führer headquarters

Hitler had by no means forgotten his old antagonist, Hammerstein. In the middle of the war, he comes back to him in his table talk:

Wolf's Lair, 21 May 1942,

The preparations for forming a government (27.1.33) were further made difficult by circles around General Schleicher, which had tried to be obstructive in every respect. Schleicher's closest collaborator and Commander in Chief of the army, General von Hammerstein, had once had the cheek to telephone and inform him 'that the Reichswehr could under no circumstances approve of him as chancellor'.

If, however, the gentlemen around Schleicher had imagined they could affect his decisions by such antics, then they were very much mistaken.

In the late afternoon (of 29 Jan.), they [i.e. Hitler and the Nazis] had been surprised by news of a quite crazy plan of the Schleicher clique.

As they had learned from Lieutenant-Colonel [Werner] von Alvensleben, General von Hammerstein had placed the Potsdam garrison on alert and authorized the order to open fire. Apart from that, they intended shunting the old gentleman [Hindenburg] off to East Prussia.

To oppose this coup attempt he, through the Berlin SA commander, Count Helldorf, had the whole of the Berlin SA put on alert. Apart from that, Police Major Wecke, who was known to be reliable, was informed that he should make the necessary preparations to occupy the Wilhelmstrasse with six police battalions. Finally, he had instructed the intended Reich Defence Minister, General von Blomberg, to proceed to the Old Gentleman immediately after his scheduled arrival in Berlin at 8 a.m. on 30 January to be sworn in, so that as Supreme Commander of the Reichswehr he would be able to suppress possible coup attempts.

This story is inaccurate—one of Hitler's obsessions. Rumours of a coup, however, had indeed been rife in the Berlin corridors on 29 January. They had arisen thanks to remarks by Werner von Alvensleben, a confidant of Schleicher, who incidentally later played an important part in the conservative opposition. He was arrested on 30 June 1934 and a second time in 1937; even after that, he kept in touch with his hunting friend Hammerstein, with Goerdeler and Beck; was arrested once more, accused and sentenced; in April 1945, the Americans liberated him from Magdeburg Prison.

Shortly before taking power, Hitler had got it into his head that the Potsdam garrison was only waiting for the order to go into action to prevent him forming a government. That was not true. Nevertheless, Hitler was very well aware that in Hammerstein he had an opponent who had to be taken into account even after his retirement.

The funeral

On 24 April 1943, before Hitler could take his revenge, Kurt von Hammerstein died in his house in Dahlem. His desk was empty—he had destroyed all personal notes, so that they would not fall into the hands of the Gestapo.

His son Ludwig remembers: 'A funeral in the Invaliden Cemetery in Berlin with all the honours due to a colonel general was rejected by the family, since the condition for it, the war flag of the Third Reich on his coffin, would be offensive.' Fierce arguments with the military authorities could not be avoided; at the responsible general command, Kunrat von Hammerstein became involved in a strange dispute:

'If the coffin is to be draped I request a naval war flag of the Imperial period or the Reichswehr flag, because my father had nothing to do with the present flag.'

'The Imperial flag is impossible.'

'Then the old Reich war flag.'

'That won't be possible either.'

'But it's still officially displayed on certain days.'

Kurt von Hammerstein's funeral in Steinhorst, 1943,
with his widow Maria and son Kunrat

'It was perhaps.'

And so on. To the general in charge, Kunrat said: 'General, you will understand that I cannot allow him [his father], now that he is defenceless, to be carried to the grave with the swastika.'

The rest of the family also intervened: 'Then I'm not entering the church,' threatened Kunrat's sister Marie Luise, and Helga suggested the funeral should take place not in the Invaliden Cemetery, where Horst Wessel and other National Socialists were also buried, but in the Hammerstein cemetery in Steinhorst. There was also an argument about the ribbon on the wreath Hitler had sent. When it was supposed to be laid down, the ribbon had all of a sudden disappeared. The relatives are supposed to have 'forgotten' it on the underground. 'So after a funeral service in Dahlem village church, Hammerstein was after all buried in the family graveyard at Steinhorst. One of Prince Solms-Baruth's huntsmen blew the signal "hunt over" for him, that was all.'

Ursula von Kardorff writes about 25 April 1943:

Was at Hammerstein's funeral. An unsentimental ceremony.

Many generals, a huge wreath from Hitler. Hardenberg and many other acquaintances. With Hammerstein, a man again passes away in whom many placed their hopes. Papa [Konrad von Kardorff] painted a good picture of him, although his illness, a tumour on the left side of his face, had already begun then.

I knew hardly anyone who so overtly rejected the regime, without any caution, without any fear. Astonishing that he was never arrested. He told anyone who wanted to hear that we could never defeat Russia, and already predicted in 1939 that we would lose the war. During the service, I couldn't help thinking about how I had experienced him at Neuhardenberg, how I sat on the shooting stand with him, held his cigar while he shot at boar—and hit them. In his simple hunting jacket, he appeared easygoing and relaxed, quite without vanity. This outward bonhomie contrasted with the biting condemnations he expressed, in a slight Berlin accent, slowly, almost by the way, but with deadly accuracy. This earned him the reputation of being embittered. How easily are such adjectives bestowed on those who see more clearly.

To me Hammerstein behaved with an almost patriarchal courtesy. 'Keep your head clear for important decisions', was the motto of this wonderfully lazy man who made no compromises.

After his father's death, Franz von Hammerstein wrote in his diary: 'Although he never talked about it, it must have been terrible for him to stand and watch Germany being destroyed without him being able to do anything. Hardly anyone predicted developments as accurately as he did.'

Kurt von Hammerstein in civilian clothes

Sixth gloss.
Remarks about the aristocracy.

A glance at any German telephone directory shows that in this country there is no shortage of Fürsten, Grafen and Freiherren—princes, counts, barons. The tenacious vitality with which this milieu has been able to assert itself through all historical upheavals and catastrophes is remarkable enough. In the Marxist sense, it has long ceased to be a class, after all, ever since it lost the basis of its existence with the end of the monarchy. Equally curious is the ambivalence with which the outside world regards the aristocracy.

The media see it primarily as a spectacle with viewer and reader figures potential; in the eyes of Americans, it's a picturesque anachronism. But there's also no lack of prejudice and resentment. It's not only the belated Jacobins of the Left who don't have a good word for the 'Junkers' and would prefer to see such 'vestiges of the past' eliminated. In the collective memory, there still survives the recollection of old experiences, of serfdom, compulsory labour and peasant wars. 'When Adam delved and Eve span, who was then the gentleman?' Such sayings express a reservation which is evidently quite compatible with a taste for the popular media and their fairy tales and scandals.

Of course, such stirrings are themselves anachronistic—for a start because the view from outside sees in the aristocracy a homogeneity which is far removed from reality. In fact, that milieu sets great store by every possible subtle gradation and distinction, precisely because everyone knows exactly whom they are dealing with even when they've never met. The *Almanach de Gotha*, with its genealogical meticulousness and its time-honoured sections, sees to that. Ancient nobility, high nobility, military nobility and nobility conferred by letters patent, court nobility and titled gentry—these are different worlds. Seniority counts for more than rank and title; what matters is when they were bestowed. Discourteous, particularly since the postwar expropriations, is any talk of 'apartment nobility', that is anyone who has no 'house' of his own; that usually means a castle and the property that goes with it. Apart from which it is precisely in the 'best' families that any appearance of conceit is frowned on.

Nonetheless, this internally diverse milieu also displays a number of common features, and it is presumably these which explain why the aristocracy's vigour has not died out after its loss of function. It is necessary to think of all kinds of old-fashioned motives and virtues. These include, in the first instance, a marked family sense across the generations. The anxious family planning of the middle classes is alien to the aristocracy; a large number of children is not the exception but the rule. (Kurt and Maria von Hammerstein made sure of an impressive progeny: no fewer than twenty grandchildren, forty-two great-grandchildren and twenty great-great-grandchildren.)

Other customary aspects have contributed to the stability of the nobility: mutual help in difficult times, a natural hospitality and an old European disdain of national borders. Although mésalliances are accepted without comment, in aristocratic circles the preference is still for marriages with one's own kind, and, even if one works as a car dealer or an estate agent, summer is spent with people like oneself in the country where one rides, collects porcelain, goes hunting and often cultivates all kinds of quirks and customs which otherwise have gone out of fashion.

There has also, however, never been a shortage of attempts to escape the 'business'. The Hammerstein clan provides striking examples of that. Yet, even the general's daughters, who displayed a remarkable predilection for Jews and Communists, never succeeded in completely shedding their origin; indeed, in that sense, it's almost possible to talk of a kind of stigma.

The antiquated virtues which for a long time survived in the parallel society of the aristocracy were by no means able to immunize them against political temptations such as German history had in store. And there's no good reason why its members should be politically more intelligent or have greater moral integrity than others; more plausible is the assumption that, in this respect, the normal distribution applies. In a dictatorship that both made use of and used up all traditions, it was precisely terms with aristocratic connotations like 'honour', 'oath of allegiance' and 'loyalty' that could be instrumentalized with particular ease.

In addition there was, as throughout western and central Europe, a deeply rooted, virtually taken-for-granted anti-Semitism. While it usually observed civil proprieties—one liked to consult one's Jewish doctor, lawyer, private banker—this posture of deliberate distance did not immunize the aristocratic elites against the Nazis' eliminatory hatred of Jews.

Interestingly, as recent publications have revealed, the high aristocracy proved to be particularly susceptible and, as the examples of the princely houses of Hesse and Schaumburg-Lippe show, not primarily from ideological motives but, rather, opportunistic ones. That is also true of large parts of the military aristocracy. The twelve years from 1933 to 1945 proved to be its political acid test.

Not a few of the generals of the Wehrmacht, who were responsible for crimes in the war of extermination against Russia, came from this background. A whole number of aristocratic officers were put on trial after 1945 for war crimes, including Field Marshal Erich von Manstein, who was sentenced to eighteen years in prison but released in 1953.

On the other hand, anyone who looks at a list of those involved in the attempted coup of 20 July 1944 will see that more than seventy aristocratic names appear there, a share which is much greater than any demographic proportion. It was their resistance that had to pay the price for the crimes of many of their own rank.

As his son Kunrat relates, Kurt von Hammerstein resigned from the Club of the Nobility (Adelsgenossenschaft) in 1933/34 when it got rid of its last non-Aryan members. He also treated the extended family with some reserve; at the family days, where usually seventy to a hundred relatives turned up, he preferred to let his wife represent him. And as for his honours—he was a Knight of the Hohenzollern Family Order and Honorary Knight of the Order of St John— he regarded them with a degree of irony and hardly ever wore them. None of that represented a break with his background—it was more a sign of his independence of mind. More important is something else: in his immediate family, there was not a single Nazi. There are not too many German families who can say that about themselves.

A room in the Bendler Block

Who was Bendler, in fact? A stonemason and site foreman from Saxony who, at the beginning of the twentieth century, got ahead in Berlin and became a local councillor and a property owner. The street in the Tiergarten district of the city was named after him.

The large group of buildings by the Landwehr Canal has been used by the military for almost a

Bendler Block, entrance, 1944

Marshal Zhukov, third from right, in the Bendler Block,
May 1945

century. German naval policy before the First World War was planned in the main building, completed in 1911 as the Reich Navy Department. After 1918, the Reich Minister of Defence, at first the Social Democrat Gustav Noske, moved into the former apartment of Grand Admiral von Tirpitz, while the Chief of Army Command had a large flat at his disposal in Bendlerstrasse, today called Stauffenbergstrasse. Hammerstein sat at his desk there for four years. In the outer office he was assisted by Margarethe von Oven, who had already taken up a post as secretary in the Defence Ministry in 1925. But the daughter of an impoverished officer's widow was no mere shorthand typist. In 1928, in the context of the secret cooperation between the Reichswehr and the Red Army, she had spent six months in the Soviet Union under a false name and was her boss's representative. Shortly after Hammerstein's retirement, she went abroad and worked for the German military attachés in Budapest and Lisbon, where she was answerable to Admiral Canaris, the head of the Abwehr, whose office was also in the main building of the Bendler Block. Much later, during the Second World War, she was the right hand of Henning von Tresckow, a key figure of the conspiracy. Carl-Hans von Hardenberg, in his memoirs, describes an episode, that probably took place in 1944:

> So, one day, Tresckow, Stauffenberg and the courageous Margarethe von Oven, who had typed appeals to nation and army on her typewriter wearing gloves so as to leave no

fingerprints, were walking down the street in Berlin, the appeals with them in a briefcase, when a police van raced up and came to a halt close by. The policemen jumped out just as the three reached the house they were going to and cordoned it off, without bothering about them. At that moment the hearts of even these three brave people stood still.

Margarethe von Oven met the Hammersteins at Neuhardenberg again; she had married Wilfried, a brother of the Count.

The buildings in the Bendlerstrasse were considerably enlarged immediately after the start of Germany's accelerated rearmament. During the killings of 30 June 1934, General von Fritsch, Hammerstein's successor, barricaded himself into the latter's former apartment behind heavily armed guards, because he feared attack by the SS; after Fritsch fell four years later, the last Supreme Commander of the Army, General von Brauchitsch, moved in.

The room in the east wing, in which Hitler made his speech on 3 February 1933, was used by Hammerstein between 1930 and 1934 as a dining room for official invitations. From 1940, it was used as an office by Colonel General Fromm, Commander of the Reserve Army.

On 20 July 1944, it was this very room that Field Marshal Erwin von Witzleben, Colonel General Ludwig Beck, General Friedrich Olbricht and General

Erich Hoeppner turned into the coordinating point of the coup attempt. They had General Fromm arrested on the afternoon of that day and detained him on the third floor, in what had been Hammerstein's private apartment.

Beck, who was earmarked as head of state after a successful assassination, was seriously wounded in an exchange of fire after the failure of the attempt. Fromm called on him to commit suicide. Since he himself was no longer in a position to do so, he was shot by a sergeant at his own request.

On 20 July, Fromm personally declared himself a drumhead court martial and ordered Olbricht, Claus Schenk Count von Stauffenberg, Albrecht Ritter Mertz von Quirnheim and Werner von Haeften to be executed in the inner courtyard.

The war was carried on from the Bendler Block until the very last moment. In March and April 1945, the last combat commander of Berlin had his headquarters there until Soviet troops captured it on 2 May. For the victor of the Battle of Berlin, Marshal Zhukov, it must have been a strange return—he knew the Bendler Block from earlier days, when he had been initiated there, in Hammerstein's Truppenamt—Army Office—into the techniques of the German General Staff.

After the war, civilian authorities were accommodated in the damaged buildings. Then the complex was rebuilt. Since 1993, the Defence Ministry is once again located there. In 1968, Hammerstein's former rooms were turned into a memorial to the German resistance. Today, during the week, one encounters classes of noisy schoolchildren in the same room where Hitler once dined with the generals for the first time. This room is dedicated to the failure of the coup.

In 1987, a radio reporter asked Ludwig von Hammerstein: 'You are now the chairman of the committee of this memorial, is it an odd feeling to return to this place of your childhood? It's hard to imagine an eleven- or twelve-year-old playing games in a military headquarters building.'—'One could in fact do that then. We went to school from there, we played there and in the evening we walked right through the army ministry, because at the other end, on Kaiserin Augusta Ufer, there was a gym we could use. As a result I knew the building pretty well and later, on 20 July, that saved my life.'

A posthumous conversation with Ludwig von Hammerstein

E: Herr von Hammerstein, can you tell me how you actually came to join the 20 July conspirators?

L: That's a long story.

E: Perhaps it has to do with your family.

L: You mean my father. Certainly, he never wanted to have anything to do with the Nazis, but he didn't recruit me to the resistance. It wasn't his way, to tell his children what they should do.

E: You were called up right at the beginning of the war.

L: Yes, at the time, on 6 September, I wrote in my notebook: 'The whole war can be described as a crime, which will destroy us all.'

E: You already saw that then?

L: That wasn't my judgement. I wasn't even twenty then. It was the conclusion I drew from everything I heard around me. In early 1941, when I was at military academy in Potsdam, I saw my father again at our home. I was present when he was talking to Colonel General Beck. They said quite unequivocally: 'The next campaign is being prepared. This time against Russia.'

E: Then you were seriously wounded on the Russian front.

L: It was a blessing in disguise — after that, I was no longer fit for combat duty. I was even able to resume my mining studies in Berlin.

E: At that time you were not yet part of the active resistance.

L: No. But Reserve Battalion 9, to which I belonged since 1940, always invited me to the officers' mess evenings in Potsdam. On 25 February 1943, two months before my father died, Fritz-Dietlof Count von der Schulenburg, whom I didn't know well, took me aside and asked me: 'Hammerstein, are you prepared to take part in an action against Hitler?' It was exactly the right moment. It was the time of the catastrophe of Stalingrad. My division was trapped there. It was then that I recklessly wrote in my pocket diary: 'National Day of Mourning for Stalingrad, it would be better to shoot the fellow.' So, naturally, I said yes.

E: And how did it go on from there?

Ludwig von Hammerstein, about 1940

THE SILENCES OF HAMMERSTEIN

L: 'When it's going to happen, we don't exactly know yet,' Fritzi Schulenburg, as we called him, explained to me, 'but make sure that you approach others, because we lack young people who can help us as ADCs.' I agreed to do so, and tried to recruit other officers. One said to me: 'Let the Nazis go under by themselves, we shouldn't intervene.' With another I had only started to sound him out — I hadn't even mentioned assassination — when he looked at me and responded: 'You know, Ludwig, you're actually a traitor to your fatherland. I should really report you.' I merely said laconically, 'Go ahead!' because I knew that among officers of that regiment it wasn't normal for them to denounce each other. And he didn't.

E: And what happened after that?

L: I met Schulenburg again in March. He told me, 'Nothing's going to happen for the time being.' What we didn't know was that Fabian von Schlabrendorff and Henning von Tresckow had attempted to blow up Hitler in his plane with a bomb disguised as a present. That had come to nothing because the fuse didn't work properly. Shortly afterwards, on Heroes Remembrance Day, Hitler wanted to visit an exhibition and Colonel von Gersdorff had prepared a bomb to kill him. But Hitler was in a hurry — he raced through the rooms without stopping. It took ten minutes until the fuse was primed, and so again nothing happened. Even before that, my regimental comrades, Ewald Heinrich von Kleist and Axel von dem Bussche, had entertained similar plans. Once, Hitler was to be shown new uniforms and Bussche wanted to use the occasion for an assassination, but the uniform patterns were burnt during an air raid and the visit was cancelled. Bussche had to go back to the front, was seriously wounded and couldn't take part any more.

So we waited, continued to serve in our units or continued our studies, like me, and limited ourselves to observing the situation. We were better informed, of course, than most others. At home we listened to the BBC and Radio Beromünster, and there we met Beck, Goerdeler and several others.

E: You no longer believed there would be an action?

L: Hardly. But then it did come.

E: When?

L: We got first indications at the beginning of July: 'Be ready!' So we started testing our revolvers and training in order to be fit. The first date that was set was 11 July. But the note that was supposed to inform me went to my brother Kunrat. He was studying in Leipzig and working for Goerdeler. He went to the agreed meeting place and waited for two hours near Bendlerstrasse. Then came the news that Goering and Himmler weren't present and the thing was called off.

On 15 July, we were again ready to go. We sat in the Esplanade hotel and waited for several hours. It was nerve-wracking. But then our contact man, Ewald Heinrich von Kleist, came and said: 'You can go home, it's all off again.' We left, went on practising with our revolvers and waited for the next deadline. On the 18th, I was in Potsdam for a very nice lunch with an elderly lady. In the evening we, Kleist and I, met Count Schwerin, who told us: 'It's going to be 20 July.'

So, at midday on the 20th, we were again sitting in the Esplanade hotel and we waited for the phone call from 1 to 4 p.m. It came at about quarter past four. 'The moment has come at last,' I thought. We immediately walked the ten minutes to the Bendlerstrasse.

THE SILENCES OF HAMMERSTEIN

E: Who were you with?

L: There were four of us: Kleist, Fritsche, Oppen and myself. We were taken to a room and there we met Schwerin, Jäger, Berthold Stauffenberg, the brother of Claus, and Peter Yorck von Wartenburg.

E: What were your tasks?

L: First, we had to disarm two SS officers. Then, I was supposed to wait in General Olbricht's anteroom for further instructions. There, I was able to listen in on the telephone conversations that were being conducted with Paris, where the readiness to join in was quite considerable: 'Hallo, *c'est bon*. It's time. Take immediate action!' I was witness to the whole thing and saw the officers of the General Staff going in and out. Then, Olbricht brought me into his room. Suddenly, his adjutant pulled open the door and shouted: 'The general's gone!' He meant Kortzfleisch, the Deputy Commanding General of Defence District III. He had refused to join in and tried to escape. I brought him back to his room. He didn't want to come, but I seized him by the jacket. He roared at me: 'To whom did you swear your oath of allegiance?' Then he was quiet and merely said he only wanted one thing: to go home and weed the garden. I reported to Beck in our old dining room, who said to me: 'He should stay where he is. We don't want to have anything more to do with him.'

E: And then?

L: Then came the news that Hitler really was still alive, that the guard regiment wasn't with us any more and that there were staff officers well-armed with sub-machine guns and hand grenades everywhere in the corridors. Suddenly, I heard shots. I took cover behind a cupboard and went for my gun. There was a lieutenant-colonel standing beside me, who said: 'Just leave it where it is — there's no point any more.' I was a complete stranger there and couldn't tell which side he was on. I didn't draw my revolver, looked down the corridor and realized that Stauffenberg was being fired at. I felt very sick. The lieutenant-colonel said: 'There is a putsch against the Führer under way here. You are at my command! Now go, cordon this off, the corridors above and below. You go upstairs!'

That was my good luck. I considered what I should do. All that mattered was to get out as fast as possible. There was nothing I could do to help anyone any more. Of course, I knew every passageway, every flight of stairs in the building, because I had lived and played there as a boy. I made a detour and ran through bombed parts of the complex. I almost got stuck in the cellars because I couldn't find the way out any more. My ears had been damaged when I was wounded and I couldn't hear very well. Then I walked across the Bendler Bridge to the nearest S-Bahn station and got on the train. Stupidly I had left my briefcase with the second revolver in Olbricht's office. I said to myself: 'It's sure to be found and then they'll be looking for you straight away.'

E: A fateful day.

L: I've often experienced blessings in disguise in my life.

E: Where did you go?

L: I went home, but my mother was in Breslau with her relatives. I told my sister Hildur, who was looking after the house: 'The *coup d'état* has gone badly. I have to go into hiding immediately because they have my name. They will be looking for me here very soon.'

Peter Count Yorck von Wartenburg, 1943

General Friedrich Olbricht, 1942

E: And your friends, Ewald von Kleist, Hans
   Fritsche and Georg Sigismund von Oppen?

L: They were arrested by the Gestapo shortly
   after. But then something strange happened:
   the People's Court abandoned proceedings
   against them for lack of evidence. We survived. That still seems like a miracle to me
   today.

Flight

The sources that bring a biography to life are like a
rivulet. They sometimes bubble up, sometimes run
dry. Very few people keep a record like Thomas Mann,
so that everyone who wants to know can find out what
he ate on particular days and who annoyed him. There
are love stories from the early nineteenth century
whose course can be reconstructed from day to day,
sometimes even from hour to hour, because, in those
days, for lack of a telephone, two people came to an
understanding or fell out by way of heatedly written
letters, which they kept carefully in their desks and
tied up with pink ribbons. In other lives, there are gaps
of years at a time and it's impossible to guess the reasons for the blackout.

In the months after 20 July, Kunrat von Hammerstein ensured that posterity has a very clear picture of
what it was like for someone on the run from the
Gestapo in summer and autumn 1944. Although he
hadn't actually taken part in the attempted coup—on
20 July itself he was in Steinhorst—he was under

investigation, presumably because of his close links with Carl Goerdeler.

These coded notebooks, written and preserved at great risk, he later expanded and published. Remarkable texts! His family says that he did have literary ambitions; and yet his writing often appears confused— an excess of details and reminiscences threatens to suffocate them. It's precisely such defects, however, that speak for their authenticity.

What follow are a number of snapshots from his flight.

On the night of 22 July, Kunrat travelled to Berlin and, at midnight, climbed into his home through an open window. His mother called out: 'Franz, come downstairs!' His brother told him: 'When he was here last night, Ludwig was in a terrible state. Goerdeler wasn't involved. You must go back to Leipzig and behave as if you didn't know anything. If two of us were involved, then we're all in trouble.' He found Ludwig at the home of a woman friend who had given him shelter. She had told him (Ludwig): 'You must not give yourself up, even if the whole family is put in a concentration camp. But it will cost you your life.'

Kunrat's situation was also precarious. It was true that because of his wound the Wehrmacht had granted him leave to study at Bonn University. He had the relevant documents. Also, he was not yet on the wanted list. But he had to anticipate that, sooner or later, the link with Ludwig would put the Gestapo on his trail. A special commission had already been set up on 21 July 1944 at the Reich Security Head Office (Reichssicherheits-hauptamt) to track down the conspirators and their helpers; within a short time, it had managed to make about six hundred arrests. There were checks everywhere: in hotels, in railway stations, on the street and in the underground.

Kunrat Hammerstein wore the black uniform of his unit, the Armoured Infantry Division Grossdeutschland; the skull on the collar patch led to confusion with the SS, which the unit had nothing to do with. In his coat pocket, he carried a loaded revolver; he was prepared to defend himself if need be.

After a few days in Berlin, moving from one place to the next, after frantic telephone conversations with trusted friends in order to be clear about the situation he hitchhiked to Leipzig—usually he was picked up by military vehicles—where he took a furnished room. He even went to lectures, 'wore uniform, spoke beside bomb craters to English prisoners of war and greeted other Germans in uniform with raised arm, as Himmler had ordered'. At the same time, he scoured the media and asked his friends for news about the fate of the conspirators. On 8 August, he learned that eight had been sentenced to death and hanged. Before that, the name Erwin Planck had also turned up again. This friend of the family had been arrested and taken to Gestapo headquarters. High on the wanted list was Goerdeler, with whom Kunrat had long been in contact, and a few days later he was betrayed by an informer and caught.

With an impudence for which he can only be envied, Kunrat made a request to his army section for university vacation; he wished to attend a summer course (which didn't exist), but first of all to visit his grandmother for a holiday break. For all of which he was given permission. He then stayed partly in Breslau with the Lüttwitzes, partly with relations in the country, constantly on his guard against military police and informers. He was conspicuous simply because he was over six foot three. He considered trying for a transfer to the Eastern Front, so as to be able to desert as soon as possible, but that would have meant even more paperwork and, by then, his name would probably have proved his undoing.

Late in August, he had to risk going to Berlin again because his leave had run out. It was an SS general who gave him a lift in his car, which resulted in nerve-wracking questioning but his skilful tactics saved him. In the capital, he secretly met his brother Ludwig again and made contact with Wilhelm Scheidt, an old friend, who held the post of 'Special Commissioner of the Führer for Military History'. They got round to talking about suicide: 'What's the best way to shoot oneself?' asked Kunrat. 'Through the open mouth at an upward angle,' answered Scheidt. He slept badly at headquarters and only with a revolver under his pillow, in order to be ready to shoot himself at any time. 'And what shall *I* do then?' asked his wife. 'Shoot

Kunrat von Hammerstein and Ewald von Kleist, about 1942

yourself too,' was the casual reply, 'otherwise you will just be tortured.'

Finally, at the end of August, Hammerstein went to Cologne where he survived in hiding until the end of the war.

In remembrance of a druggist

Such reports reveal that within the 'Volksgemein-schaft'—the national community—of the Third Reich there existed a tiny but alert and tenacious civil society with its own rules. In a way which is hard to grasp, one recognized who belonged to it and who did not. In the late phase of the regime at any rate, this agreement could no longer be defined by adherence to a class, a political programme or a particular family back-ground. One went more by a gesture, a shrug, a nuance in the choice of words. In Kunrat's account, in the space of six weeks, in addition to officers and estate owners from Hammerstein's own background, there appear the following helpers: a former nurse, a senior civil servant, a metalworker, a lawyer, a French driver, a country doctor, a building contractor, a half-Jewish Czech shorthand typist, a military judge, a former Communist, a baroness, a gardener, a Polish servant girl and a masseuse. Even a policeman and a Gestapo member helped him during his flight, at least by being in no hurry to act or by doing nothing at all.

What counted after the failed coup was not dramatic actions like sabotage or plans for new assassination attempts but a stamp on documents here or a warning there or a bed for the night. Those who were in danger quickly developed a sixth sense for the people they were dealing with. Small indicators, code words, intonation served as marks of identification.

Ludwig von Hammerstein, unlike his brother, had of course been directly involved in the clashes in the Bendler Block and the pressure of the search was all the greater on him. Two days after the failed assassination, he went to the district of Kreuzberg on the last underground, and walked to 36 Oranienstrasse, to the home of the wife of an officer he had known at military academy. On the same floor lived a druggist by the name of Hertha Kerp, whose husband had been killed in action. She had hidden a Jewish woman in her store when the deportations began. She was immediately willing to take in Hammerstein who slept on the floor the first night. From the evening of 22 July until the day of liberation, 26 April 1945, he spent most of the time in her apartment; it was his 'headquarters' till the end. It doesn't take much thought to imagine what that meant for his hostess, who also still had her drug store to look after. It appears that Hammerstein not only felt safe with her and her mother but also at ease. He read physics books which relatives sent him. When, however, he asked for hair lotion but sent back what had been delivered because it was not the right one, the patience of his sister Helga snapped. 'We would soon all be in a fix, if we went on like that,' was the message she passed on.

There were more urgent problems. Without papers, Hammerstein couldn't survive for any length of time. From earlier years, Helga knew a graphic artist and painter who didn't want to go to war for Hitler and had been living illegally in Berlin under the name Oskar Huth. He specialized in forging documents. When he came to visit, he brought food ration stamps with him. Hammerstein didn't want to accept them because Huth was himself on the run and not registered anywhere, but he replied: 'Go on, take them, I made them myself.'

One of Huth's friends, who worked on the staff of an anti-aircraft gun training school in Schulzendorf, was able to steal a number of blank service record books from the orderly room. Ludwig had grown a moustache and sideburns and had himself photographed wearing the uniform of a friend. Huth stuck the photo in the record book, stamped it and entered the following false information:

Surname: Hegemann

First names: Karl, Ludwig

Birthday: 25 August 1917

Place of birth: Casa Santa Teresa (Uruguay)

Nationality: German Reich and Uruguay (Remigrant)

Although it was extremely dangerous, the supposed Herr Hegemann often went out in the evening,

I. Angaben zur Person		
1	Familien-name	Hegemann
2	Vornamen (Rufname unterstreichen)	Karl, Ludwig
3	Geburtstag, -monat, -jahr	25. August 1917
4	Geburtsort Verwaltungs-bezirk (z. B. Kreis, Reg. Bezirk)	Casa Santa Teresa (Uruguay)
5	Staatsan-gehörigkeit (auch früher)	Deutsches Reich u. Uruguay (Rückwanderer)
6	Religion	evg.
7	Familien-stand	led.
8	Beruf (nach Berufs-verzeichnis)	erlernter stud. phys. ausgeübter Bergbau-Assistent
9	Eltern	Vater Georg Hegemann (Rufname, Familienname) Botaniker Beruf (nach Berufsverzeichnis) (wenn verstorben: † und Sterbejahr)	Mutter Katharina Hegemann (Rufname, Familienname) Künstel Mädchenname (wenn verstorben: † und Sterbejahr)

Forged service record book used by Ludwig von Hammerstein, 1944, personal description

Sonderausgabe

zum

Deutschen Kriminalpolizeiblatt

Herausgegeben vom Reichskriminalpolizeiamt in Berlin

Erscheint nach Bedarf · Zu beziehen durch die Geschäftsstelle Potsdam, Kaiserstraße 3

17. Jahrgang	Berlin, den 22. Dezember 1944	Nummer 5067 a

Nur für deutsche Behörden bestimmt!
Die Sonderausgaben sind nach ihrer Auswertung sorgfältig
zu sammeln und unter Verschluß zu halten.

Mitteilungen zur Kriegsfahndung

Postausweise keine amtlichen Lichtbildausweise!

Nach dem RdErl. d. RFHuChdDtPol. vom 10. 11. 44 (MBiV. S. 1131) gelten Postausweise fortan nur noch im Verkehr mit den Postanstalten. Sie werden als amtliche Lichtbildausweise im öffentlichen Verkehr, insbesondere bei polizeilichen und militärischen Personalkontrollen, nicht mehr anerkannt.

Alle in der Kriegsfahndung tätigen Kräfte sind hierüber zu unterrichten.
Bei feblenden können im Zusammenhang mit anderen Ausweispapieren Postausweise auch weiterhin zur Feststellung der Person herangezogen werden. In Händen von Ausländern sind Postausweise in keinem Falle als Personalpapiere oder als Ersatz von Personalpapieren anzuerkennen.

1012/44 — C 1 b —,   16. 12. 44.   Reichskriminalpolizeiamt, Kriegsfahndungszentrale

---

A. Neuausschreibungen

I. Raubmord durch ‖-Angehörigen in Chynorany (Slowakei)

In der Nacht zum 9. 12. 44 wurde in Chynorany (Slowakei) 76jähr. Landwirtin und deren 40jähr. Tochter in ihrer Wohnung mit Beil ermordet. Hinzukommenden Sohn fesselte unbek. Täter auf Stuhl. Geraubt wurden: 3 Anzüge (schwa., gra., bla.); slow. Gendarmerie-Reithose; bla. Wintermantel; hellgra. Ballonseidenmantel; 2 P. schwa. Damenstiefel; 2 P. schwa. Herrenstiefel, 830 Kronen; Herrenfahrrad „Pelikan", Nr. 424449; Koffer. Als Täter kommt der Schütze der ‖-Einheit „Dirlewanger" in Frage, der sich bei der Familie 3 Tage einquartiert hatte. Er war im Besitze eines Marschbefehls, auf dem der Ort Dvornik verzeichnet war. Offenbar ist richtige Ortsbezeichnung Dvorec bei Banovce (Slow.), da dort bezeichnete Einheit gelegen hat. Beschr.: Etwa 19 Jahre, etwa 1,68 m, ov. voll. Gesicht, bra. gewellte Haare, dklbra. Augen, ausgebogene kl. Nase; Wehrmachtschiffchenmütze mit schwa.-weiß-rot. Kokarde, Tarnjacke mit weiß. Futter, Feldbluse ohne Spiegel, rot. eingefaßte Schulterklappen, lg. gra. Militärhose, schwa. Stiefel, Aermelstreifen der Einheit „Dirlewanger".

Energische Fahndung! Festnahme!

C 2 a Nr. 76/44.   20. 12. 44.   Reichskriminalpolizeiamt

II. Fahnenflüchtige Wehrmachtangehörige

Wegen Fahnenflucht sind festzunehmen: Ludwig von Hammerstein, Stud. des Bergbaues, 17. 11. 19 Berlin, zul. Berlin-Zehlendorf, Breisacher Str. 19, bis Anfang September in Berlin illegal aufhältlich gewesen, will ins Ausland. Beschr.: 1,86 m, fast schwa. Haare, schlank; Narbe über r. Auge.

Kunrat von Hammerstein, stud. jur., 14. 6. 18 Berlin, zul. aufhältl. in Leipzig, jetzt möglicherweise im Rheinland (Köln, Bonn, Koblenz). Beschr.: 1,92 m, dklblo. Haare, schlank, kurzsichtig. Es handelt sich um Brüder. **Sie sind hierunter abgebildet.**

Festnehmen!

IV 1 b (S K IV) 422/44 g.   29. 11. 44.   StapoLSt Berlin

Ludwig von Hammerstein   sind festzunehmen.   Kunrat von Hammerstein

Wanted notice, 1944

in civilian clothes but with his revolver in his pocket. He arranged to meet good friends, in order to find out who had been arrested and how the situation was being assessed. He was even foolhardy enough to go home once again in November to see his sister Helga. It took some time before the Gestapo's investigations had got to the point when the two brothers could be officially listed as wanted in the *Sonderausgabe zum Deutschen Kriminalpolizeiblatt* (Special Dupplement to the German Criminal Investigation Paper) of 22 December 1944.

The reaction

The attempted assassination put an end to the strange indecision which the regime had displayed with regard to the Hammerstein family. The period of grace was now over.

On 21 July, a certain Frau Theile, a neighbour in Steinhorst, where Maria von Hammerstein was staying, had already reported Kunrat and his mother. A Gestapo man who came from Wolfsburg to investigate thought the informer perhaps hysterical or 'he just didn't want to find anything'; no house search took place.

Three weeks later, the Gestapo did search the Hammersteins' Berlin home in Breisacher Strasse and questioned the general's widow at the Prinz Albrecht Palais, their headquarters in central Berlin. That same day, just before midnight, Gestapo men rang the door-bell of step-grandmother Lüttwitz in Breslau and asked about the two brothers. Although Kunrat had been in the house only a little while before, the maid tried to deny it. The house search produced no results and the two brothers were not traced.

After that, the Gestapo turned their attention to other relatives, first of all to Franz von Hammerstein, the youngest brother, who had been spared call-up. 'I only see with one eye,' he says, 'I'm blind in the other. That's probably why I survived.' He had trained as an industrial manager and was working for Krupp. The Gestapo arrested him at work. He was suspected of having participated in the coup attempt and it was also hoped that, with his help, his brothers would be tracked down.

> Thank God, he remembers, that we soon didn't know where my brothers were hiding. From August 1944, I was in solitary confine-ment in the Gestapo prison in Moabit, with-out books, newspapers, wireless. There were regular interrogations by the Gestapo and there were bedbugs. But I was relieved of any further guilt as a soldier or in the armaments industry, relieved of any shared responsibility for the terrible war crimes.

Then Helga was also arrested. She, however, was released after two weeks—dumped in the street at night with a fever and left to her fate. Finally, it was the turn of Maria von Hammerstein and her youngest daughter; on 1 December, they were both taken to the women's prison in Moabit. Later, they were held for three months in the women's prison in Kantstrasse in Charlottenburg. The Gestapo was firmly convinced that the mother knew her sons' hiding place, and didn't want to release her until she divulged it. Her brother Smilo wrote to Field Marshal Keitel and asked him to ensure that his sister and her children would soon be released. After three weeks, Keitel had a subordinate in the personnel office reply: 'Your letter to Field Marshal Keitel is the first complaint we have received in relation to family liability [Sippenhaft]. All others have communicated their gratitude for such measures to us. Heil Hitler!'

'We all lied,' says Hildur, and, in a secret message she was able to send to her sister Helga, she writes: 'Mummy is extremely incautious and gets me into the most impossible situations. She will probably never learn how to talk in prison. Please send something for the bedbugs.'

Family liability

On 1 March 1945, Franz von Hammerstein was surprised to see his mother and sister Hildur again in a green police van taking them to the Anhalt Station. Also in the party were Reinhard Goerdeler, a son of

Carl Goerdeler; his father had been executed in Plötzensee Prison in February. The arrested did not know their destination: Buchenwald concentration camp.

In November 1944, a 'Family Liability' section had been set up at Reich Security Head Office. 'By family [*Sippe*] is understood: spouse, children, siblings, parents and other relations, if anything unfavourable is known about them.' Those concerned were detained without a warrant and only informed orally about the reasons for arrest. There was an opaque combination of vindictiveness and calculation involved in the operation. It was based on a plan long contemplated by Himmler. He had seized the hostages in order to use them as security; he had the mad idea that at the last minute he could negotiate with the victorious powers behind Hitler's back in order to gain advantages for himself. Hence, it was necessary to place the arrested family members out of reach of advancing Allied forces. A further aspect was the deluded notion of a redoubt in the mountains, the so-called Alpine fortress.

Hans-Günter Richardi has researched the abduction of the prominent prisoners in detail. The largest number were relatives of the protagonists of the German resistance, and so, among members of the Gisevius, Goerdeler, von Hassell, von Plettenberg, von Stauffenberg and other families there were also Maria, Franz and Hildur von Hammerstein. In addition,

Himmler had seized a number of other hostages from seventeen nations—politicians, senior officers and civil servants, industrialists and clerics whom he hoped to use as counters in negotiations. They included the former French Prime Minister Léon Blum who understood very well why the Nazis had incarcerated him in Buchenwald: 'Because to them I was more than a French politician, that is, a Socialist Democrat and a Jew. The same reasons that made me a loathsome enemy also made me a valuable hostage. The attempt is made to obtain an appropriate return for them. Such negotiations always involve threats and blackmail, and the life of the hostage is at stake.'

Some more names:

Alexander Schenk Count von Stauffenberg,

Otto, Marquart and Marquart Jr Schenk Counts von Stauffenberg

Alexandra, Elisabeth, Inez, Maria and Marie Gabriele Schenk Countesses von Stauffenberg

Franz Halder, Chief of the General Staff until 1942

Alexander von Falkenhausen, Military Commander in Belgium and northern France until 1944

Bogislav von Bonin, Colonel, Army Supreme Command

Hjalmar Schacht, Reich Economics Minister until 1937, President of the Reich Bank until 1939

Hermann Pünder, Permanent Secretary (retd)

Martin Niemöller, pastor of the Confessing Church

Fritz Thyssen, major industrialist, and his wife
Amélie

Wilhelm von Flügge, Director of the IG Farben
chemicals combine

Friedrich Leopold, Prince of Prussia

Philip Prince of Hesse, German Ambassador in Italy
until 1943

Fey von Hassell, daughter of Ambassador Ulrich
von Hassell in Rome

Isa Vermehren, cabaret artist from Werner Finck's
satirical cabaret *Katakombe* in Berlin

Kurt von Schuschnigg, Austrian Chancellor until
1938 and his wife

Prince Xavier de Bourbon, brother of Zita, the last
Empress of Austria

Mario Badoglio, son of the Italian Field Marshal

Johannes van Dijk, Dutch Defence Minister until
1940

Hans Lunding, head of the Danish intelligence
service

Alexander Papagos, Commander in Chief of the
Greek Army

Ivan Bessonov, Red Army General

Miklós von Kállay, Hungarian Prime Minister until
1944

Miklós von Horthy, son of the Hungarian Vice-
Regent

Sigismund Payne Best, Captain in the British secret
  service
Sante Garibaldi, Italian General

The necrosis of power

In the chaos of the last months of the war, the prisoners began a bizarre odyssey which led from Buchenwald and Dachau concentration camps to the imaginary Alpine fortress and the South Tyrol. The SS guards had orders to murder them if necessary.

Arriving at Weimar Station, they faced a night march. 'After walking for two and a half hours, the first barriers, lit up in red, appeared before us and an eerily illuminated sign with the skull and crossbones,' says Isa Vermehren, and Franz von Hammerstein relates:

> At Buchenwald, we stood at the gate, trembling, not knowing what was going to happen. But we weren't driven through the gate into the camp—instead, we ended up outside the camp, in a hut with a wall around it, and found ourselves isolated there in astonishing company: Amélie and Fritz Thyssen, with whom I then played chess, several Stauffenbergs, old and young, Gertrud Halder, the Kaisers, Fey von Hassell, Annelise Gisevius, the Goerdeler family and more adults and children, each family in a small room with bunk beds.
>
> Only gradually did it become clear to me that there were not only family members of

those involved in 20 July there, but also 'liable family members' of the National Committee for a Free Germany in the Soviet Union, relatives of deserters and all kinds of other forms of resistance. All had already been through arrest, prison, various concentration camps like Stutthof or Ravensbrück.

Fey von Hassell writes: 'For me, there was a happy meeting with Maria Hammerstein, her daughter Hildur, called "Puppe" [doll], and one of her many sons, Franz. As a young girl, Maria had been one of my mother's best friends. They had gone to court balls together.'

On 3 April, when artillery fire could already be heard from the front—American troops were only twenty-five miles from Weimar—the order came to move out. The confusion of chains of command, the contradictory orders, the disrupted transport and communications links meant that an orderly withdrawal was no longer possible. Prisoners from other camps joined the convoy; others, for reasons that no one understood, were not taken along. The night-time journey of the remainder led first of all to Flossenbürg, but the camp commandant refused to accept the prisoners. At Regensburg too they were turned away, a sign that the command structures were breaking down. The guards didn't know what to do. As Frau von Hassell relates, the transport commander, an SS Untersturmführer—lieutenant—was 'quite desperate, and actually asked us where they should take us.

Simply unbelievable!' Finally, the commandant of Dachau concentration camp declared he was willing to admit the hostages.

Marie Gabriele von Stauffenberg describes the sight the German provinces presented: 'Everywhere, columns of disintegrating army units, a melancholy sight, refugees on the roads. Landshut is burning. Constant air raid warnings—frequent halts and driving slowly with dimmed lights. The sky everywhere red from fires.' Frau von Hassell:

> Our night-time journey was accompanied by constant air raids. Burnt-out vehicles, dead horses and homeless people lined the road. Then we drove through Munich—I was shaken. From a distance, everything looked intact. But the closer we came, the more clearly we saw: nothing but walls and facades, yawning emptiness behind them, a few people wandering around. There were no cars any more. Munich had become a ghost town where deep silence held sway.

Captain Payne Best, a British special prisoner, describes the arrival in Dachau:

> There were no seats, we were hungry and tired and, for about an hour, we just hung about there, our spirits getting lower every minute. At last, a portly SS colonel made his appearance and, with great politeness, introduced himself as Obersturmbannführer Weiter, Commandant of Auschwitz. With a

Pragser Wildsee hotel (Lago de Braies).
1930s' postcard

most obliging air he made us a regular speech, even gallantly attempting, but failing, to kiss Mrs von Schusnigg's hand. He was very sorry that we had been kept waiting for so long, but Dachau was very crowded and it had really been most difficult to find suitable accommodation for such distinguished guests. He had done what he could but, even so, realized that the quarters to which he would now conduct us were very far from being such as we expected and deserved, but, really, they were the best that he could provide, and he hoped that we would forgive their shortcomings.

His astonished listeners could conclude from this greeting that their guards were very nervous. There were constant air raids and, in Dachau too, the artillery fire of the advancing American army could already be heard in the distance.

Our SS guards [says Isa Vermehren] grew old and grey during those days. They only turned up for duty sporadically, and were so caught up in their own worries that it was hardly worth bothering them with any question. The hectic rushing around of all the SS people reminded me of the desperate attempts at escape of a captured animal.

Imprisonment in Dachau lasted less than three weeks. On 17 April, the first of the heavily guarded hostages left for Innsbruck on buses and trucks. Franz

American troops enter Niederdorf, South Tyrol
4 May 1945

von Hammerstein was separated from his mother and his sister Hildur and stayed behind, supposedly because there was no more room in the vehicles for him and four other family hostages; they were sent south on foot. On 27 April, a convoy with 139 prisoners left Innsbruck heading for the South Tyrol. This transport had assembled the most prominent hostages whom Himmler had managed to get hold of. No one knew where the journey was intended to end. Only at the last moment did the prisoners find out that their destination was a remote grand hotel close to Niederdorf in the Dolomites. There it turned out that three Wehrmacht generals with their staffs had installed themselves in the Pragser Wildsee hotel, which had been earmarked as accommodation for the hostages who now had to make do with provisional quarters in the village. The inhabitants, in the words of Hermann Pünder, 'were not a little surprised when they saw our motley band: gaunt gentlemen in general's trousers, civilian jackets and slouch hats, ladies in high soldiers' boots, shivering figures with scarves to keep them warm, elderly ladies and gentlemen with a shabby rucksack on their back.'

In such a situation, the easing of conditions of imprisonment alternate with threats. The eighty-six men of the SS and SD escort are demoralized. Colonel Bogislav von Bonin resolves to act. He manages to have a secret priority telephone call with the headquarters of Army Group Italy. He asks for help because of the danger that the hostages will be liquidated by the SS. Finally, on 30 April, shortly before the capitulation of the German troops in Italy, a Wehrmacht company, under Captain Wichard von Alvensleben, arrives in Niederdorf. He places the hostages under his protection and forces the SS to withdraw without resistance. That same evening he billets the prisoners in the Pragser Wildsee hotel. Their captivity is over. On the morning of 4 May, an advance party of the American army reaches the village. It's soon followed by a vast baggage train of jeeps, trucks, radio vehicles and field kitchens, and, at the same time, the first reporters and photographers.

Now it was German soldiers who began the march to a prison camp. A brigadier-general of the US army appeared and ordered the departure of the distinguished guests. His instructions were to take them by way of Verona to Naples and from there to the island of Capri. Only after weeks of waiting were Maria and Hildur von Hammerstein able to leave their gilded cage and return to a devastated Germany to find out where their relatives were.

Berlin, at the end

While his mother and her youngest daughter were on their wanderings through the Alps, Ludwig von Hammerstein witnessed the end of the war in the home of the druggist in Kreuzberg:

On 21 April, the first Russian shells fell on our city. There was no electricity any more. Consequently, no wireless news from London, Beromünster and Moscow. Instead, ever more rumours of every kind. On 23 April, the warehouses at the East Harbour were opened for 'looting'. People dragged barrels of butter and half oxen home. There were wild scenes. The Warsaw Bridge was already cordoned off and being prepared for blasting. Only soldiers were falling back and completely exhausted lads of the 'children's anti-aircraft service'. There were bodies lying in the street with a cardboard sign 'We still have the power'. Terror to the very last minute.

On 25 April, I tried to phone friends in the suburb of Zehlendorf. But it was already a Russian voice that answered. On 26 April, Mother Kerp cooked a magnificent lunch. A bottle of red wine with it. Everyone was full of hope again after the bombs and shells. Then, at about three o'clock, the first Russian infantrymen appeared in Oranienstrasse. The inhabitants stood in the entries to the houses and were happy that the whole mess was over at last. I didn't see anyone offering resistance. The last of our own soldiers had already slunk across our back court in the morning.

The Russians stuck their weapons in our faces and collected watches and jewellery. Then they distributed tobacco and cigarettes from the shop at the corner and searched the houses for hidden German soldiers. In the darkness, one fell down the shop stairs of the drug store, fortunately didn't do himself any harm, but lost his temper and wanted to shoot me who had had to accompany him. I showed him 'hands up' and smiled at him—there was nothing else I could do—he calmed down and merely punched me in the face. To the question whether I was a soldier, I replied, 'Nix soldier, nix Fascist.' Earlier, I had only just in time hidden my revolver, supposed to protect me from the Gestapo, in a refuse bin.

As long as it was daylight, the Russians were reasonably well behaved. At night, it was a different matter. Groups of soldiers forced their way into cellars and homes. Pistols drawn, they fetched women and girls. Only elderly and resolute women—like Mother Kerp—were any kind of protection—the soldiers usually showed them some respect. Some of the officers even tried to prevent excesses. But they couldn't be everywhere.

A colonel had meanwhile taken up quarters in the drug store and we all dossed in the shop [squashed together] like herring. On 3 May, I was arrested as a suspected soldier and placed in the courtyard under guard. Else Kerp then argued with the colonel for so long that he sent me to the local commandant, to have my particulars checked. There I had to come clean about who I really was, including the 'first lieutenant'. It went well. The commandant spoke German and had presumably heard something about 20 July. He wrote something in Russian on my driver's licence. It was the only genuine identification I possessed.

I couldn't read the entry, but it was respected everywhere. I got to Zehlendorf unscathed. On 8 May, I was able to enter our house again, but no one was talking about the capitulation of the German Reich. There was no wireless news and no newspapers. All we knew: the war in Berlin is over. In the evening, the Russians often fired in the air a lot. They knew more. What interested me, first of all, was who had survived. In Berlin, it was everyone who had helped me to escape the Gestapo and risked their neck doing so. We did not get the good news about my mother, my youngest sister and my brother, whom the Gestapo had arrested, and about my older brother who had gone into hiding in Cologne, until July.

The return

Maria von Hammerstein and her daughter Hildur arrived in Frankfurt am Main on 16 June 1945. She knew nothing of the fate of the rest of the family and, first of all, set out on the difficult journey to Munich to see Butzi who was living in Prien on the Chiemsee lake.

Marie Luise had already left the Münchhausen estate, which had employed Polish and Ukrainian forced labour during the war; she wasn't interested in agriculture and she didn't feel comfortable with the role of lady of the manor. Also the Gestapo, who had obtained her files from Berlin, began to search the house again and to interrogate her for hours. The couple had in any case drifted apart, and, in 1942, when Münchhausen came home to Herrengosserstedt on leave, he discovered that his wife had gone away with the children.

'I left my husband's home against his will,' writes Marie Luise, 'and with my three children moved to Prien in Upper Bavaria, where an old school friend took me in although I was under surveillance by the police.' Marie Luise was not safe from the attentions of the Gestapo there either. (The friend, born Irmgard Wegener and from Kassel, had already had a hand in politicizing the Hammerstein sisters in the 1920s, as Maria Therese relates; she says Irmgard had been Marie Luise's 'evil genius', and so her and Helga's 'evil genius' as well, meaning Irmgard Wegener's political influence on the sisters. Meanwhile, Irmgard had married Franz Josef Schöningk, later one of the publishers of the liberal *Südddeutsche Zeitung* newspaper, and had moved to the Chiemsee.)

In the final weeks of the war, Captain von Münch-hausen's unit was transferred from Italy to Bohemia. On the way, he was able to visit his wife in Bavaria. She advised him: 'Stay here, I'll hide you.' He, however, did not want to let his men down, as he said, and with his company was taken prisoner by the Russians. His estate, Herrengosserstedt, was expropriated immediately after the war.

Hardly were hostilities over when the two friends attempted to build up a Communist cell in idyllic Prien and campaigned for the Communist Party in the first elections to the Bavarian parliament to be held since the Nazis seized power. Anyone who knows the area around Chiemsee will not be surprised to learn that their efforts were not crowned with success.

Not until autumn 1945 could the Hammerstein family gather in Steinhorst by Celle, where Maria had already found shelter with the children after the First World War. In one of her first letters, she invited her daughter Maria Therese to return to Germany. In Steinhorst, her daughter's family could, first of all, relax:

> The housing difficulties are of course great. Accommodation possibilities are to be created as soon as possible, huts and better things. One can live quite well in decently built huts. We discovered that in Buchenwald and Dachau, where we stayed during our captivity. In Berlin, all valuable things have, of course,

gone missing. But one can also live simply—
it's better for work, in fact.

But her daughter didn't want to come back to the
bosom of the family now as poor as a church mouse.

In February 1946, my mother returned to
Berlin where the house in Breisacher Strasse
had more or less survived Gestapo, bombs,
conquest and looting. The journey took four
days because she had to pass through a
refugee camp at the zonal border. Not until
1949 did she finally move back to Berlin.
(Ludwig)

At the end of the 1940s, in the crowded
house in Dahlem, at 19 Breisacher Strasse.
Franz lived in the cloakroom, Hildur behind
a cupboard in the hall; in the kitchen, Ama fed
'Hütchen', the master of forged documents
[who, in the Nazi years, had saved many
people with the help of his products]; Kunrat
was flat on his back because of a weak chest;
Ludwig was working at the *Welt* newspaper
during the day; only Helga, living respectably
on the upper floor with her husband and little
adopted son Horst, had a housekeeper, inher-
ited from her Jewish friends the Magnuses,
who had emigrated. The first to move out of
this overcrowded house was Ludwig, who
joined the staff of the CDU politician Jacob
Kaiser in Bonn. Next to leave was Hildur who
had a grant to study in Zürich, then Franz and
Hildur, both of whom went to the USA.
(Verena von Hammerstein)

The mother

From 1952, Maria drew her widow's pension, more than 1,000 marks, and was from then on the wealthiest in the family and was happy to be able to help others. She summoned an elderly Hungarian tailor, who addressed her as Your Excellency and measured Franz, who as a newly ordained pastor earned only 250 marks, for a black suit. For herself, she continued her improvised lifestyle and made only the most essential purchases—apart from an elegant hat for an aristocratic wedding, which she lost on the way home. In the 1960s, several of her grandsons would spend nights at the house and they learned that school should not be taken too seriously. They were often allowed to stay with her in the morning and she wrote a sick note, which the teachers immediately recognized as coming from the grandmother. (Verena v. H.)

She wasn't tall, but imposing in her manner. She always had a sharp tongue, whether she was speaking in German or English. She had a cherry tree in her garden. Under her watchful eyes, the children were allowed to pick the fruit. I was always a little intimidated by her. (Carol Levine Paasche, daughter-in-law of Maria Therese)

She was in the habit of walking barefoot on the grass of the parks in Dahlem early in the morning. A park warder drew her attention to the fact that this was not allowed. She looked at him dumbfounded and replied: 'My God, young man, how narrowminded you are.' So that Herr Huth had some money, she often asked him to come and restore her furniture; she always gave him a princely reward. One day it was the turn of her bureau, in which she presumably kept some of her jewellery. She told my mother that afterwards her valuable earrings were missing. Her comment was: 'Huth took them no doubt, he needs them more than I do. Why should an old goat like me still be sticking on these fancy things!' (Verena v. H.)

Asked about her good health, she said: 'If, like me, you had been born in a roadside ditch in Hungary [she means Silesia] and ate as much garlic, you would feel much better too.' (Christian Count zu Lynar)

She often drank a little bottle of sparkling wine. For her afternoon nap, she didn't lie down in bed but rested undressed over a broomstick. On Sundays, she went to Catholic mass at seven in the morning and to the Christengemeinschaft (a Protestant community influenced by anthroposophy) or to the Protestant church at ten. (Joan Paasche, daughter of Maria Therese)

Finally, she lived alone on one floor at 7 Breisacher Strasse which Helga had furnished for her. Being alone didn't agree with her.

Until then, she had always managed to attract young people to her. But she was no longer looking after herself properly. She didn't want a help, a lady companion, not even Pari [Caspari, the old nanny at the Bendlerstrasse]; she couldn't bear even her beloved granddaughter Bettina for long. Helga, who lived in the same street, kept an eye on her. But the solution was these schoolchildren who spent the night with her in turn and whom she didn't perceive as carers but who would report if something was wrong. She was still riding around on her bicycle, after all, when she was over eighty. It was taken away from her. She bribed a grandson who brought it back to her.

In her last years, she was very restless. She still set out on a round of visits, to Munich, Bonn or Hamburg. Once, at Tempelhof Airport, she lay down on a bench before her flight, because she was hardly able to go on. Otherwise, she wore her age well. She wrote a huge number of postcards, and it's no coincidence that, in 1970, she collapsed at a letter-box in Mutlangen when she was taking a cure at the Paracelsus Sanatorium. Her best friend in her old age, the widow of Count zu Lynar, kept her company. She was taken to a Catholic hospital in Mutlangen and cared for by nuns. All the children came to visit her. There was laughter at the hospital bed. Ama mixed up her children with her siblings and delivered her dry maxims. When she realized

Maria von Hammerstein, around 1968

that she was paralysed on one side, she refused to eat and the nuns let her be. Having received the last rites, she passed away peacefully in her sleep on 9 March 1970, two days before her eighty-third birthday. She was buried next to her husband in the family cemetery in Steinhorst. (Verena v. H.)

Journeys back to normality

In 1945, Franz von Hammerstein had been separated from his relatives in Dachau and had to set out southward on foot. 'We had a horse and cart for our luggage and spent the night with farmers or in barns. On 30 April, we were shut in the cellar of an isolated farmhouse. When we came out on 1 May, the SS had disappeared, the farmers gave us breakfast, the Americans were driving past outside and took us to Munich.' On the way back home, not far from Steinhorst, he relates, 'a tramp came towards me, and I was immediately afraid that he would try to steal my bicycle, my last possession. But as he came closer I recognized him as my brother Kunrat, whom I'd long thought lost. He met me here by chance on the road, hundreds of miles from Berlin.'

'Franz gave up the idea of becoming a businessman,' writes his mother, 'after his difficult experiences.' She meant his experiences of captivity and flight. Perhaps, the influence of the Confessing Church

Franz von Hammerstein, about 2000

in Dahlem also played a part in his decision to study theology, first in Bethel, near Bielefeld, then in Göttingen. In 1948, he continued his studies in Chicago where he got to know Jewish culture. 'At school there were still Jewish boys, at home there were Jewish visitors, my older sisters helped Jews escape but I didn't have a clue about Jewish history, Jewish religion, synagogue life.' He was helped to rectify that by German-Jewish émigrés like Bergsträsser, Rothfels and Schuber who taught in Washington and Chicago.

At Howard, a Black university in Washington DC, he was confronted with the problems of race; his parish disapproved of his association with Blacks. In 1950, he returned to Berlin where he was ordained by Bishop Dibelius. In 1952, near Zürich, he married a Swiss woman, Verena Rordorf. It was not until later that he met Leo Baeck and Martin Buber, the subject of his doctoral dissertation [*Das Messiasproblem bei Martin Buber*—The Problem of the Messiah in Martin Buber (1958)], in Jerusalem. After a second stay in America, he took over the newly established Social Pastorate in Berlin and became one of the founders of Aktion Sühnezeichen (a reconciliation programme involving young people from Germany and other countries). Since then, Franz von Hammerstein has been especially committed to reconciliation with Poland, former Czechoslovakia and Russia. He also worked for the World Council of Churches. In 1973, he returned fairly exhausted from Moscow where he had attended the World Peace Conference. From 1976, until his retirement in 1986, he was head of the Protestant Academy in Berlin.

Ludwig von Hammerstein was perhaps the most level-headed of the Hammerstein children. His brief biography of his father is distinguished by restraint and clarity. He participated without hesitation in building up the Federal Republic (West Germany). Shortly after the end of the war, in 1946, he joined the editorial staff of the daily *Die Welt*; for a decade from 1950, he was Press Officer in the Ministry of All-German Affairs. He was spied on by the East German State Security Service (Stasi) but the result of their researches was meagre: 'He is a close friend of Minister Kaiser and his wife, goes on many official trips, smokes rarely, likes to drink, private life unknown, approx. five foot eleven inches tall, slim, narrow head, wears glasses, black, slightly wavy hair, always dressed English style.'

In 1961, he was appointed Deputy Director of North German Broadcasting and in 1974, Director of the RIAS Berlin radio station. After his official retirement, he helped to set up Deutschland Radio. The 20 July Foundation also owes him a great deal—he did what he could to help surviving relatives and made a big contribution to putting an end to their defamation. In 1950 he married Dorothee Claessen. He died in Berlin in 1996.

Hildur's life is not marked by extravagances either. In 1952, after studying in Munich, she married Ralph

Ludwig von Hammerstein, 1944

Zorn, an American pastor whom she accompanied to the United States the following year. He first had charge of a Lutheran parish in Yonkers, New York, then went to the southern states. In 1962, the Zorns returned to Berlin with five children. They had fallen out with their very hidebound Lutheran church in Missouri because Blacks were unwelcome in the congregation there. The Zorns were unwilling to accept that. Hildur's mother approached Bishop Dibelius, whom she knew well, and asked him to appoint Ralph as a pastor in Berlin.

A beginning in the New World

Maria Therese left Japan in 1948 and, with her husband Joachim (John) Paasche and their four children, emigrated to the United States, to San Francisco. Jacob Wuest, who had been US military attaché in Berlin, and other friends who have always remained loyal to the Hammersteins, procured the immigration documents, the affidavit and stood surety for them. Their son Gottfried says: 'Coming more or less as both German and Japanese to the USA during the cold war was hell.' It was very far from being a return to a familiar civilization. 'The Americans were almost as alien to us as the Japanese,' said Maria Therese. 'Their polite smiles only serve to conceal an abyss.'

Shadowed in Germany, under suspicion in Japan, the couple were now in the sights of the FBI. Joachim

Paasche, like his wife, spoke Russian and studied Slavonic languages. On top of that he had known the notorious Dr Sorge, and his wife's sisters had worked for the Communists. That was enough.

Joachim Paasche did not find a position as a scholar in America and had to get by as an ordinary worker. Under these difficult conditions, he also began to study Chinese. His wife supported the family as a cook and a cleaner. At the time, Paasche's brother-in-law, Franz von Hammerstein, wrote: 'It's not so easy for him, because on the one hand he is not yet a citizen of the United States and on the other he has not completed an academic education. In addition, he is sensitive and doesn't like to be put under time pressure in a piece of work which, unfortunately, is normal in America.' The marriage also suffered. 'My father was a man of integrity, but impractical and easily hurt,' says Gottfried Paasche, 'and my mother loved strong characters.'

Maria Therese's mother already managed to visit her relations in America in 1954: Hildur who lived in New Jersey, her grandson Gottfried in Vermont and the Paasches in California. She stayed in the USA for almost six months and also renewed her old Berlin friendship with Jacob Wuest.

Not until 1957 did Paasche get a post in the China Department of the Library of Congress. He died in 1994.

John Paasche, 1950

Maria Therese with her three daughters
Joan, Michaela and Vergilia,
California 1949

Maria Therese hardly spoke to her children about her experiences in the resistance. She died at the age of ninety in a Jewish old people's home. Her ashes were interred in the family grave at Steinhorst.

The sleeper awakes

Marie Luise had been living in Dahlem since 1947; her house had survived the war. Her Communist convictions, despite two marriages to aristocrats, had also steadfastly outlasted the Third Reich. Since she profoundly distrusted the new West German state, 'because of its many brown spots', she sold the house in the west and, after the establishment of the German Democratic Republic, moved to the 'democratic sector of Berlin' with her three children.

Her mother was very concerned when Friedemann von Münchhausen returned after five years' captivity in the Soviet Union and Butzi expected him to live with her in East Berlin. He refused. Later he became a permanent secretary in Düsseldorf, in the regional government of North Rhine-Westphalia.

Marie Luise devoted herself to the new East German state with noteworthy radicalism. Officially, at least, she didn't have a good word to say about her family. Asked about it, she replied in 1951 in her personal file as follows: 'Six siblings, all in West Berlin and West Germany, apart from one sister in the USA. Activities and employment not known, since all contact broken off some time ago.' As far as her husband was concerned, she added: 'It is to be expected that the divorce will follow with the blame on my side alone as I refuse to continue the marriage for political reasons.' And to make a complete clean sweep, she renounced her title: 'Since moving to the democratic sector [of Berlin], I have dispensed with the *von* in front of my name and had my ID made out accordingly'— a decision she never revised. Immediately after the move, she became a member of the SED, took up her law studies again, qualified, lived in the northern suburb of Wilhelmsruh and worked in joint chambers in Pankow. Until the end of the 1950s she also dealt with criminal cases; she defended 'absconders from the Republic' and in some cases managed to achieve a mitigation of sentences.

It was not only politically that she picked up the threads again that had been broken in 1934—she also maintained lively contacts with the small Jewish community in East Berlin. Above all, she took an interest in the Jewish Communists of her generation who had returned from the Soviet Union after the war. She was a close friend of Ernst Scholem, a nephew of Werner, who died a Stalinist. They often met at the Jewish cemetery in Weissensee in Berlin. The writings of Gershom Scholem, whom she admired, meant a great deal to her. She is also said to have protected Jewish clients from the accusation of Zionism which the Party was all too willing to raise.

After the Wall was built, she gave up acting as defence counsel in criminal cases and restricted herself to family, inheritance and copyright law, probably out of fear of possible reprisals and so as not to put her children at risk. Nevertheless, in 1976, when the defence lawyer Robert Havemanns was to be expelled from the lawyers' college, she was the only one at the meeting of the Party members of the body who voted against the resolution.

Although there could be no doubt about her loyalty, and although as a victim of the Nazi regime she enjoyed a degree of protection, she was under constant surveillance by the organs of the state. In their files there exists a document which appears to show that after the war she also worked for the KGB.

Head Section XX Berlin 04.12.1976

BstU 000100/101

Investigation Report

von Münchhausen, Marie-Luise,

née von Hammerstein

Born: 24.09.1908, Berlin

Resident: Berlin-Wilhelmsruh, 5 Lessingstrasse

Lawyer, member of the College of Lawyers of Greater Berlin

Member of SED, FDGB [trade union] and of the League of Culture

Descended from an old, aristocratic officers' family. Her father, Colonel-General von Hammerstein, was Chief of Army Command of the Reichswehr from 1930-1936 [in fact 1934].

THE SILENCES OF HAMMERSTEIN

She herself already joined the KPD in 1928 during her legal studies. With her help, according to information, available documents about the construction of cruisers are said to have come to the attention of the KPD.

Brothers of Münchhausen living in the Federal Republic were involved in the events of the 20 July 1944 but were able to evade the subsequent proceedings while other family members were arrested.

From 1950—1960, M. was unofficially active for the Soviet security organs.

M. is divorced. Her former husband, active as a jurist in the Federal Republic, visited her regularly.

One son absconded from the Republic in 1958 [in fact 1956] and lives in the Federal Republic.

One daughter, a teacher, was smuggled out of the GDR in 1960 [in fact 1969] with husband. To what extent contact exists between M. and these children is not known.

In the 1960s, M. was unofficially assessed as an energetic person, loyal to the GDR, who, because of her background, her bourgeois education and many West contacts, is not free from prejudices and petty-bourgeois ways of thinking.

As a lawyer, M. was exclusively concerned with civil law cases.

From the available documents, it appears that, in 1959, she was a member of a legislative commission on copyright law of the Ministry of Culture. In addition, she was the legal consultant of the Association of Fine Artists.

Section XX of the former VFS [Administra-
tion for Training] of Greater Berlin noti-
fied in 1969 that M. maintained links with
persons in the circles around Havemanns
and Biermann.

In 1970, M. came to the attention of Sect.
II of the Potsdam BV [District Administration of
State Security] because she was in contact with
a US citizen sentenced for malicious agitation against the state. [This is not the case: it
was her daughter Cecil who was friends with an American.]
In an operative check by Head Section II,
no indications of a hostile activity were
compiled.

Marie Luise's daughters, Bettina and Cecil, vehe-
mently deny that Marie Luise worked for the Soviet
secret service. The only thing that is certain in such
cases is that the dossiers of State Security are never to
be trusted without reservation.

Border issues

Ama's last two decades [1950–70] were governed by the rhythm of her weekly trips to
Wilhelmruh, with plastic bags inside her coat
full of freshly pressed orange juice, and ban-
knotes and forbidden printed matter hidden
in her pockets. On 17 June 1953 [i.e. during
the Uprising of that month], when there was
shooting in the city centre, Ludwig had to
hold her back by force from her usual errand.
She was well-known to the members of the
People's Police after all. (Verena v. H.)

THE SILENCES OF HAMMERSTEIN

Operative conclusive result about the person:

von Hammerstein, née Baroness von Lüttwitz, first name Marie-Luise, born 11.3.86 in Schweidnitz, resident Steinhorst by Celle, Lower Saxony, pensioner.

Facts of the case:

H. appeared on 5.6.67 at about 11 a.m. for entry into the capital of the GDR. She was accompanied by the West German citizen Franz v. Hammerstein. At customs inspection, 20 DM/German Fed. Bank were ascertained which she had not declared. On further customs inspection, 50 marks [East] were ascertained in the coat pocket of H — as she allegedly wanted to buy somewhat cheaper in 'East Berlin'. It should also be mentioned that she attempted, during the customs inspection, to *eat* the marks, which she was prevented from doing by the Customs. The aforementioned currency was confiscated by the Customs and H. punished by a fine of 50 DM/West. She further said that she could not understand that as a woman she was constantly so strictly inspected. She had already been in a concentration camp before 1945.

signed Kunze, captain

Hänsel, sergeant

From time to time, she asked young border policemen to carry her heavy bags because she was an elderly lady and so got them through the inspection unchallenged. Even years later, border policemen, when they read the name Hammerstein in the passport, would still ask after the old lady who had crossed the Bornholm Bridge checkpoint so often. (Ludwig)

'Marie Luise lived in another world, we knew that,' said her mother. That is also evident from a brusque letter which she wrote to her brother Kunrat in 1954. In complete agreement with the SED, she sees in West Germany a police state which reminds her of the 1930s:

> I was never interrogated before 1933 by the 'Secret State Police' [i.e. Gestapo] because of my membership of the Communist Party but certainly in 1934, 1942/43 and 1944. That would perhaps soon happen to me again over there [in the West]. In addition to which, people I had contact with and my post were kept under surveillance the whole time. As a result, I only wrote love letters. I forgot [to mention] 1 May 1929, when demonstrators standing next to me were shot down and I was arrested. That could also happen again today. So don't tell any jokes, at least not if I'm around.

Marie Luise's sister-in-law, Verena, notes that the loyalty and warmth of her mother softened the ideological hardness of the daughter which had often taken hurtful forms. Apart from, that Butzi had also had her own problems with the Party she had placed her trust in.

In later years, she is said to have distanced herself more and more from the state apparatus and urged her children to be cautious; she even compared State Security (the Stasi) to the Gestapo. She found it ever harder to reconcile such fears with her independence of mind, her spirit of defiance and her loyalty. The contact with her family, or with her divorced husband who never let her down, at no time completely broke off. In 1954, there was even a family meeting in West Berlin, in the Paris Bar, where Marie Luise's birthday was celebrated.

Her favourite child Kai did not flourish in the East; he already got into difficulties as a student of agriculture. 'You're cutting the ground from under your feet,' said his mother. 'Go to your father and continue in the West!' In 1956, he followed her advice and went to West Germany, although he was and remained a Communist. After the building of the Wall, he was followed by Marie Luise's daughter Bettina. In spring 1968, her husband met a Czech diplomat who offered to help the couple flee the republic. One year later, twelve hours apart, he took the couple across the inner German border in his car. 'It was heart-stopping for all those involved, it was bad for those who remained in the East,' says Bettina von Münchhausen. 'For the two of us, the world was at our feet and we were spared the last twenty years in the GDR.' She and her husband, an expert in tropical agriculture, then worked in development aid throughout the world. Today, they live in retirement in Essen.

Marie Luise's youngest daughter, Cecil, remained in the East. She cared for her mother, who had lost her memory and no longer spoke, at home until her death in late autumn 1999.

A posthumous conversation
with Marie Luise von Münchhausen

E: I have talked to your brothers and sisters,
    Frau von Münchhausen, and I've been told that
    you are reluctant to talk about your experi-
    ences. But there are things which only you can
    tell me about.

M: I know what you want to ask me.

E: Well, what?

M: Always the same thing. First my parents, then
    my husband, my brothers and sisters, finally
    the children.

E: You probably don't trust me.

M: Oh, I know quite well who you are. I saw your
    play about Cuba at the Berliner Ensemble. That
    must have been in the early 1970s.

E: 'Play' is probably claiming too much. It was
    more a documentation.

M: Your past.

E: Yes. But I'm interested in yours.

M: Put crudely: you're snooping on me.

E: One could call it that. Your family doesn't
    talk about everything. I've looked in the
    archives. Werner Scholem's papers, cadre files
    in Moscow and Berlin.

M: Do you believe everything in those documents?

E: Not necessarily.

M: And what do my relatives say? Nothing good, I
    assume.

E: You are said to have turned your back on your
    brothers Ludwig and Kunrat — although they
    were in the resistance, to you they were ide-
    ologically suspect as officers. Franz was evi-
    dently the only one who found favour with you
    because, during the war, he displayed no mil-
    itary ambition of any kind and later joined
    the Society for German-Soviet Friendship.

THE SILENCES OF HAMMERSTEIN

M: No wonder that I was seen as exotic by the family. You presumably believe that being determines consciousness?

E: Not a particularly new insight. But applied to you the sentence really doesn't seem very plausible. You broke away very early, after all. Nathan Steinberger says you were the first to go underground, even before your sister Helga.

M: That's a long time ago.

E: I do ask myself how you got through the twelve years of Nazi rule. Two marriages within your social class and life as lady of the manor . . .

M: I got through it. There's nothing more to be said about it.

E: It doesn't seem to have changed your political convictions. Otherwise, you would hardly have decided for the SED.

M: It wasn't the easiest option.

E: Your commitment must have been very great. You not only worked for the SED, but also for the Soviets, more precisely for the KGB.

M: Who told you that?

E: Head Section XX, Ministry of State Security.

M: I can hardly believe that.

E: In the meantime, almost anyone who wants to can look at these files. The bureaucracy doesn't forget.

M: Don't you have anything better to do?

E: No. With all respect for your constancy — it's not easy to remain loyal to a lost cause for twenty, thirty, forty years. Only — did it have to be the KGB on top of that?

M: That's what you say.

E: That's what State Security says.

M: In which you evidently have every confidence.

E: Far from it. That's why I'm asking you.

M: You want to interrogate me? — but I've been through enough interrogations in my life. Let me set a trap for you. What would you say if at that time I had thought: if I do make a commitment, then a complete one. Why go to the branch office, which has hardly any say? Why not go straight to the head? Or, if this is something you'd rather hear: perhaps I sought to cover myself, in order to avoid being made an informer for the State Security of the GDR? You see, there are more possible reasons for such a note in the files than you could dream of. But how should you know? You live in normal times.

E: There are no normal times. You know what the Italians say? *Nel peggio non c'è fine* — there's no end to the bad.

M: Not everyone can accept that. I did what I could.

E: Like your father.

M: In his own way. We were never in agreement. In the end, we both lost. But I sometimes think that he was right in the end. And with that I've already said too much to you, a stranger. Write what you like, but leave me alone and don't come again.

Helga's final years

At the end of the 1940s, Helga was living with her husband in her mother's home. She dearly wanted a child, but the marriage remained childless. She adopted a five-year-old boy who had survived typhus in a children's home.

An old friend from the early 1930s got in touch once again. Hubert von Ranke writes:

> I have remained friends with her, our constant contact interrupted only by the vicissitudes of war. She had her own heavy load to bear. When we saw each other again after the war, it was wonderful to feel that each of us, in our own way, had gone through the same development. I visited her last summer. It is as if our conversation had broken off only yesterday—we still speak the same language.

Walter Rossow, her husband, didn't remain an ordinary gardener—he became an expert in the field of landscaping, and played an important part in restoring Berlin's Tiergarten park. Nevertheless, he was not appointed professor in the city because he did not have a school-leaving certificate. Consequently, the family moved to Stuttgart where Rossow established the Institute of Landscape Planning at the Technical University; he became Chairman of the Deutsche Werkbund and was awarded the order Pour le mérite (now no longer a military distinction). He detested kitsch and sentimentality, and his aesthetic approach is said to have assumed tyrannical features. For him, form, colour and design were governed by inexorable laws.

Helga had to look after three households: her mother's old home in Berlin, which accommodated her husband's planning office, their apartment in Stuttgart and a farm near Ravensburg which her husband had acquired and which was run on anthroposophical lines.

Later, health problems accumulated. She suffered from diabetes and could no longer cope with her medication alone. When her husband died quite suddenly at the beginning of 1992, she was in a hospital with the ominous name *Forest Peace*. Helga remained alone in Berlin and fell into a deep depression. She moved to an old people's home in Esslingen near Stuttgart. Then, increasingly confused, she had to be looked after in St Vincent, a geronto-psychiatric care home in Plattenhardt.

She often rambled and talked nonsense. Once, she described how she had travelled on the Trans-Siberian Railway via Moscow (!) to visit her sister Maria Therese in Japan. In 2004, the last year of her life, her nephew Gottfried Paasche visited her. She could no longer move and hardly spoke. She sat in a wheelchair and when he mentioned her friend Leo Roth she stared at Gottfried for a moment; then she said that Leo Roth, a good person, had been the most important man in her life.

Seventh gloss.
The silence of the Hammersteins.

It's not as if the survivors of the family clammed up at the questions of a stranger. They received him with exceptional courtesy and patience, perhaps also with a touch of irony, like Hildur Zorn, the general's youngest daughter, by then an eighty-four-year-old lady. Because she doubts whether history in general and that of her family in particular can be recounted by an outsider. Not only because memory deceives, because every witness remembers in his or her way and because every record is full of differing versions and contradictions. Her scepticism is not based on epistemology alone. Nor is it a matter of that discretion which is part of good manners in a Prussian family. One doesn't get the impression that she is concerned about avoiding unpleasant incidents. The facts, in so far as they are clear, are communicated in matter-of-fact words.

But there remains the doubt whether later generations have sufficient imagination to do justice to what happened many decades ago. 'People today can't understand it any more, because they think they know everything,' says Hildur Zorn in her dry way.

However that may be, the Hammersteins display a silence of a special kind. If someone has to learn in a time of dictatorship that it can be dangerous to say everything that goes through one's head, then such a training may become second nature and it may not be easy to desist. That's also true of the behaviour of many survivors of the genocide who remained silent about their experiences for decades.

In the case of the Hammersteins, however, other elements probably play a part. All the children said the same thing about their father—that at table he hardly said a word, and it's certain that he passed over his daughters' risky escapades in silence. 'He didn't say much at all, and so we had to guess everything, which we preferred to do anyway.' That's Maria Therese's comment. She, incidentally, refused all her life to talk about her actions to save the persecuted. As for Helga and Maria Luise, they never talked about their militant past; more than that, they fell completely silent years before they died. Kunrat, too, is said to have withdrawn completely from the outside world.

The two Hammerstein brothers were very reticent, if they said anything at all, about their actions in the resistance. To the question whether the 20 July conspirators could count on him, Ludwig merely replied, 'Yes, of course,' without giving any further reason.

'None of them wanted to be a hero,' says Hildur. 'It was just that nothing else was possible. They simply did what had to be done.'

Altogether the Hammersteins display a deep-rooted aversion to complaining about the trials to which they were exposed or even to making a show of their own services and conflicts. 'We didn't want it all to be dwelt on,' says Hildur, and, as early as 1946, her mother declares in a letter: 'Our itinerary belongs to the past and doesn't need to be mentioned any more.'

The decisions of each individual were not questioned, but accepted, even when, as in the case of

Helga and Marie Luise, they were hard to understand or involved political risks. Hildur Zorn says: 'Why should they explain their lives?' In that attitude, one can perhaps find again something of the general's generosity. In any case, the silence of the Hammersteins rests on a mutual agreement which is not accessible to any outsider. There remains an unspoken remnant, which no biography can clarify. And perhaps it is this remnant that counts.

Why this book is not a novel.
Postscript.

I

What does the public care how an author comes by his subjects. At most, someone who has to write an MA thesis makes some inquiries about it. Otherwise, there is a lot to be said for sparing the reader such details. I would like to contravene this unwritten rule—not out of any concern for myself but for the story of other people, who deserve, I think, to be remembered.

I first heard about a general called Hammerstein more than half a century ago, in the old Stuttgart broadcasting building in Neckarstrasse. In 1955, Alfred Andersch, a man to whom I owe a great deal, took me into his radio-essay department at South German Radio, a first job and a very interesting one— in those days radio was a leading medium with degrees of freedom which have become inconceivable nowadays. The director of the station left us in peace. His name was Fritz Eberhard and he had been in the resistance and forced to flee to England in 1937; after the war, he made an important contribution to building democratic structures.

Authors like Wolfgang Koeppen, Arno Schmidt and Theodor W. Adorno were Andersch regulars.

Beyond that, he was also one of the very few then who stood up for the writers who had gone into exile, in whom the culture business of the day showed no interest and who had got by abroad, usually in wretched circumstances.

One day, there appeared in the Stuttgart office, at Andersch's invitation, an elderly man, in poor health, from San Francisco, small and shabbily dressed but with a pugnacious temperament. At the time, Franz Jung was one of the forgotten men of his generation. A few swiftly sketched details from his biography can provide only a faint idea of his life:

> Before the First World War, friendship with Erich Mühsam and Oskar Maria Graf. Contributor to the Expressionist periodicals *Der Sturm* and *Die Aktion*. In 1914, deserts the army, is confined to a fortress, sent to a mental hospital. A double life: earning a living with business journalism and stock exchange reports, secret political activity. Co-editor of *Club Dada*, close relations with George Grosz, Richard Huelsenbeck and John Heartfield. In January 1919, fights in the Spartakus Uprising in Berlin. Arrest and flight. Membership of the KPD, expelled 1920. Travels to Moscow, commandeering a fishing steamer on the way. In prison again for 'piracy on the high seas'. In 1921, expelled to the Soviet Union after the March Uprising of that year in central

Germany. Sets up a match factory near Novgorod. In 1923, returns to Germany under the false name Franz Larsz. Once again, active as business journalist and entrepreneur. Opaque currency dealings. In addition, dramatist; collaborates with Piscator. After 1933, publisher of a subscriber service on economic questions; at the same time, active in an underground group, 'The Red Fighters'. Arrested once again. Flight to Prague, Vienna and Geneva. Expelled for economic espionage. 1939, insurance agent in Budapest. Again arrested. 1944, flight to Italy, interned in Bozen concentration camp (South Tyrol). 1948 emigration to the United States.

That biography so impressed Andersch that he wanted to help, as far as was possible, Jung in his precarious situation. He agreed to some broadcasts with him. The visitor made suggestions, and I still remember that Hammerstein and his daughters were also mentioned. I was fascinated by what Jung told us and scented an exemplary story. In my naivety, I also took everything I was told at face value and overlooked the cheap novel elements of Jung's hints and suggestions. As with countless other projects of his, nothing came of the planned broadcast.

Franz Jung died in Stuttgart in 1963, in absolute poverty. His rediscovery had come too late. The publication of his powerful, mercilessly honest, autobiography *Der Weg nach unten* (The Way Down, 1961) did nothing to change that. It was not until its republication eleven years later under the title *Der Torpedokäfer* (The Torpedo Beetle) that interest in him was aroused. Since then, two voluminous collections of his work have appeared, even an edition of his letters.

Jung's totem, the torpedo beetle, which he invented, can stand as an emblem for the many interrupted biographies of the 'short twentieth century':

The beetle picks up speed, shoots forward, all the time accelerating towards the goal . . . Time flashes past in panic-laden suspense, eyes shut. Hits resistance—and then the fall . . . It is the biological peculiarity of the torpedo beetle that it flies towards the goal and falls . . . Once on the floor, all strength is gone. The observer is already sure: the beetle won't make it. But it does make it. Back to the point it started from . . . I have experienced the flight countless times in myself, by day and by night. The end has always been the same: impact, fall, crawling around on the floor, getting back to the point of departure, the starting position—only with difficulty, and each time it's more of an effort . . . The wall the beetle is flying at is solidly built. Generations of humanity stand behind it. The narrow

Franz Jung, around 1950

opening which is the target, and which even
lights up from time to time, is perhaps only an
illusion and in reality does not exist at all.

II

At the end of the 1950s I got to know Walter Maria
Guggenheimer. He worked on the left-wing *Frankfurter Hefte* and was an editor at the Suhrkamp publishing house; he was one of the few in those days who
provided any kind of orientation. Guggenheimer was
a Jewish *gentleman*, who had led an adventurous life
in exile. During the Third Reich, he went to Tehran.
In 1941, he joined de Gaulle's Forces Françaises Libres
for which he undertook intelligence missions in the
Near East, in North Africa, Italy and France. Apart
from his political acuity, there was little that betrayed
that past. He confined himself to his work as a critic,
translator and commentator. But he had a breadth of
horizon which was rare in those cheerless years. He
drew my attention to Hannah Arendt and to Czesław
Miłosz's *The Captive Mind* (1953) and one day pressed
Ruth Fischer's book *Stalin and German Communism*
(1948) into my hands. It had appeared earlier but had
hardly been noticed.

This intelligent, ambitious, pugnacious woman is
one of the key figures of the German Left in the 1920s.
She had at least eight different names, but was actually
called Elfriede Eisler and belonged to an Austrian
family which also produced the composer Hanns

Eisler and the later East German official and propagandist Gerhart Eisler, her brothers. Ruth Fischer was one of her numerous Party and cover names. In November 1918, in Vienna, she founded the first Communist Party in western or central Europe and had the membership number 1 of the KPÖ (Austrian Communist Party). One year later, she went to Berlin. In 1924, she was voted into the leadership of the German party and briefly determined its political course. Shortly afterwards, she had to defend herself in Moscow because of her ultra-Left positions.

Not long before, in Berlin, she had met Arkadi Maslow, with whom she lived until his death. Originally called Isaak Chemerinsky, he was born the son of an impoverished scholar in a small town in southern Ukraine who later emigrated to Germany with his mother. As a twenty-year-old he showed considerable musical talent; he undertook concert tours as a pianist. Then he studied mathematics in Berlin with Planck and Einstein. In 1918, he joined the Spartakus League, meeting Ruth Fischer in 1919. 'We were happy in 1919 and 1920,' he wrote later, 'when we were young and stupid and took appearance for the thing itself.' From that time on, he was a professional revolutionary, and rose, just as she did, into the leadership of the KPD.

While he was being tried by the Reich Court in Leipzig for high treason, Ruth Fischer was summoned to Moscow by Stalin with whom she had a heated discussion. She was accommodated, of course, in

Ruth Fischer, around 1920

the Hotel Lux. It was a kind of house arrest. Stalin declared to the plenum of the Comintern: 'Of all the undesirable and negative groups in the Communist Party, the Ruth Fischer group is the most undesirable and most negative.' She was not able to return to Germany until 1926. That same year, she, with Maslow, was expelled from the Party for 'persistent factional activity'.

In 1933, they both had to flee Germany. They went to Paris and, until 1936, as 'involuntary renegades', worked with Trotsky. In a secret trial in Moscow, they were both condemned to death in absentia for allegedly plotting to murder Stalin. Thanks to a sham marriage, Ruth Fischer had become a French citizen and now called herself Maria Elfriede Pleuchot. Pursued by both Nazis and Communists, the couple managed to escape across Spain to Lisbon before the German occupation of France. There, they lived on funds transferred to them by Franz Jung. While Ruth Fischer reached New York in 1941 on a Danish passport, Maslow was stuck in Havana because he was refused an American visa. After a few months he was found unconscious in the street and, on 21 November, died in hospital of causes unknown. Ruth Fischer was always convinced that the Soviet secret service played a part in his death. She consequently also suspected her brother Gerhart. Charlie Chaplin is supposed to have said: 'Relations between the members of the Eisler family are like those of the royals in a Shakespeare history play.'

In America, Ruth Fischer was very active as a journalist with the aim of fighting Stalinism. She got a
well-paid post at Harvard University as an expert on
Communism and acquired American citizenship. In
1947, she gave evidence against her brothers Gerhart
and Hanns to the House Committee on Un-American
Activities. 'I regard him as an extremely dangerous
terrorist,' she said about her brother Gerhart. Her enemies said she had links with the American secret services but she was merely a consultant to the State
Department for a while and an academic at Harvard.
In 1955, she returned to Paris. In her final years she
again drew closer to the militant positions of her ultra-
Left phase and was enthusiastic about Mao Zedong.
She thereby even put at risk the compensation payments to which she was entitled from Germany.

I visited her in Paris in March 1961 shortly before
her death. She was living in the Rue Montalivet, in an
elegant, spacious pavilion, situated in a garden and set
back from the road. There she looked after a large
library and an extensive private archive. She told me
two things that afternoon. First: that in 1938 her companion Arkadi Maslow had written a novel about the
'Hammerstein Case', which was never published. The
manuscript bears the title *The General's Daughters*
and is in the Houghton Library of Harvard University,
which holds Ruth Fischer's papers.

Maslow evidently wrote the text for money—
he was hoping for a film version of the sensationally
written-up material. His literary talent was not that

great, however, and he wasn't much concerned with the facts. Hindenburg, Schleicher, Ribbentrop and Goering crop up in passing as caricatures. Kurt von Hammerstein has the name Franz von Bimmelburg and appears as a narrow-minded, caste-fixated reactionary; his wife as a prudish spouse, Gerhard Scholem, with whom Maslow had once been friends, as a philanderer, Marie Luise as a naïve, insipid, little blonde, who in the end dies cruelly under the guillotine . . . The political analysis is flimsy, and the plot in large part entirely invented.

III

I could have left it at that, had Ruth Fischer not told me about her long friendship with Franz Jung. The two had known each other since 1919 and remained in touch even in exile. It was Ruth Fischer who, in 1941, obtained an entry visa to the United States for him. In 1960, he visited her in Paris, and, irrespective of all their political differences, their friendship held. He didn't want to know about her renewed rapprochement with Communism. 'The same people are the heroes again,' he wrote to a friend in Italy, 'a complete submission, even to the goatee [i.e. Walter Ulbricht] in the Zone. I don't understand it.' No doubt it's a kind of second youth for her, he can see all that, but he doesn't want to be part of it any more.

Nevertheless he proposed a new collaboration to her. Ruth Fischer had let him see Maslow's novel and he developed an extended treatment from it. It has the title 'Concerning: *The Hammersteins*. The Struggle for the Control of Command Authority in the German Army 1932–1937' and was supposed to serve as the basis of a book and a TV film. Stylistically, this text takes the form of a documentary report, and Maslow's fictitious persons now have their historical names. Jung's political analysis is much less amateurish than Maslow's, presumably not least because, in 1938, the latter did not have sufficient information available to him. He has largely eliminated the elements of cheap literature. Nevertheless, his plot incorporates numerous completely fictitious stories from Maslow's version. It's said of Helga von Hammerstein, for example, that, on returning from Paris, she was arrested at the border and was 'missing' ever since; and that Marie Luise was put on trial as a spy and sentenced to death. The melodramatic conclusion is mixed up with a quite different affair, the case of Renate von Natzmer, who, in 1935, was executed in Plötzensee Prison in Berlin for spying for Poland—to mention only a few of Jung's many other errors and fictions.

A third author who has devoted some attention to Hammerstein and his daughters is Alexander Kluge. In his stories in *The Devil's Blind Spot: Tales from the New Century* (2004), he deals boldly, not to say unscrupulously, with the facts; but here it is not a matter, as with Maslow, of propaganda or sensationalism but of the imaginative reconstruction of historical moments. Kluge's source is a fictitious Chinese biographer at Beijing University who comes to very intelligent conclusions. What Hammerstein and his daughters experienced was 'always an abyss next to life, a second life, as it were, and next to that an abyss again. The year 1931 is the year of multiple lives.' Even someone who scrapes past the facts can, as Kluge shows, certainly come to correct insights. Factography is not the only useful procedure.

IV

Nevertheless I decided to get to the bottom of the thing, even if it was very late, perhaps too late, with many of the witnesses no longer alive. It seems to me necessary because via the story of the Hammerstein family it is possible to find and describe in a small space all the essential motifs and contradictions of the German emergency: from Hitler's bid for total power to Germany's reeling between East and West, from the destruction of the Weimar Republic to the failure of the resistance, and from the attraction of the Communist utopia to the disappointment of the dream and the end of the cold war. Not least, this exemplary German story is about the last signs of life of the German-Jewish symbiosis and the fact that, long before the Feminist movement of recent decades, it was the strength of women on which the survival of the survivors depended.

Such a task, of course throws up a number of problems of an epistemological and literary kind.

J. L. Motley, a nineteenth-century American historian, had very radical ideas about that. 'There is no such thing as human history,' he wrote.

Nothing can be more profoundly, sadly true. The annals of mankind have never been written, never can be written; nor would it be within human capacity to read them if they were written. We have a leaf or two from the great book of human fate as it flutters in the stormwinds ever sweeping the earth. We decipher them as best we can with purblind eyes; but it is all confused babble, hieroglyphics of which the key is lost.

I would not want to go as far as that; Motley's scepticism suffers from an excess of Romantic poetry. Yet in a case like the one we are concerned with here, scruples and reservations are very much in order. As every detective knows from bitter experience, the statements of witnesses cannot always be taken at face value. Even well-meaning reports turn out to have gaps or to be contradictory. A craving for admiration or a desire to gloss things over can cause confusion just as much as a poor memory or downright lying. Things are no better when it comes to written sources. The word *document* suggests a credibility which is often very far from justified. Memoirs written long after the event show the marks of forgetfulness. Deliberate falsification is the least problem: that can be uncovered. More disturbing is the specific mixture of pedantry and slipshodness usual in developed bureaucracies. Politically motivated distortions have an even more dangerous effect. Very special care is called for where, as at many points in this story, evidence from secret service sources is concerned. It is not only plots and the urge to create an image that intrude but also the paranoia of the milieu. Entirely unreliable are the statements of the accused in the political trials of the 1930s and '40s which were often extorted by torture.

Despite these difficulties, I have tried to distinguish between facts and inventions. There was much that could not be completely clarified. Often, several different versions of one and the same event exist. A thorough verification of the sources is something I must leave to the experts.

Nevertheless, this book is not a novel. To draw a risky parallel: it proceeds analogously to photography rather than to painting. I wanted to separate what I could verify from written and oral sources from my own subjective judgements which appear here in the shape of glosses. In addition, I have made use of the venerable literary form of the conversation with the dead. Such posthumous conversations make possible a dialogue between those alive today and earlier generations—a discussion which inevitably has to cope with diverse difficulties of comprehension, because those who have got away lightly, historically speaking, often believe that they know better than those who lived in a permanent state of emergency and risked their necks.

Even though it is not a novel, this work does not make scholarly claims. For that reason I have abstained from footnotes, page references and suspension points. Anyone who wants to know more can consult the bibliography. Beyond that, I was able to draw on a store of unpublished materials: lengthy documents from the archives listed, interviews with surviving family members and handwritten letters and notes which they made available to me. I owe a large debt of gratitude to all those who were willing to talk to me. Without the help of the historians and the archivists, I would not have got beyond the first steps; yet it was never my intention to trespass on their territory. Everyone, even a writer, does as best he can.

Translator's notes

The *Reichswehr* was the official title of the German army from 1919 to 1935, when it was renamed the *Wehrmacht*.

Freikorps were unofficial military units consisting mainly of veterans and which were used to suppress left-wing movements and in disputed border areas in the months and years immediately after the end of the First World War.

The *Harzburg Front* (1931) was a short-lived coalition of the 'national opposition' that was opposed to the government of Heinrich Brüning. The principal organizations involved were the veterans' organization *Stahlhelm*, the conservative *Deutschnationale Volkspartei* (German National People's Party) and the Nazi Party.

'*Battle as Inner Experience*'—*Der Kampf als inneres Erlebnis*—the title of a book of essays by the right-wing author Ernst Jünger, best known in English for his autobiographical account of his service on the Western Front, *Storms of Steel*.

Annaberg. The Battle of Annaberg May 1921 in disputed Upper Silesia was the scene of a victory of German Freikorps over Polish irregulars. At the time, and in the years that followed, the engagement was accorded mythic status by the Right wing in Germany.

Herbert Wehner was already a prominent member of the KPD before 1933. After that, he was underground in Germany and subsequently a leading Comintern agent. Arrested and sentenced for spying in neutral Sweden during the Second World War, he broke with Communism. Returning to Germany in 1946, he joined the Social Democratic Party, becoming, in the 1960s, along with Willy Brandt and Helmut Schmidt, one of its most powerful figures.

Sources

ARCHIVES

Berlin. Behörde des Bundesbeauftragten für die Unterlagen des Staatssicherheitsdienstes der ehemaligen Deutschen Demokratischen Republik (Office of the Federal Commissioner for the Documents of the State Security Service of the Former GDR)

Berlin. Gedenkstätte Deutscher Widerstand (German Resistance Memorial Centre)

Berlin. Family archive, Franz von Hammerstein

Berlin. Stiftung Archiv der Parteien und Massenorganisationen der DDR im Bundesarchiv (SAPMO-DDR) (Foundation Archive of the parties and mass organizations of the GDR in the Federal Archive)

Cambridge, MA. Houghton Library, Harvard University, Ruth Fischer Files; there Arkadi Maslow, *Die Tochter des Generals*. Outline. Novel ms. 249pp. Doc. 2775–2777

Hamburg. Family archive, Juliane Kutter

Hamburg. Hamburger Institut für Sozialforschung. Copies of documents in Berlin and Moscow archives

Hanover. Archiv des Instituts für Politikwissenschaft, Hanover University

Koblenz. Federal Archive. Shelf mark ED 902

Moscow. Russian State Archive of Social Political History (RGASPI)

Moscow. Central State Archive of the Soviet Army (ZGASA)

Munich. Institut für Zeitgeschichte (Institute of Contemporary History)

Washington. National Archives

PUBLICATIONS

BRACHER, Karl Dietrich, Wolfgang Sauer, Gerhard Schulz. *Die nationalsozialistische Machtergreifung. Studien zur Errichtung der totalitären Herrschaft in Deutschland.* Cologne: 1962.

BRÜNING, Heinrich. *Memoiren 1918–1934.* Stuttgart: 1970.

BUCKMILLER, Michael and Pascal Nafe. 'Die Naherwartung des Kommunismus–Werner Scholem', in Michael Buckmiller, Dietrich Heimann and Joachim Perels (eds), *Judentum und politische Existenz. Siebzehn Porträts deutsch-jüdischer Intellektueller.* Hanover: 2000.

—— and Klaus Meschkat (eds). *Biographisches Handbuch zur Geschichte der Kommunistischen Internationale.* Berlin: 2007.

CARSTEN, Francis L. *Reichswehr und Politik 1918–1933.* Cologne: 1964.

——. 'Die Reichswehr und die Diktatur', in Gotthard Jasper (ed.), *Von Weimar zu Hitler 1930–1933.* Cologne and Berlin: 1968.

FEUCHTWANGER, Franz. 'Der militärpolitische Apparat der KPD in den Jahren 1928–1935. Erinnerungen'. *Internationale wissenschaftliche Korrespondenz zur Geschichte der deutschen Arbeiterbewegung,* 4 (1981).

FISCHER, Ruth. *Stalin and German Communism. A Study in the Origins of the State Party.* Harvard: 1948.

—— and Arkadij Maslow. *Abtrünnig wider Willen. Aus Briefen und Manuskripten des Exils* (Peter Lübbe ed.; with a foreword by Hermann Weber). Munich: 1990.

FLEXIUS, Walter. *Das Blutbad im Dritten Reich. Authentische Darstellungen nach den Mitteilungen geflüchteter SA-Führer.* Pamphlet published by Heimatbund Saarland. Saarbrücken: 1934.

FOERTSCH, Hermann. *Schuld und Verhängnis. Die Fritsch-Krise im Frühjahr 1938 als Wendepunkt in der Geschichte der nationalsozialistischen Zeit.* Stuttgart: 1951.

GROEHLER, Olaf. *Selbstmörderische Allianz. Deutsch-russische Militärbeziehungen 1920–1941*. Berlin: 1992.

HAMMERSTEIN, Kunrat von. 'Schleicher, Hammerstein und die Machtübernahme 1933'. *Frankfurter Hefte*, 11 (1956).

——. *Spähtrupp*. Stuttgart: 1963.

——. *Flucht. Aufzeichnungen nach dem 20. Juli*. Olten and Freiburg im Breisgau: 1966.

HAMMERSTEIN, Ludwig von. 'Kurt Freiherr von Hammerstein-Equord 1878–1943', in *Familienblatt des Familienverbandes des Freiherrn von Hammerstein* (19 December 1961).

——. 'Notizen', in Johannes Steinhoff, Peter Pechel and Dennis Showalter (eds.), *Deutsche im Zweiten Weltkrieg. Zeitzeugen sprechen*. Munich: 1989.

——. *Der 20. Juli 1944. Erinnerungen eines Beteiligten*. Saarbrücken: 1994.

HARDENBERG, Reinhild Gräfin von. *Auf immer neuen Wegen. Erinnerung an Neuhardenberg und den Widerstand gegen den Nationasozialismus*. Berlin: 2003.

HASSELL, Fey von. *Niemals sich beugen. Erinnerungen einer Sondergefangenen der SS*. Munich: 1990.

HASSELL, Ulrich von. *The von Hassell Diaries 1938–1944. The Story of the Forces Against Hitler Inside Germany*. New York: 1947 (also later editions).

HEDELER, Wladislaw. *Chronik der Moskauer Schauprozesse 1936, 1937 und 1938. Planung, Inszenierung und Wirkung* (with an essay by Steffen Dietzsch). Berlin: 2003.

HERING, Sabine and Kurt Schilde. *Kampfname Ruth Fischer. Wandlungen einer deutschen Kommunisten*. Frankfurt/Main: 1995.

JUNG, Franz. *Briefe* (Klaus Behnken ed.). Salzhausen: 1981.

——. *Briefe und Prospekte. Dokumente eines Lebenskonzeptes* (arrangement and commentary by Sieglinde and Fritz Mierau). Hamburg: 1988.

KAHLBERG, Friedrich P., Rudolf G. Pichoja, Ljudmila V. Dvojnych, *Reichswehr und Rote Armee. Dokumente aus den Militärarchiven Deutschlands und Russlands 1925–1931.* Koblenz: 1995.

KARDORFF, Ursula von. *Berliner Aufzeichnungen.* Munich: 1992 (new edition).

KAUFMANN, Bernd et al., *Der Nachrichtendienst der KPD 1919–1937.* Berlin: 1993.

KOBE, Gerd. *Pflicht und Gewissen. Smilo Freiherr von Lütt-witz. Lebensbild eines Soldaten.* Mainz: 1988.

KLUGE, Alexander. *Die Lücke, die der Teufel lässt. Im Umfeld des neuen Jahrhunderts.* Frankfurt/Main: 2003. [The story referred to by Enzensberger, 'Lebendigkeit von 1931', pp. 25–30, is not contained in the shortened English edition, Alexander Kluge, *The Devil's Blind Spot: Tales from the New Century* (Martin Chalmers and Michael Hulse trans.). New York: 2004.—Trans.]

KOENEN, Gerd. 'Hitlers Russland. Ambivalenzen im deut-schen "Drang nach Osten" ', *Kommune*, 1 (2003).

——. *Der Russland-Komplex. Die Deutschen und der Osten 1900–1945.* Munich: 2005.

KOESTLER, Arthur. *Darkness at Noon* (various editions).

KROSIGK, Ludwig Schwerin von. *Es geschah in Deutschland. Menschenbilder underes Jahrhunderts.* Tübingen: 1951.

LUKÁCS, Georg, Johannes R. Becher, Friedrich Wolf et al., *Die Säuberung. Moskau 1936: Stenogramm einer geschlossenen Parteiversammlung* (Reinhard Müller ed.). Reinbek: 1991.

MANSTEIN, Erich von. *Aus meinem Soldatenleben 1887–1939.* Bonn: 1958.

MAYENBURG, Ruth von. *Blaues Blut und rote Fahnen. Ein Leben unter vielen Namen.* Vienna and Munich: 1969.

——. *Hotel Lux. Mit Dimitrow, Ernst Fischer, Ho Tschi Minh, Pieck, Rakosi, Slansky, Dr. Sorge, Tito, Togliatti,*

Tschou En-Lai, Ulbricht und Wehner im Moskauer Quartier der Kommunistischen Internationale. Munich: 1978.

MEISSNER, Hans Otto and Harry Wilde, *Die Machtergreifung. Ein Bericht über die Technik des nationalsozialistischen Staatsstreichs.* Stuttgart: 1958.

MÜLLER, Klaus-Jürgen. *Das Heer und Hitler. Armee und nationalsozialistisches Regime 1933–1940.* Stuttgart: 1969.

MÜLLER, Reinhard. *Die Akte Wehner. Moskau 1937 bis 1941.* Berlin: 1993.

——. 'Hitler's Rede vor der Reichswehr und Reichsmarineführung am 3. Februar 1933. Eine neue Moskauer Überlieferung'. *Mittelweg,* 4 (2000).

——. *Menschenfalle Moskau. Exil und stalinistische Verfolgung.* Hamburg: 2001.

——. *Herbert Wehner. Moskau 1937.* Hamburg: 2004.

OTT, Eugen. 'Ein Bild des Generals Kurt von Schleicher aus den Erfahrungen seiner Mitarbeiter dargestellt. *Politische Studien,* 10 (1959).

PAASCHE, Maria Therese. *Our Thanks to the Fuji-San* (interview by Sandra Marshall Finley). San Francisco: 1984 (private publication).

—— and John Paasche, *Diverse Antecedents* (Sandra Marshall Finley ed.). San Francisco: 1986 (private publication).

PAPEN, Franz von. *Vom Scheitern einer Demokratie 1930–1933.* Mainz: 1968.

PICKER, Henry. *Hitlers Tischgespräche im Führerhauptquartier 1941-1942* (re-edited by Percy Ernst Schramm et al.). Stuttgart: 1963.

PUFENDORF, Astrid von. *Die Plancks. Eine Familie zwischen Patriotismus und Widerstand.* Berlin: 2006.

RICHARDI, Hans-Günter. *SS-Geiseln in der Alpenfestung. Die Veschleppung prominenter KZ-Häftlinge aus Deutschland nach Südtirol.* Bozen: 2006.

SANDVOSS, Hans-Rainer. *Widerstand in Mitte und Tiergarten.* Berlin: 1994.

——. *Die 'andere' Reichsshauptstadt. Widerstand aus der Arbeiterbewgung in Berlin von 1933 bis 1945.* Berlin: 2007.

SCHÄFER, Kirstin A. *Werner von Blomberg, Hitlers erster Feldmarschall.* Paderborn: 2005.

SCHLABRENDORFF, Fabian von. *Offiziere gegen Hitler* (Gero Schulze-Gaevernitz ed.). Zürich: 1946 (revised 1951).

SCHLÖGEL, Karl. *Berlin-Ostbahnhof. Russen und Deutsche in ihrem Jahrhundert.* Berlin: 1998.

——. 'Moskau 1937. Eine Stadt in den Zeiten des grossen Terrors'. *Jahrbuch des Historischen Kollegs,* 12 (2006).

SPEIDEL, Helm. 'Reichswehr und Rote Armee'. *Vierteljahreshefte für Zeitgeschichte,* 1 (1953).

STEINBERGER, Nathan and Barbara Broggini, *Berlin-Moskau-Kolyma und zurück. Ein biographisches Gespräch über Stalinismus und Antisemitismus.* Berlin and Amsterdam: 1996.

STRENGE, Irene. *Kurt von Schleicher. Politik im Reichswehrministerium am Ende der Weimarer Republik.* Berlin: 2006.

VERMEHREN, Isa. *Reise durch den letzten Akt. Ravensbrück, Buchenwald, Dachau: eine Frau berichtet.* Reinbek: 1979.

VOGELSANG, Thilo. 'Neue Dokumente zur Geschichte der Reichswehr 1930–1933'. *Vierteljahreshefte für Zeitgeschichte,* 2 (1956).

——. *Reichswehr, Staat und NSDAP. Beiträge zur deutschen Geschichte 1930–1933.* Stuttgart: 1962.

WEBER, Hermann and Andreas Herbst, *Deutsche Kommunisten. Biographisches Handbuch 1918 bis 1945.* Berlin 2004.

WEHNER, Herbert. *Zeugnis* (Gerhard Jahn ed.). Cologne: 1982.

WOHLFEIL, Rainer and Hans Dollinger, *Die deutsche Reichs-wehr. Bilder, Dokumente, Texte zur Geschichte des Hunderttausend-Mann-Heeres 1919–1933.* Frank-furt/Main: 1972.

ZEIDLER, Manfred. *Reichswehr und Rote Armee 1920–1933. Wege und Stationen einer ungewöhnlichen Zusam-menarbeit.* Munich: 1993.

Acknowledgements

I am grateful above all to the members of the Hammerstein family who opened their private archives to me and entrusted me not only with their photographs but also their memories:

Franz and Verena von Hammerstein, Berlin

Hildur Zorn, Berlin

Gottfried Paasche, Toronto

Cecil von Münchhausen, Berlin, and

Juliane Kutter, Hamburg.

No less indispensable was the generous assistance provided by Reinhard Müller, an authority on the history of German Communism, who tracks down the most remote sources and hidden archives. Without his researches in Berlin and Moscow, much of what occurred in the 'Apparatus' would have remained obscure. His work on a film version of the Hammerstein story will be equally indispensable should one be made.

Finally, I owe thanks to:

Michael Buckmiller, Hanover

Renée Goddard, London

Christine Haselmayr von Ranke, Munich

Andreas Herbst, Berlin

Olga Mannheimer, Munich

Hartmut Mehringer, Munich

Hans-Rainer Sandvoss, Berlin and

Johannes Tuchel, Berlin

The photographs

Unless otherwise stated, the photographs come from the von Hammerstein, Paasche, Kutter and Höslmayr families.

PAGES 30, 71, 97, 132, 184, 194, 206, 221, 231, 234, 239, 260, 273: Hamburg Institute for Social Research;

PAGES 38, 41, 42, 139, 166, 265, 295, 296, 307, 308, 317, 318: German Resistance Memorial Centre;

PAGES 101, 181: from Ruth von Mayenburg, *Blaues Blut und rote Fahnen*;

PAGE 375: from Sabine Hering and Kurt Schilde, *Kampfnahme Ruth Fischer*;

PAGES 328, 330: from Hans-Günter Richardi: *SS-Geiseln in der Alpenfestung*;

PAGE 372: Deutsches Literaturarchiv Marbach.

Any holders of rights who have not been traced should contact the publisher.

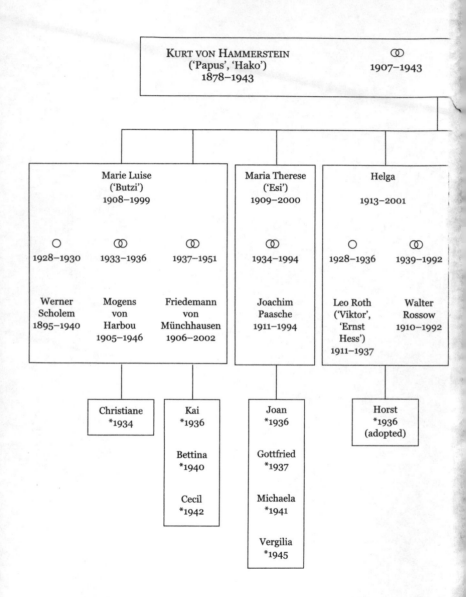

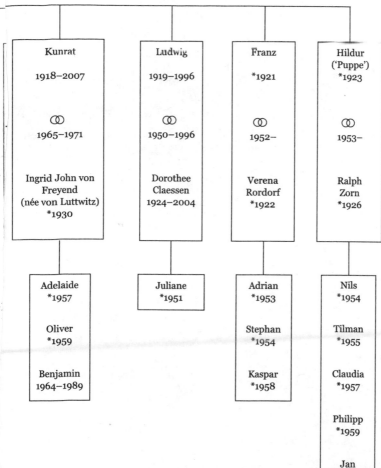

MARIA VON HAMMERSTEIN
(née von Luttwitz)
('Ama', 'Mietze')
1886–1970

Kunrat	Ludwig	Franz	Hildur ('Puppe')
1918–2007	1919–1996	*1921	*1923
⊕	⊕	⊕	⊕
1965–1971	1950–1996	1952–	1953–
Ingrid John von Freyend (née von Luttwitz) *1930	Dorothee Claessen 1924–2004	Verena Rordorf *1922	Ralph Zorn *1926

Adelaide *1957	Juliane *1951	Adrian *1953	Nils *1954
Oliver *1959		Stephan *1954	Tilman *1955
Benjamin 1964–1989		Kaspar *1958	Claudia *1957
			Philipp *1959
			Jan *1960